WORLD WAR 3
GLOBAL ISLAMIC JIHAD

G. A. Mohr,
P. E. Mohr & R. S. Mohr

WORLD WAR 3
GLOBAL ISLAMIC JIHAD

G. A. Mohr,
P. E. Mohr & R. S. Mohr

TRI

Transworld Research & Innovation
9 Hampstead Drive
Hoppers Crossing VIC 3029
AUSTRALIA

G. A. Mohr, P. E. Mohr & R. S. Mohr
World War 3:
Global Islamic Jihad

TRI

Transworld Research & Innovation
9 Hampstead Drive
Hoppers Crossing VIC 3029
AUSTRALIA

ALSO BY G. A. MOHR

Finite Elements for Solids, Fluids, and Optimization

A Microcomputer Introduction to the Finite Element Method

The Pretentious Persuaders:
A Brief History & Science of Mass Persuasion

Curing Cancer & Heart Disease,
Proven Ways to Combat Aging, Atherosclerosis & Cancer

The Variant Virus, Introducing Secret Agent Simon Sinclair

The Doomsday Calculation: The End Of The Human Race

The War of the Sexes: Women Are Getting On Top

Heart Disease, Cancer, & Ageing:
Proven Neutraceutical & Lifestyle Solutions

2045: A Remote Town Survives Global Holocaust

The History & Psychology of Human Conflict

Elementary Thinking for Modern Management

The 8-Week+ Program to Reverse Cardiovascular Disease

The Scientific MBA;   Mohr's Law of Hierarchies

The DIY Cardiovascular Cure,
A Comprehensive Program to Reverse Atherosclerosis

Combating Cancer, Proven Neutraceutical & Lifestyle Remedies

The Psychology of Life; The Psychology of Depression

ALSO WITH R.S. MOHR/RICHARD SINCLAIR & P.E. MOHR/EDWIN FEAR

The Evolving Universe: Relativity, Redshift and Life from Space

World Religions: The History, Psychology, Issues & Truth

World War 3, When & How Will It End?

The Brainwashed, From Consumer Zombies to Islamic Jihad

Human Intelligence, Learning & Behaviour

New Theories of The Universe, Evolution, and Relativity

The Population Explosion

World Religions: From to Animism to Mohronism

Human Conflict: An Attitudinal Psychology Model

Brainwashed Zombies: Religious, Political & Consumer Persuasion

The Psychology of Hope;   The Psychology of Success

TABLE OF CONTENTS

PREFACE

It has been estimated that in the period 1820 to 1990 there were at least 100 wars involving at least two nations. In the last century there were two world wars, the second killing 60 million people, mostly civilians. In the period 1946 to 1990 there were more than 100 wars in 60 countries or territories, killing another 16 million, mostly civilians.

The 15 chapters that make up Part 1 of this book give an overview of man's long history of conflict.

Part 2 discusses worldwide conflict in the Middle East, Africa, Asia, Europe, North America, Central and South America, and Australasia.

The first chapter of Part 3 (Chapter 23) discusses the 'seeds of conflict' that threaten our very survival, including our grossly excessive population, resource depletion, and climate change, many other such seeds having been discussed in my 2012 book *The Doomsday Calculation*.

Chapter 24 discusses modern economic, infrastructure, and cyber warfare, whilst Chapters 25 and 26 discuss NBC warfare (nuclear and biochemical warfare).

Chapter 27 discusses continuing conflicts of 'socialism vs. oligarchy' that continue in the warm ashes of the Cold War.

Chapters 28 and 29 discuss Islamic Jihad and 'World War 3', which the authors feel began with establishment the state of Israel in 1948 in what had been the UN-mandated British protectorate of "Palestine", and 'WW3' continues to this day.

Then, when Osama Bin Laden formally declared war on the US in 1998, calling for removal of the state of Israel, and reduction of US forces and influence in the Middle East, that could be seen as yet another Islamic tyrant and terrorist jumping on the bandwagon of what was already WW3.

Thus OBL simply joined the dozens of other Islamic terrorist groups such as the PLO in Islamic jihad aimed at taking over the entire world and turning it into a massive caliphate in which all are oppressed except those high in the corrupt Islamic hierarchy who still have the modern equivalent of harems (i.e., 4 wives + sex slaves), as did their predecessors centuries ago, some of whom had thousands of women slaves in their harems to keep their insanely sick minds amused at night after yet another day of slaughtering Christians and any other "unbelievers."

Over centuries, countless millions have been brutally slaughtered by Islamic terrorists.

Now things look worse, however, and we agree with Benjamin Netanyahu that Iran might well already have their first nuclear bomb, or will have it soon.

Worse still, we note that Islamic State, the most brutal and powerful group of organized Islamic slaughterers in modern history, have got together top scientists in order to make advanced chemical and biological weapons.

It is in such a scenario, WW3 having already simmered since 1948, and it now having heated up quite a bit of late, Armageddon might not be far away as the last stage of WW3 begins with the use of NBC weapons, a far more serious situation than WW2 ending with just 2 relatively small nukes being dropped on Japan.

I hope this book will make people more aware of mankind's disastrous history of conflict and of how to reduce hostility and conflict at every level of society so that we can focus on improving our survival prospects as a species.

As for 'could it [WW3] happen' – yes we think it could, and it would be far worse than in the novel *The Third World War* (Hawksey, 2003), where the worst that happens according to the blurb on the back cover is that a "US military base is hit by a North Korean missile" with a nuke, destroying everything within a one-mile radius.

If ISIS manage to produce biological weapons such as the Marburg Variant U that Russia put atop its SS16s (Alibek, 1999) the results could be devastating and, perhaps, exterminate humanity, as suggested possible in the book *Our Stolen Future,* with a forward by Nobel prize winner Al Gore, (Colborn et al., 1996). He worries about the "synthetic chemicals that we have spread across this Earth". I worry about viruses than can transform to an alternative and worse form, e.g. smallpox into something far worse, and I have this happening in the fiction novel *The Variant Virus,* but in real life/death we won't have the heroic Simon Sinclair to mitigate the damage and thus save the day (Mohr, 2012c).

Finally, I am grateful to my co-authors for helpful discussions and ideas which have helped make this book a little more complete. Once again, I am also grateful to the publishers and their editors and other staff for, once again, doing an excellent job in finally bringing this book to print.

Geoff Mohr, November, 2018

PART 1
A LONG HISTORY OF WAR

Chapter 1

TRIBAL HOMO SAPIENS

Tribalism is the strongest force in the world today.
Vine Deloria, U.S. Native American leader,
Custer Died for Your Sins: An Indian Manifesto (1969), ch. 11.

Introduction

Humans are animals, of course, but simply with an enlarged cerebral cortex to store the semantic memory needed for our advanced languages. Nevertheless, we evolved from animal origins and, therefore, possess the same physical and behavioural characteristics as most of the larger land-based animal species.

Physically, we eat, we sleep, we defecate, and so forth. Behaviourally, besides our language, which we take so long to learn in infancy, we make various other communicative noises, we still encourage the despicable alpha-male phenomenon (for example in such animalistic sports as rugby), our male sports stars still bare and beat their chests after victory, just as apes might do, and, of course, we have a sorry history of conflict ranging from interpersonal conflict to world wars.

Indeed, our history of wars and other disasters is such that we might, indeed, wonder whether we are not, perhaps, in many ways the most stupid of animals.

Evolution of tribal man

Chimpanzees, with which we share circa 96% of the same genes, are sociable animals that live in groups of 20 to 60, forming into subgroups of adults (male and female), all-male groups and groups of mothers and offspring. African gorillas also live in bisexual groups of between 2 to 30 but which do not comprise smaller subgroups.

The best known studies of chimpanzees were conducted by Jane Goodall and associates in the Gombe National Park on the edge of Lake Tanganyika in Tanzania (Goodall, 1971).

Ultimately, Goodall was quite disillusioned to find that *tribes* of chimps were led by an alpha male and would occasionally have small wars with neighbouring tribes, these resuming at intervals over periods of many years. She concluded that they were all too much like humans!

Comparisons of blood proteins and the DNA of the African great apes with that of humans indicates that the line leading to modern people did not split off from that of chimpanzees and gorillas until comparatively late in evolution, perhaps 6 million to 8 million years ago.

Fossils of the first *hominines,* the *australopithecines*, dating to 5 million years ago have been discovered. This genus seems to have become extinct about 1.5 million years ago, but before doing so one of seven species of australopithecines, *Australopithecus africanus*, evolved into the genus *Homo* between 1.5 and 2 million years ago.

The earliest evidence of stone tools comes from sites in Africa dated to about 2.5 million years ago. These tools seem to be associated with all hominine species.

Around 1.7 to 1.9 million years ago two new species of large brained, small-toothed hominines emerged, *Homo ergaster* in Africa and *Homo erectus* in Asia.

Later *H. erectus* skulls possess brain sizes in the range of 1100 to 1300 cc (67.1 to 79.3 cu in), within the size variation of *Homo sapiens*.

A number of archaeological sites dating from the time of *Homo erectus* reveal a greater sophistication in tool making than was found at earlier sites. Evidence found at the cave site of "Peking Man" in northern China, suggests that *Homo erectus* used fire.

The remains of the foundations of an oval structure built by a *Homo erectus* group were found at the Terra-Amata site in France, and within this structure, there was a fireplace (Weiss and Mann, 1978).

The *Homo* species spread widely and by 350,000 years ago planned hunting, fire making, wearing of clothes, and probably burial rituals, were well established.

Between 200,000 and 300,000 years ago, *Homo sapiens* evolved.

The Neanderthals or *Homo sapiens neanderthalensis* had similar DNA to modern man and occupied parts of Europe and the Middle East as early as 120,000 years ago. They lived only in family groups, the men being hunter-gatherers to feed the family.

The Neanderthals left cave paintings that were an important evolutionary advance. These often depicted a simple activity, perhaps a precursor to the highly pictorial hieroglyphic script of the ancient Egyptians (Egerton-Eastwick, 1896).

Though Neanderthals had 10% larger brains than modern man has, there is some evidence that the part of the cerebral cortex devoted to language and thinking in modern man was underdeveloped in Neanderthal man, casting some doubt on whether Neanderthal man was capable of modern spoken language.

Thought by some to be a different evolutionary branch, the Neanderthals disappeared from the fossil record about 30,000 years ago.

Differing in appearance, modern humans or *Homo sapiens sapiens* evolved in southern Africa or the Middle East perhaps 90,000 to 200,000 years ago and 70,000 years ago began to spread to all parts of the world, reaching Europe about 40,000 years ago, soon outnumbering, perhaps interbreeding with, and finally supplanting the local, earlier *Homo sapiens* populations.

Like chimpanzees, Homo sapiens sapiens formed tribes and there is evidence of religion, recorded events and art dating from 30,000 to 40,000 years ago implying the advanced language and ethics required for the ordering of social groups.

Evolution of religion

Around the same time Homo sapiens developed cave art, about 100,000 years ago, he would have developed language and, eventually some form of 'pictorial' communication which eventually evolved into hieroglyphic script, then cuneiform script, and finally the symbolic writing we now use.

Typically, each tribe had a leader, a religion, and a common language and culture.

The first forms of religion involved such beliefs and practices as:

(a) *Animism*, belief that plants, inanimate objects and natural phenomena had souls or spirits.

(b) *Polytheism,* belief in multiple Gods, sometimes attributing certain acts of nature to each.

(c) *Ancestor Worship* teaching that a tribe's people were descended from a common ancestor.

(d) *Immortality* or belief that the dead live on as spirits, promises of immortality to the faithful still being amongst the 'blackmail' tactics preachers use today.

Eventually these religions evolved into the *monotheism* that dominates the world today.

Thus, at the outset it was the tribal elders who passed on tribal beliefs from one generation to another, a situation that still exists amongst a few primitive people today. Along the way *shamans* or 'witch doctors' claiming some special connection with the spirits appeared, along with religious rites and ceremonies.

In groups of hunter-gatherers, just as with many other species of animals, the 'dominant' males were, of course, responsible for protection of the group from external threats which, just as with chimpanzees, often took the form of other 'tribes' or groups.

At the same time, however, the supposedly wiser elders still indoctrinated the young into religion and had considerable influence, if not control, over the 'dominant males.' Their weapons for control ranged from rhetoric to dire threats of a vengeful spirit or God.

Thus, from the ancient Greeks through to the middle ages a study of *rhetoric* was considered important because of its use to bullshit people into doing as political and religious leaders wished. Francis Bacon (1561 - 1626), for example, studied Elizabethan logic and rhetoric at Cambridge University for two years, leaving at the age of 14 (note that people got married at this sort of age then).

Conflict

No doubt there was occasional conflict within the family groups that Homo sapiens lived in, perhaps, for example, over decisions about where to search and hunt for food.

Indeed, such arguments may have led to conflict over who leadership of the group should be trusted to.

There may, of course, have also been occasional conflict with other family groups over territorial issues or, in effect, 'hunting and searching rights' in certain areas which more than one group lived near.

Once tribes were established, questions of leadership may have become more important. No doubt the stronger males were likely to be chosen as leaders in both regular hunting and occasional conflicts between neighbouring tribes.

Indeed, tribal conflicts are 'war' and, of course, some American Indians still ceremonially perpetuate the practice of covering their faces with 'war paint' that traditionally preceded a tribal conflict.

In addition, the elders would often, at least, have had some influence, whilst their role in passing on tribal folklore would certainly have involved tales of conflicts past with other tribes and thus encouraged acceptance and continuance of such conflicts.

In addition, tribal witch doctors or shamans would have had considerable influence, their superstitious view of things no doubt causing other tribes to be considered 'heathen' and viewed with suspicion, if not hostility.

Thus they increased the 'differences' between their tribe and others, an important factor in ethnic conflict which is further discussed in Chapters 8 and 10.

Indeed, it was often supposed that the Neanderthals were wiped out by invading Homo sapiens sapiens from the South, but is now believed that, in fact, the two closely related species interbred and thus those of us with European lineage have some Neanderthal DNA.

No doubt the invaders also killed a great many Neanderthals as well, perhaps mostly the more threatening males. In other words, in war kill the men and rape the women, something that has not changed since then in the brutality of war.

Conclusion

Primitive man was not far different from modern man, having large groups sometimes in conflict, supposedly stronger leaders to lead or dictate those conflicts, religious leaders to create ethnic differences to encourage mistrust and tribal conflict, and elders to keep alive and thus help continue a history of conflict.

An example of the latter today, some people call one of the major Australian TV channels 'The Hitler Channel' because it so often airs documentaries about Hitler and his associates to keep us reminded of one of the greatest villains in relatively recent history, and keep us mentally prepared to blindly accept the political propaganda and bullshit that will precede the next war some of us are ordered to participate in.

Thus, when I saw repeated pictures of Saddam Hussein holding a rifle in the media in the months before the post 9/11 US invasion of Iraq, I knew that the US would go to war with that country, however mistakenly. As usual, they did far more harm than good and, in effect, lost because, of course, they certainly didn't win anything but lost a great deal of money yet again, as they did in Vietnam and Korea.

The US also lost WW2 (to Joseph Stalin) but made a great deal of money using Lend Lease to sell badly needed weapons to several countries including England, France, the Netherlands, and Russia.

Finally, and farcically, we still perpetuate the absurd tribal practices of sports with a conflict connotation, for example shooting, archery, and rugby (do as told and charge the enemy as in the trench warfare of WW1).

Primitive tribal man did likewise but with spears and perhaps knives and rocks.

Modern man, thanks to advanced technology, has far more brutal weapons and thus could be argued to have become far more brutal, just one factor in our 'reverse evolution' discussed in a recent book (Mohr, 2012b).

Chapter 2

THE AGRICULTURAL REVOLUTION & CITY-STATES

> *Clearly, then, the city is not a concrete jungle, it is a human zoo.*
> Desmond Morris, *The Human Zoo* (1969), Introduction.

The Agricultural Revolution

About 12,000 years ago the Agricultural Revolution, in part enabled by development of primitive forms of permanent housing, led to the growth of human societies from small tribes to those of settlements of hundreds and eventually, as farming became more productive, thousands of people.

More efficient farming allowed more specialization, for example millers, bakers and weavers. In these growing societies religion became increasingly important as a means of imparting ethics and standards.

These larger societies now had houses and farms to defend, however, so that the need for stronger males for territorial defence grew and with it the influence that their leaders had upon society. This may have led to the appearance of leaders of towns or regions involving a few nearby towns and, eventually, monarchs.

In some societies, however, priest-kings emerged, but generally 'church' and 'state' have remained, ostensibly at least, separate entities to this day, both doing their utmost to control their societies.

In the rest of society the mercantile infrastructure of the consumer society that we have today began to evolve with open air markets largely giving way to shops and barter systems giving way to currency.

Regular armies

With towns and surrounding farms to defend from intrusion and theft of agricultural products, the task of defence would have fallen into the hands of ordinary local citizens, particularly the outlying farmers whose fields were most vulnerable to intrusion.

Eventually, as towns grew in size, and the occupations of the citizens in them continued to diversify, small citizen territorial armies may have been formed on an occasional basis to protect towns and their surrounding farms.

Ultimately, however, increasingly powerful leaders formed regular armies, their power increasing with each conquest during which, no doubt, they were able to seize valuables and slaves from captured towns.

Mesopotamia

Mesopotamia, the area between the Tigris and the Euphrates, was conventionally divided in two: Upper Mesopotamia, the home of the Assyrians, extending from Baghdad to eastern Turkey, and Lower Mesopotamia.

Sumer, the part of Lower Mesopotamia between Babylon and the Persian Gulf, was the place where the world's first urban civilization evolved. Eridu, Ur and Uruk were amongst the greatest Sumerian city-states dating as far back as 4000BC.

Political primacy passed from one city and its kingly dynasty to another, for example the Alkadians (first under Sargon I circa 2350BC), the Amorites (whose laws, codified by Hammurabi circa 1792-1750BC, have biblical parallels), and the Assyrians, with interludes by the Hittites, Kassites, and Mitannia (World Almanac, 1998).

Surviving art forms date from 2500BC, and include stone statues of Gudea and coloured bas-reliefs.

Gudea, the fourth ruler of the Sumerian dynasty of Lagash, ruled from circa 2144 to 2124BC. Lagash was a powerful city-state on the present-day site of Telloh near the Persian Gulf in southern Iraq. Gudea built 15 temples in Girsu, an administrative centre of Lagash, including the massive temple Eninnu which was devoted to the city god Ningursu. Gudea had military victories over the nearby settlements of Anshan and Elam.

Later came Babylonia, the region in Lower Mesopotamia around the ancient city of Babylon, around which was centred two extensive but short-lived empires (Chambers, 1993).

The first was created by the Amorite King Hammurabi (c. 1795 – 1750BC) and covered the whole of Mesopotamia but was destroyed by the Hittites circa 1595BC. The second resulted from the Babylonian overthrow of Assyria in 612BC and under its greatest monarch, Nebuchadnezzar (605 - 562BC), it stretched as far east as the Mediterranean. It was conquered by Persia in 539 – 538BC.

Egypt

Agricultural villages along the Nile were unified by 3300BC into two kingdoms, Upper and Lower Egypt, which were unified circa 3100BC by the pharaoh Menes. Hieroglyphic writing appeared by 3200 BC and a bureaucracy supervised construction of canals and monuments, construction of the first pyramids beginning circa 2700BC.

A powerful priesthood in Memphis served a hierarchical order of gods, including totemistic animals, and believed in the afterlife.

Control over Nubia to the south was gained from 2600BC. After a period of dominance by Semitic Hyksos from Asia (1700 – 1550BC), the New Kingdom established an empire in Syria. Egypt became increasingly embroiled in Asiatic wars and was conquered by Persia in 525BC (World Almanac, 1998).

India

Between 3000 and 1500BC urban civilization with an as yet undeciphered writing system stretched across the Indus Valley and along the Arabian Sea, and the entire region may have been ruled as a single state.

The cities of Harappa and Mohenjo-Daro in Pakistan were geometrically well-planned with underground sewers and large granaries.

Religious life mainly derived from fertility cults and Indus civilization was destroyed by Aryan invaders from the north-west, speaking an Indo-European language from which most languages in Pakistan, north India and Bangladesh derive. Led by a warrior aristocracy the Aryans spread east and south, bringing their sky gods, elaborate Brahman rituals, and the roots of the caste system.

Greece

On Crete, the Bronze Age Minoan civilization emerged circa 2500BC, reaching its peak in 1500BC, the economy prospering by seaborne commerce.

Mycenae and other cities in mainland Greece and Asia Minor such as Troy preserved Minoan culture until circa 1200BC. Cretan Linear A script (c. 2000 – 1700BC) remains undeciphered but Linear B script (c. 1300 – 1200BC) records an early Greek dialect.

Sparta, in the south Peloponnesus, was one of the leading city-states of ancient Greece, having expanded its power by subjugating the neighbouring Laconians and Messenians as serfs. Government was oligarchic and led by two hereditary kings whose duties were primarily military and religious.

The revolt of Messenia in 650BC led to military and social reforms aimed at preventing further uprisings. By the 6th century BC Sparta was the greatest military power in Greece, its leadership of the Peloponnesian League helping it defeat Athens in the Peloponnesian War of 431 – 404BC.

Thereafter Sparta's military power declined and was never to be revived after defeat by the Thebans at the Battle of Leuctra in 371BC (Chambers, 1993).

China

North and south-east China had long had Neolithic cultures when the Shang dynasty (c. 1523BC) formed the first large political state in which a writing system with 2,000 characters was in use. Shang kings called themselves Sons of Heaven, and presided over cults of human and animal sacrifice to ancestors and nature gods.

The Chang dynasty, which started circa 1027BC, expanded the area of the Sons of Heaven's dominion, but feudal states still had most temporal power.

The Americas

Circa 1500 BC Olmecs settled on the Gulf of Mexico and developed the first civilization in the Western hemisphere. Temple cities dated from 1200BC and a crude calendar and writing system existed. Olmec religion, based on a jaguar god, and Olmec art forms are said to have influenced all later Central American cultures.

Rome

Legend has it that Rome, the greatest city-state in history, was founded in 753BC by Romulus and Remus, the twin sons of Rhea Silvia, a vestal virgin and daughter of Numitor, king of Alba Longa, a nearby City in ancient Latium. Alba Longa was founded by Ascanius, son of the Trojan leader Aeneas, who was founder and first king of Alba Longa.

Romulus was the first of 7 kings in Rome's 'regal period' from 753 to 510BC. The king, or rex, was chosen by the Senate, or Council of Elders, from the ranks of the patricians, who constituted the *populus*, or people, whose dependants (often slaves), known as clients or the plebs, had no political rights.

The king called out the populus for war and led the army himself. He was the supreme judge in civil and criminal suits and the Senate gave its advice only when the king chose to ask for it.

Later in the regal period, when the plebs had been allowed to acquire property and wealth, both patrician and plebeian property holders were compelled to serve in the army, their rank depending upon their wealth.

Over time, of course, Rome grew in power, ultimately forging a great empire covering much of the globe, as will be discussed in Chapter 4.

Conclusions

In the early city-states, their growing societies and the organizations within them, especially the army and the church, took on hierarchical forms and the main weapons of control ranged from verbal persuasion to threats throughout a chain of command to see that the rest of the population towed the line.

Unfortunately, however, the ambitious, aggressive, and assertive people who literally fight their way to leadership positions through impatience, stupidity and deceit have done far more harm than good and our unending history of conflict and war attests to this.

In the early city-states these wasteful leaders required grand residences and temples to be built, had large numbers of domestic slaves, and organized large armies of soldiers.

As we have seen throughout history, these armies were used all too often, often for little or no good reason, and some attempt to bring a little science to the understanding of mankind's seemingly endless history of conflict is made in following chapters of this book.

Chapter 3

MONARCHY & OLIGARCHY

> *In all ages, hypocrites, called priests, have put crowns*
> *upon the heads of thieves, called kings.*
> Robert G. Ingersoll, *Prose-Poems and Selections* (1884).
>
> They that are discontented under *monarchy*, call it *tyranny;*
> and they that are displeased with *aristocracy*, call it *oligarchy;*
> so also, they which find themselves grieved under a *democracy,* call it
> *anarchy,* which signifies a want of government;
> and yet I think no man believes, that want of government,
> is any new kind of government.
> Thomas Hobbes, *Leviathan* (1651), pt. 2, ch. 1.

Introduction

Throughout history man has had many kinds of leadership, some of the historically most common forms of leadership or government having been:

1. Autocracy is government by a single individual and WordWeb 6 defines autocrat as: *A cruel and oppressive dictator.* The Concise Oxford Dictionary (edn 9) defines dictator as: *1 a ruler with (often usurped) unrestricted authority.*

2. Representative democracy is government by a collection of freely elected representatives of the people. In direct democracy the public participates directly in government, as in some ancient Greek city-states.

3. Fascism, according to Encyclopaedia Britannica Ready Reference 2003, is: *a philosophy of government that stresses the primacy and glory of the state, unquestioning obedience to its leader, subordination of the individual will to the state's authority, and harsh suppression of dissent.*

4. Monarchy is government led by a monarch, the Concise Oxford Dictionary (edn 9) defining monarch as: *a sovereign with the title of king, queen, emperor, empress, or the equivalent.* To this list *pharaoh* may be added for the case of ancient Egypt.

WordWeb 6 defines monarchy as: *An autocracy governed by a monarch who usually inherits the authority.*

5. Oligarchy is defined by Encyclopaedia Britannica Ready Reference 2003 as: *Rule by the few, often seen as having self-serving ends,* adding that: *Aristotle used the term pejoratively for unjust rule by bad men.*

Here the 'few' is unspecified in nature and more specific terms are:

(a) Aristocracy, according to the Concise Oxford Dictionary (edn 9) is:

1a the highest class in society; the nobility. **b** the nobility as a ruling class.

2a government by the nobility or a privileged group. **b** a state governed in this way.

(b) Plutocracy is defined by the Concise Oxford as:

1a government by the wealthy. **b** a state governed in this way.

2a wealthy elite or ruling class.

6. Theocracy is defined by Encyclopaedia Britannica Ready Reference 2003 as: *Government by those regarded as divinely guided. The government's leaders may be clergy, or that state's legal system may be based on religious laws. Theocratic rule was a constant of early civilizations. The enlightenment marked the end of theocracy in most Western countries. Present-day examples include Saudi Arabia, Iran, Afghanistan, and the Vatican.*

7. Totalitarianism is defined by the Concise Oxford as: ***adj.*** *of or relating to a centralized dictatorial form of government requiring complete subservience to the State.*

In relatively early history there were sometimes Priest-Kings, this being a form of theocracy relating back to the tribal witch doctors and shamans of primitive man.

Whatever form of leadership, however, mankind has throughout history continued to suffer dreadful spates of conflict and war, and almost invariably the blame for this must lie with the leaders for, of course, common man struggling to provide for his family, has little or no spare resources. To despicable leaders, however, the common working man is a *resource* to be used at their whim should they, yet again, find reason to engage in yet another war.

The Greek and Roman empires and war

As noted in Chapter 2, man's early civilizations were invariably at war, the early Greek and Roman Empires being perhaps the best examples as in these the king had the exclusive power to call the populace out to war.

As discussed in Chapter 4, Alexander the Great, regarded by many as one of the greatest generals in history, was almost always fighting one war or another in seeking to expand his empire.

There are few better examples of the absurd and underhand politics of war than that of Cleopatra's dealings with Rome. To save Egypt from annexation by Rome she bore a son to Julius Caesar, who supported her claim to the throne against her brother in 47BC. Mark Antony, by whom she had three children, restored to her portions of the old Ptolemaic Empire and gave their joint offspring parts of the Roman East in 34BC.

Eventually Marc Antony fell into disfavour in Rome and his and Cleopatra's combined forces suffered defeats by those of Octavius, he and later Cleopatra both committing suicide in 30BC.

The mighty Roman Empire always had trouble holding its borders in the West which lasted from 31BC to 476AD, but it lasted to 1453 in the East as the Byzantine Empire when the eastern capital Constantinople fell to the Ottoman Turks.

The long history of conflict associated with both the Greek and Roman empires is detailed in Chapter 4.

Europe's mad monarchs

Early man's tribes were led by chiefs, defined by the Concise Oxford Dictionary (edn 9) as: *1 a a leader or ruler. b the head of a tribe, clan, etc.*

Originally man's tribal leaders were the bravest, strongest and smartest.   With monarchy came the establishment of hereditary thrones which, thanks to the premature demise of the monarch, were often occupied by children who were advised by often untrustworthy people.

Worse still, many royal families married their own cousins and sometimes even their own sisters or brothers, perhaps seeking to ensure that they married royalty. The result was the odd half-witted monarch thanks to genetic defects.

The bottom line is, as Joy Masoff points out, that through history there have been many "cruddy kings, stupid shahs, evil emperors, and flat-out crazy Caesars" (Massof, 2006).

Thus in the time of Henry Tudor "one thing kings did back then was go to war. France and England were always at each other's throats" (Massof, 2006).

After a brief alliance with Francis, the French king, Henry signed a treaty with Charles V, ruler of the Holy Roman Empire which included what is now Germany, Switzerland, Hungary, Austria, and the Netherlands. Within a month England and France were at war and kept at it on and off for the next 200 years.

Indeed, for hundreds of years, some part of Europe has, more often than not been at war with another, culminating in WW1 and WW2, whilst more recently we saw war in the former Yugoslavia.

China

In 221BC, the king of Qin proclaimed himself Shihuangdi, or First Emperor of the Qin dynasty (221-206BC). The name China is derived from this dynasty (Encarta, 1999).

The First Emperor welded a loose configuration of quasi-feudal states into an administratively centralized and culturally unified empire. The hereditary aristocracies were abolished and their territories divided into provinces governed by bureaucrats appointed by the emperor.

The Qin capital, near the present-day city of Xi'an, became the first seat of imperial China. A standardized system of written characters was adopted, and its use was made compulsory throughout the empire.

The First Emperor also attempted to push the perimeter of Chinese civilization far beyond the outer boundaries of the Zhou dynasty (c. 1027-256BC), his armies marching south to the delta of the Red River, in what is now Vietnam. In the southwest the realm was extended to include most of the present-day provinces of Yunnan, Guizhou, and Sichuan. In the northwest his conquests reached as far as Lanzhou in present-day Gansu Province. In the northeast part of what today is Korea was added to the empire.

The centre of Chinese civilization, however, remained in the Huang He valley. Aside from the unification and expansion of China, the best-known achievement of the Qin was the completion of earthen fortifications that centuries later came to be known as the Great Wall.

The foreign conquests of the Qin and the wall building and other public works cost a great many lives and drained the public coffers.

The increasing burden of taxation, military service, and forced labour caused resentment against the Qin rule amongst the common people and finally rebellion resulted in the establishment of the Earlier Han Dynasty (206BC – 8AD) and by the middle of the 2nd century BC almost all Han territory was under direct imperial rule.

The Han established Confucianism as the official ideology, incorporating ideas from many other philosophical schools into it. In staffing the bureaucracy the Han emperors followed the Confucian principle of appointing men on the basis of merit rather than birth and written examinations were used to find the best people. In the late 2nd century BC an imperial university was established, in which prospective bureaucrats were trained in the five classics of the Confucian school (Encarta, 1999).

The power of the Earlier Han peaked under Emperor Wu Ti's reign (from 140 to 87 BC) and almost all of what today constitutes China was brought under imperial rule.

The short-lived Hsin Dynasty (AD 9-23) followed after a period of discontent. This was followed by the Later Han (25-220) which suffered considerable internal disunity and external rebellion from religious sects.

The Han Empire began to disintegrate as large landholding families established their own private armies. Finally, in 220 the son of Ts'ao Ts'ao seized the throne and established the Wei dynasty (220-264).

Soon other leaders with dynastic claims established three other kingdoms in regions of China and these waged incessant warfare against one another.

Many other dynasties were to follow but, typical of man's history, disunity and conflict reappeared periodically.

The Re-established Empire reunited China during the Sui dynasty (589-618). The brief Sui reign was a time of great activity. The Great Wall was repaired at an enormous cost in human life. A canal system, which later formed the Grand Canal, was built to carry the rich agricultural produce of the Yangtze delta to Luoyang and the north.

Under Sui rule Chinese control was reasserted over northern Vietnam and, to a limited degree, over the Central Asian tribes to the north and west. A prolonged and costly campaign against a kingdom in southern Manchuria and northern Korea, however, ended in defeat. With its prestige seriously tarnished and its population impoverished, the Sui dynasty fell in 618 to domestic rebels led by Li Yuan.

Founded by Li Yuan, the Tang dynasty (618-907) was an era of strength and brilliance unprecedented in the history of Chinese civilization. Its system of civil service examinations for recruitment of the bureaucracy was so well refined that its basic form survived into the 20th century. Under the Tang, Chinese influence was extended over Korea, southern Manchuria, and northern Vietnam. In the west, by means of alliances with Central Asian tribes, the Tang controlled the Tarim Pendi and eventually made their influence felt as far afield as present-day Afghanistan (Encarta, 1999).

Oligarchy

A democracy exits whenever those who are free and are not well-off, being in the majority, are in sovereign control of government, an oligarchy when control lies with the rich and better born. Aristotle, *The Politics* (343 BC).

The administration of the Roman Empire was largely oligarchical, the Senate being comprised of the wealthiest men in Rome who elected the emperor and charged him with the task of extending and defending the empire.

Indeed, from man's earliest tribal days there has always been a tendency for the strongest and thence more powerful to control the affairs of a tribe, town, city, or nation. Thus European kingdoms usually established an aristocracy to govern them, with the king as the head of state, an example being England's House of Lords.

In more recent times both the UK and USA are strongly oligarchical, a good example being the Trilateral Commission funded by David Rockefeller in the 1970s.

In 1975 it held a meeting of multinational corporate executives to consider the "excess of democracy" afflicting advanced capitalist countries and to "rationalize the US economy through capitalist dominated planning and in conjunction with other leading capitalist nations to reassert US authority on a world scale" (Crough et al., 1980).

In both the USA and UK big business largely runs the government, particularly their massive arms industries, the world's two biggest (Thomas, 2007).

Indeed, as discussed in Chapter 25, it was the fears of big business in the UK and US that led to the immensely prolonged and costly Cold War against the USSR, the immense stockpiles of nuclear and biochemical weapons, for example, helping to keep the barons of the arms industry filthy rich.

Conclusion

The Greek and Roman Empires were, it seems, at war as often as not, the same applying to some of the European states and empires of the last millennium, particularly England.

For over a thousand years China too had conflict as often as not, much of it a result of internal dissent, and its empire did not expand a great deal compared to that of Rome at its peak.

In much of this history one is tempted to associate the territorial ambitions of leaders with those of alpha males in the animal kingdom, and no better example of this might have been Alexander the Great (see Chapter 4).

Today still we still suffer bad and/or mad leaders and the oligarchies usually associated with them.

A case in point is the President of the USA who is chief of the army and has the sole power to kick start a nuclear war at the push of a button.

Indeed, no doubt influenced by the Rockefellers et al., the USA is still busy trying to be the 'world's only superpower' and exert that power, a history of mistaken and lost wars growing with every decade and including Korea, Vietnam, Iraq and now Afghanistan and resulting in the death of circa 10 million innocent civilians, a result even Hitler would not have dreamed of.

There is nothing very democratic about this.

We elect people with party power behind them, that being funded by large handouts from big business and the public purse. We do not elect the party leaders, however, and nor do we have any real say in policy.

Worse still, what little firm policy parties announce before an election is as likely as not to be changed within a few years, a good example being Australia's Prime Minister John Howard announcing before an election in the 1990s that he would never introduce a GST. Re-elected, he did just that within a few years.

As for war, normal adult people with families to care for want peace and enough money to get by on without too much suffering. Most of them dare not even dream of the prosperity that bullshit artist politicians so often talk of.

More importantly, normal sane people do not want to fight wars sometimes thousands of miles away from their homes, wars which only sent their nations 'broke' in the end in any case.

As we have already seen in only 3 chapters of this book, it seems that wars are usually in the interests of lousy leaders and their oligarchies rather than the populace, and this needs change. Indeed, it seems that this practice became something of a habit for national leaders thousands of years ago, one that to a large extent, at least, remains to the present day. What we need is for warring leaders to kill each other and leave it at that!

Chapter 4

EMPIRE BUILDING

> *An empire founded by war has to maintain itself by war.*
> Baron Montesquieu, Considérations sur les causes de la
> grandeur des Romains, et de leur dècadence (1734), ch. 8.

The Empires of Athens and Macedon

The first known European empires resulted from the unification of city-states in Greece to deal with invading Persians who were turned back in 480BC at the land battle of Thermopylae and the naval battle of Salamis. From 478BC the alliance was centred in Athens but the empire collapsed in the Peloponnesian Wars of 431-404BC when some of the city states rebelled against Athenian rule (Cowie et al., 1994).

Alexander ascended to the Macedonian throne in 336BC when his father was assassinated. A student of Aristotle, he quickly executed domestic opponents, quickly restored Macedonian rule to a rebellious Thessaly, and was elected by a congress of state at Corinth.

In 335BC he led a successful campaign against defecting Thracians, reaching as far as the Danube River.

On return to Greece he crushed threatening Illyrians in just a week. Then he took the revolting city of Thebes by storm, razed it, and took the 8,000 survivors prisoner as slaves.

In 334BC he went to war with Persia with an army of 35,000 Macedonians and Greeks and defeated an army of 40,000 Persians and Greek *hoplites* (mercenaries), legend having it that he lost only 110 men in the process. After this battle all the states of Asia Minor submitted to his authority.

In 333BC he defeated what legend has it was a huge Persian army led by Darius at Issus in north-eastern Syria, but Darius escaped, leaving his family behind.

After a 7 month siege he captured the strongly fortified seaport of Tyre, moving on to Gaza and then Egypt, gaining control of the entire eastern Mediterranean coastline.

In 332BC he founded the city of Alexandria at the mouth of the Nile River. Soon afterward Cyrene, the capital of the ancient North African kingdom of Cyrenaica, submitted to Alexander and he then extended his dominion to Carthaginian territory.

After a spell in Egypt he headed northward again towards Babylon with an army of 40,000 infantry and 7,000 cavalry. Crossing the Euphrates and Tigris he defeated another huge army led by Darius at the battle of Gaugamela on Oct. 1st, 331BC. Again Darius fled but was eventually assassinated by two of his generals.

Babylon surrendered after Gaugamela, and the city of Sûsa with its enormous treasures was soon conquered.

Then, in midwinter, Alexander forced his way to the Persian capital Persepolis and plundered and burned it, completing his destruction of the ancient Persian Empire.

Alexander's domain now extended along and beyond the southern shores of the Caspian Sea, including modern Afghanistan and Baluchistan, and northward into Central Asia. It took Alexander only three years, from the spring of 330BC to the spring of 327BC, to master this vast area.

In order to complete his conquest of the remnants of the Persian Empire, which had once included part of western India, Alexander crossed the Indus River in 326BC, and invaded the Punjab but then the Macedonians rebelled and refused to go further.

Alexander then constructed a fleet and passed down the Indus, reaching its mouth in September 325BC. The fleet then sailed to the Persian Gulf. With his army, he returned overland across the desert to Media. Shortages of food and water caused severe losses and hardship among his troops.

Alexander then spent about a year organizing his dominions and completing a survey of the Persian Gulf in preparation for further conquests but in June 323BC he contracted a fever and died, willing his empire "to the strongest," a testament that led to conflicts for 50 years.

The Roman Empire

The powerful city state of Rome's 'regal period' (753 - 510BC) was briefly outlined in Chapter 2.

In the period 510 – 264BC there were many administrative and social changes, the senate including both patricians and plebeians and electing two consuls as leaders with only a one-year term.

Rome had acquired leadership of Latium before the end of the regal period. Now the military policy became more aggressive and, assisted by their allies, the Romans fought wars against the Etruscans, the Volscians, and the Aequians. In 390BC the Romans were defeated by the Gauls at Allia and Rome was captured and burned.

Nevertheless, Rome continued to overtake Etruria and by the middle of the 4th century BC all southern Etruria was kept in check by Roman garrisons and denationalized by an influx of Roman colonists. Eventually the whole country was assimilated by the Romans circa 200BC (Encarta, 1999).

Victories over the Volscians, the Latins, and the Hernicans gave the Romans control of central Italy and brought them into conflict with the Samnites of southern Italy, who were defeated in a series of three wars, extending from 343 to 290BC. A revolt of the Latins and Volscians was put down and resistance elsewhere was also eventually overcome.

Circa 270BC the Romans completed their conquest of southern Italy and thus gained control of the entire peninsula as far north as the Arno and Rubicon rivers.

In 264BC Rome engaged in struggle with Carthage, the foremost maritime power in the world at that time, for control over the Mediterranean Sea.

In the First Punic War (264-261BC) Rome gained its first foreign possession, the Carthaginian part of Sicily, and Sardinia and Corsica were annexed soon after this.

Carthage responded by taking over part of Spain and using it as a military base.

In the Second Punic War (218 – 201BC) Hannibal crossed the alps and invaded Italy from the north and ravaged it for years but was recalled to fight Scipio Africanus, the Roman general who had invaded Carthage, and who defeated Hannibal at Zama in 202BC. Rome forced Carthage to cede Spain and its Mediterranean islands and pay a huge indemnity.

In the Third Punic War (149-146BC) the Romans, led by Scipio the Younger, captured the city of Carthage, razed it to the ground, and sold the surviving inhabitants into slavery.

Meanwhile, in the preceding years Rome had increased its holdings in Europe, Asia Minor and Greece.

After two wars with Macedonia, it was made a province in 146BC.

A series of Spanish campaigns ended with the capture of Numantia in 133 BC. In the same year Attalus III of Pergamum (in what is now western Turkey) died, ceding his kingdom to Rome, and soon after this the territory was formed into the province of Asia (Encarta, 1999).

By now Rome's power had spread from the Italian Peninsula to cover much of the world.

From 133 to 27BC there was much internal conflict as wealthy families sought to increase their power. In that period, however, Rome continued to gain more territory in Africa, Gaul and Northern Italy.

In 67BC Julius Caesar began to rise to prominence as leader of the popular party, becoming consul in 59BC. Given extensive military commands competition between he and other leaders led to a five-year civil war from which Caesar emerged victorious.

Conflict with his remaining political opponent, Pompey, continued for some time, however, but Caesar finally defeated him and was made dictator for life in 45BC, only to be assassinated a year later.

Further battles for control of Rome ensued, Octavian eventually becoming undisputed ruler of the Empire in 29BC.

The following 200 years were prosperous and Rome's empire expanded considerably, extending as far as Britain where in 122 Hadrian ordered construction of the wall named after him.

The years 193-476 were those of the decline and fall of the Western Roman Empire but Rome's influence continued from 330 until 1453 in the East as the Byzantine Empire when the eastern capital Constantinople fell to the Ottoman Turks.

The Vikings

The Vikings were pagan pirates, traders and settlers who between the late 8c and the mid-11c conquered and colonized large parts of Britain (Dublin, est. 831), Normandy (settled 911), and Russia (8c – 11c).

They also attacked Spain, Morocco and Italy; traded with Byzantium, Persia and India; and discovered and occupied Iceland (874) and Greenland (986). They also reached the coast of North America circa 1000 and led by Duke William of Normandy conquered England in 1066 (Chambers, 1993; World Almanac, 1998).

The Islamic Empire

The Islamic Empire that emerged in the 7th century AD derived its cohesion from a religious belief. Early in the 8th century BC Muslim forces occupied Spain and threatened France, being repulsed at Tours only 300 km from Paris (Cowie et al., 1994).

The Ottoman Empire was a dynastic state centred in what is now Turkey. It was founded circa 1300 in Asia Minor. Ottoman forces entered Europe in 1345, conquered Constantinople in 1453, and by 1520 controlled most of south-eastern Europe, including part of Hungary, the Middle East, and North Africa.

From this peak the Ottoman Empire was eroded by the ambitions of Russia and Austria in south-east Europe, the ambitions of France, Britain and Italy in North Africa, and the emergence of the Balkan nations.

By the early 1900s the Ottoman Empire only controlled Asia Minor (the Anatolia region of present-day Turkey) and parts of the Balkans and the Middle East.

The empire lost further territory during WW1 and was occupied by Allied troops until 1922. These were driven out by nationalist forces and the Republic of Turkey was proclaimed in 1923 (Chambers, 1993; Encarta, 1999).

The Aztecs and Incas

By 1519 the Aztecs had built a Meso-American empire with its capital in Tenochtitlán (founded 1325) the centre of a cult requiring enormous levels of human sacrifice

Most of the civilized areas of South America were ruled by the centralized Inca Empire (1476 – 1534) which extended from Ecuador to NW Argentina.

The Spanish Empire

Besets by revolts, the Aztec and Inca Empires fell to gold-seeking Spanish forces based in the Antilles and Panama, Cortez taking Mexico (1519-21), and Pizarro taking Peru (1532-35) and founding its capital Lima.

From these centres land and sea expeditions claimed most of North and South America for Spain, most Indians being reduced to poverty whilst their cultures were destroyed by Christian missionaries and the new upper class of whites and mestizos (World Almanac, 1998).

Spain overtook Portugal in 1580 but a national uprising began in 1640. This soon gained French naval and military support. In 1660 the marriage of Catherine of Braganza to Charles II of England ensured British help. After repeated failures by the Spanish to subdue the rebellion the Treaty of Lisbon (Feb. 1668) restored Portugal's independence.

The Spanish-American Wars of Independence (1810 – 1826) involved Venezuela, New Granada, Quito, Argentina, Chile and Peru. Peru was liberated in 1824 and the last Spanish garrisons surrendered to the patriots in 1826.

After the Spanish-American War of 1898 Spain lost the final remnants of its empire, Cuba, Puerto Rico and the Philippines, to the USA, signalling the emergence of the USA as an imperial power. The 'Disaster of 1898' triggered a protracted internal crisis that culminated in the fall of the monarchy in 1931 (Chambers, 1993).

The Portuguese Empire

The Portuguese reached Brazil by 1500 and settled after 1530. Portuguese explorers established a commercial empire in the Indian Ocean based on trade and war, rather than on taking large amounts of land and dominating its people. At first they had little competition because the Chinese called their fleets home and Indian and Arab ships did not carry guns.

By the early 16th century the Portuguese had established a string of strategic bases, including Hormuz at the tip of the Persian Gulf, Goa on the west coast of India, and the Straits of Molucca, the gateway between the Indian Ocean and the China Sea. From these bases the Portuguese controlled the sea-trade of the entire region and dominated the slave trade in the 16th century.

When larger European nations arrived in the area, however, Portuguese naval supremacy vanished.

The Dutch Empire

The urban Calvinist provinces of the northern Netherlands rebelled in 1568 against Hapsburg Spain and founded an oligarchic mercantile republic. After Spain absorbed Portugal in 1580, the Dutch seized Portuguese possessions and created a vast but generally short-lived empire in Brazil, the Antilles, Africa, India, Ceylon, Malacca, Indonesia and Taiwan.

Belgium gained its independence from the Netherlands in April 1839 after a revolution in 1830, followed by successful Dutch retaliation in 1831, and then an armed standoff and bitter negotiations for several years.

The French Empire

France founded permanent colonies in Canada (1608), the Caribbean (1626) and India (1674).

France's coastal blockade of Europe failed to neutralize Britain and Napoleon's 1812 invasion of Russia was a disaster. After his exile at Elba in 1814 his armies were defeated at Waterloo in 1815 by British and Prussian troops.

At the Congress of Vienna (Sept. 1814 – June 1815), the monarchs and princes of Europe revised their boundaries, Prussia making gains in Saxony and the Ruhr, Austria in Illyria and Venetia, Russia in Poland and Finland.

British conquest of Dutch and French colonies (South Africa, Ceylon and Mauritius) was recognized and France retained its expanded 1792 borders. This settlement gave Europe 50 years of peace.

After World War 2 former French colonies were reclassified as departments of France or overseas territories, most of which rapidly gained their independence in the following two decades.

China

The Great Wall of China was begun using 300,000 troops in 221BC during the Qin dynasty to repel attacks from northern nomads. It was improved during the Han (202BC – 220AD) and the Ming dynasties (1368 – 1644) and stretches 2150 miles from the Yellow Sea to the central Asian desert.

The Manchu invaded from the north-east in 1644 and created the Qing dynasty (1644 – 1912). This expanded Chinese control to its greatest extent in central and south-east Asia and established cautious diplomatic and trade contacts with Europe. It was overthrown by revolution.

Russia

Under Peter I (r 1682 – 1727) and Catherine II (r 1762 - 1796) Russia's borders continued to expand in all directions and trade and cultural contact with the West increased from the new Baltic Sea capital of St Petersburg (est. 1703).

Alaska was a Russian colony for 126 years until sold to the USA in 1867.

In 1898 Russia leased Port Arthur from China with the intention of making it the base of Russian naval power in the Pacific. Russia poured troops into Manchuria during the Boxer Uprising in 1900 but, faced with the Anglo-Japanese alliance of 1902, promised to leave Chinese territory.

The promise was not kept and in June 1903 Japan proposed an agreement with Russia recognizing Japan's interests in Korea and Russia's in Manchuria, and insuring the integrity of China and Korea.

Russia refused and on of February 8, 1904, the Japanese navy launched a surprise attack on Port Arthur and blockaded the damaged Russian fleet.

Hostilities continued for several months and, after Russian defeats at Shenyang and Tsushima, on September 5, 1905, the Treaty of Portsmouth was signed. Russia surrendered its lease to Liaoyang and Port Arthur, ceded the southern half of Sakhalin, evacuated Manchuria, and recognized Korea as a Japanese sphere of influence (Encarta, 1999).

African colonies

After 1880 the vast African interior was rapidly colonized by European nations and West African Muslim kingdoms (Fulani), Arab slave traders (Zanzibar) and Bantu confederations (Zulu) were subdued. Only Christian Ethiopia, which defeated Italy in 1896, and Liberia, resisted the invasion successfully.

The major beneficiaries were France (West Africa) and England ('Cape to Cape and the Boer War, 1899 – 1902).

The slave trade

The African and Caribbean colonies of several European nations developed a plantation economy where sugarcane, tobacco, cotton, coffee, rice, indigo and lumber were grown commercially by slaves.

The Portuguese dominated the slave trade in the 16th century, the Dutch in the early 17th, whilst the late 17th century was a period of intense competition between these two nations and the French, British, Danes and Swedes.

The trade peaked in the second half of the 18th century from which point the East African slave trade become predominant.

The British formally abolished the slave trade in 1807, and the institution of slavery in 1833. Then Britain formed Royal Navy anti-slavery squadrons on the west and east coasts of Africa.

The best estimates are that from circa 1650 to 1850 circa 12.5 million slaves were transported to work in the New World, this keeping the African population static for over two centuries (Chambers, 1993).

The Austro-Hungarian Empire

An agreement between the Habsburg Emperor of Austria, Francis Joseph I, and the Magyar rulers of the kingdom of Hungary, created the Austro-Hungarian Empire in 1867. The empire extended over more than 675,000 sq km in central Europe, and included Austria, Hungary, Slovakia, and the Czech Republic, as well as parts of present-day Poland, Romania, Italy, Slovenia, Croatia, Bosnia and Herzegovina, and the Federal Republic of Yugoslavia.

Austria-Hungary was regarded as a great European power along with France, Germany, Russia, and Britain, but the empire was ultimately destroyed by defeat in World War 1 (Encarta, 1999).

Hitler's Third Reich

Adolf Hitler rose from humble beginnings to leadership of the National Socialist German Worker's Party, or Nazi party, becoming Chancellor of Germany in 1933.

An ethnic German born in Austria, Hitler set about unifying Germany and Austria to form an empire he named *The Third Reich* by external pressure, eventually ordering his army to march into Austria, proclaiming the official union of Austria and Germany on March 12th 1938.

In 1936 he established the Rome-Berlin 'axis' with Mussolini, pursuing an aggressive foreign policy which resulted in Czechoslovakia ceding ethnic German parts of the country, particularly *The Sudetenland* in the west.

In March 1938 Hitler's forces occupied most of Czechoslovakia, breaking the Munich Pact.

Next they annexed part of Lithuania.

Offering Stalin a share of any conquests in Eastern Europe, on August 23rd 1939 Hitler signed a pact with the USSR ensuring that it would not stand in his way.

The invasion of Poland began on September 1st 1939, causing Britain and France to declare war on Germany and beginning World War 2.

Much of the terrible history of that war is well known, particularly the mass murder of millions of Jews by the Nazis, a process aided by IBM's German subsidiary Demohag, which collected data on Jewish families in Germany, and Du Pont, which made the Zyklon B gas used to kill them.

Like Napoleon before him, Hitler made the mistake of taking on Russia, the turning point being the prolonged Battle of Stalingrad during which the Russians dropped tularemia on the German Panzer divisions, the first large scale use of biological warfare in history.

The war was finally ended with the nuclear bombing of Hiroshima (Aug. 6) and Nagasaki (Aug. 9) in 1945.

The British Empire

British privateers such as Drake (1540 – 96) challenged Spanish control of the New World, establishing the North American colonies of Jamestown (1607) and Plymouth (1620), and penetrated Asian trade routes, taking Madras in 1639.

Britain founded colonies in the Caribbean and North America in the 17th century, losing the American colonies after the American War of Independence (1775 – 1783).

Much of India was conquered (1757 – 1857) and islands and trading posts were acquired from Aden to Hong Kong.

Settlements were established in Canada, Australia, New Zealand and the Cape in South Africa, each of which became 'dominions' in 1910.

Towards the end of the 19th century other 'dependent territories' were established in Africa such as Rhodesia.

In addition Britain also had an 'informal empire' over which it had considerable industrial and commercial influence, including parts of South America, the Middle East, the Persian Gulf and China.

After WW1 Britain, heavily in debt, could not control its extensive empire and the dominions gained effective independence in 1931.

After WW2 Britain had run up huge debts, much of this to the USA via lend-lease, and India gained independence in 1947, most of the rest of the empire was decolonized in the 1960s, whilst Rhodesia became independent in 1980.

The USA

After losing the Crimean war (1853 – 1856) against the British and French the Russian government thought it could no longer afford an American colony. Thus, in 1867 Alaska was sold to the USA for $7.2 million.

By winning the Spanish-American War of 1898 the USA gained control of Cuba, Puerto Rico and the Philippines.

Hawaii was also annexed by the USA in 1898.

Involved in allied victories in WW1 and WW2 the USA continued to grow in economic strength, power and influence to the point that the 20th century was called by many "The American Century."

Conclusions

According to Cowie et al. (1994):

The oldest and most repeated justification for imperial activity was the Christian mission to go into the world and preach the Gospel, bringing salvation to the 'heathen'. Early imperialist activities by the Spanish and Portuguese carried the pope's blessing for this endeavour.

Rudyard Kipling extolled the virtues of such imperialism as being a responsibility:

Take up the White Man's burden -
Send forth the best ye breed -
Go, bind your sons to exile
To serve your captive's need;
To wait in heavy harness,
On fluttered fold and wild -
Your new-caught, sullen peoples,
Half-devil and half-child.

R. Kipling, *Rudyard Kipling's Verse,* Inclusive edition. Hodder & Stoughton, London (1949) pp 371-372.

Indeed, Baden Powell, creator of the Boy Scouts movement, originally considered calling it *Young Knights of the Empire*, a good example of the imperialist and warmongering spirit of the UK at the time.

As noted in Chapter 1, early tribal man was influenced by religious superstitions which allowed leaders to declare other tribes 'heathen' and justify conflict.

According to World Almanac 1998, the notions of Kipling's "white man's burden" or a "civilizing mission" justified the European conquests of Africa.

The quotation that opens this chapter rings very true in the pages that follow it. That is, empire building requires war, in turn provoking opposition and thence further war.

Thus conflict seems to be a human habit, as with almost all other animal species (particularly if you call eating other animals a hostile act), and war comes with organization into misguided groups.

The difference with humans is that we are led like lemmings into one disaster after another by bullshit spouted by lousy leaders (Mohr, 2012a).

All too often these lousy leaders are none too clever, whilst some are quite clearly crazy, for example:

[1] Alexander the Great considered himself divine.

{2] Early in his reign Nero had a rival poisoned. In 59 he had his mother killed because she had criticized his mistress, who he later married, then killing his ex-wife. His second wife he kicked to death and then married another woman after killing her husband.

After a plot against Nero 18 of 41 Romans implicated in it perished, including his former tutor Seneca.

Eventually the Senate declared Nero a public enemy and he committed suicide.

[3] Some think Hitler contracted syphilis from a Jewish prostitute in WW1, in part explaining his hostility to the Jews (in addition to the centuries old prejudice against their proclivity for running pawnshops, banks etc.). Syphilis was relatively untreatable without antibiotics and Hitler was no doubt psychotic, a symptom of tertiary syphilis.

Part of the problem with lousy leaders may be Mohr's Law of Hierarchy (Mohr, 2014), that is, they do little real work, and thus have plenty of time to dream up stupid, if not disastrous ideas.

Another is that all too often government is oligarchical, never truer than today in such countries as the USA and UK where powerful industrialists, most notably in the arms industry, have great influence on policy.

Some effort to suggest solutions to our ongoing problems of overpopulation, bad government, and war will be made in the final chapter of this book.

Chapter 5

TRIBAL & TERRITORIAL CONFLICT

> *Altogether, national hatred is something peculiar.*
> *You will always find it strongest and most violent*
> *where there is the lowest degree of culture.*
> Johann Wolfgang von Goethe, quoted by Johann Peter Eckermann,
> *Conversations with Goethe,* Mar. 14, 1830.

Introduction

The best known studies of chimpanzees, with which we share 96% of our genes, were conducted by Jane Goodall and associates in the Gombe National Park on the edge of Lake Tanganyika in Tanzania (Goodall, 1971).

Ultimately, Goodall was quite disillusioned to find that *tribes* of chimps were led by an alpha male and would occasionally have small wars with neighbouring tribes, these resuming at intervals over periods of many years. She concluded that they were all too much like humans!

The first definition given by the 9th edition of the Concise Oxford Dictionary for tribe is: *a group of (esp. primitive) families or communities, linked by social, economic, religious, or blood ties, and usu. having a common culture and dialect and a recognized leader.*

The first use of the word *tribe* in English referred to the 12 tribes of the ancient Hebrews, 10 of which were named for the sons of Jacob, and 2 for sons of Jacob's son Joseph. After Israel was conquered by Assyria in 721BC only 2 tribes remained, the others being referred to by posterity as 'the 10 lost tribes of Israel'.

Early Greek and Roman tribes

In ancient Greece (circa 1200BC) tribes were distinct by location, dialect, and tradition, and included the Ionians, Dorians, Achaeans and Aetolians. In Attica in 508BC (the region in which Athens is now located) Cleisthenes replaced four Ionian tribes with 10 new ones, each named after a local hero. All 140 villages or demes were represented in The Council of Five Hundred or *Boule* according to their size. At first this council's main function was in dealing with two invasions of the new state, but it may have been the crude beginning of democracy.

The first Roman tribes were the Titienses, Ramnenses and Luceres. These were later replaced by 4 urban and 16 rural tribes, the number of the latter increasing to 35 by 241BC. Provincial communities and people granted Roman citizenship of the empire after 27BC were all enrolled in a particular tribe, these serving as units for the purposes of census taking, taxation, and military conscription.

The German tribes

The Germanic peoples originated at the beginning of the Bronze Age (circa 1800BC) from the mixing of Battle-Ax people from the Corded Ware Culture of middle Germany with the megalithic culture on the eastern North Sea coast.

They spread over southern Scandinavia and into Germany but during the Iron Age (which lasted until the Roman period) they were cut off from the Mediterranean by the Celts and Illyrians. Increasing population and worsening climate forced them further south and before 200BC Germanic tribes had reached the lower Danube.

Circa 110BC the Germanic Cimbri and Teutonic tribes combined to invade the Roman province of Transalpine Gaul and then defeated a Roman army sent to deal with them at the Battle of Arausio on Oct. 6th, 105BC. They were eventually defeated by the Romans in 101BC in the region of the Upper Po River.

Land-hungry German tribes continued to advance, however, but were stalled by Julius Caesar in 58BC after they had crossed the upper Rhine, and from about 70AD the Germans were pushed back. Eventually the Germans advanced again, by 150 threatening Italy itself.

The Goths reached the Black sea circa 200, plundering the Balkan Peninsula and Anatolia as far as Cyprus.

Circa 260 – 300 the Alemanni and Franks moved towards Gaul and Italy.

After 375 the Huns from central Asia also became a force competing for space in Europe but the German tribes continued to advance, crushing the Romans at Adrianople in 378, after which the Roman Empire began to shrink.

Finally, in 476 the German leader Odoacer deposed emperor Romulus Augustulus at Ravenna, ending the Western Roman Empire and becoming the first barbarian ruler of Italy.

Mongolian invasions

Born in 1162 into a clan that had a tradition of power and rule, Genghis Khan's success in tribal warfare resulted in him being made ruler of Mongolia. From 1207 to 1215 his armies probed deep into North China, taking the Chin capital Chung-tu (modern Peking). Then he moved westward, taking over Turkistan and then northern Iran.

Leaving his sons and generals to continue campaigns into Russia and Eastern Europe, Genghis Khan launched a successful campaign against the Hsi Hsia, a Tangut tribe near the northwest border of China but died during it.

India

Excavations place the Indus valley civilizations back at least 5,000 years. Sanskrit-speaking Aryan tribes invaded from the northwest circa 1500BC, merging with the inhabitants.

Asoka, the third Mauryan king of Magadha, ruled most of the Indian subcontinent in the 3rd century BC, establishing Buddhism as the main religion. Hinduism eventually revived, however, and predominated.

Arabs invaded the West and established a Muslim foothold in the 8th century, Turkish Muslims gaining control of North India by 1200.

Vasco de Gama established Portuguese trading posts circa 1500 and the Dutch also established a presence. The British gained trading concessions in 1609 and the East India Company eventually gained control of most of India.

The Americas

Families of Indians of the Americas joined to form local *bands* of 20 – 500 people, their size depending upon how many people the nearby area could support.

Tribes were a collection of bands in the same general area and there were hundreds of tribes in the Americas when Columbus arrived. Some tribes in North America joined in *federations*, it is thought to prevent inter-tribal conflict.

The Aztecs in Mexico and Incas in Peru were advanced civilizations that developed empires and systems of government. In Middle America large Mayan cities with tens of thousands of people ruled over the surrounding areas.

In the Indian Wars (1622 – 1890) Europeans invaded, conquered and settled the USA, the native Indian population being reduced from about 1 million at first contact to about 250,000 at the end of the 18th century (Chambers, 1993).

The Tasmanian aborigines

The Tasmanian aborigines had three groupings:

[1] The 'hearth group' of a husband and wife, their children, and other relatives that cooked and camped around a single fire.

[2] The 'band', a landowning group consisting of several hearth groups. Bands could allow or deny others from foraging in their territory.

[3] The 'tribe' of 250 to 700 people from bands with adjoining territories. There were nine Tasmanian tribes, each with their own language or dialect and cultures.

In 1768 Captain James Cook set out on a 3-year voyage that was to awake England's interest in Australia, and his further two voyages in the 1770s cemented that interest. With the invasion of white settlers from Britain, however, the Tasmanian aborigines were completely exterminated.

Palestine and Israel

According to Bell and Hall (1991):

It is also estimated that since World War 2 there has been 100 wars, fought in more than 60 countries or territories. During no year has there been less than four wars, and in some years as many as 18 wars have been fought.

Perhaps the best example of territorial conflict at present is the ongoing conflict between Israel and Palestine. The Palestinians do have great cause for grievance, Palestine having been mandated as a British protectorate which was then divided between Jordan and Israel. Subsequently Egypt, Jordan, Syria, Lebanon, Iraq and Saudi Arabia invaded but were repelled by the Jewish state which gained territory.

Separate armistices were signed with Arab nations in 1949, Jordan occupying the West Bank and Egypt occupying Gaza. Neither granted Palestinian autonomy.

Israel, with the brief help of British and French forces, invaded Egypt in 1956 after repeated terrorist attacks. A cease-fire was arranged by the UN on November 6th.

With the help of a UN Emergency Force an uneasy truce lasted until 1967 when the UN force withdrew at Egypt's demand. Egypt reoccupied the Gaza Strip and closed the Gulf of Aqaba to Israeli shipping.

On June 5th the 6-day war began and Israel took the Gaza Strip, the Sinai Peninsula to the Suez Canal, East Jerusalem, Syria's Golan Heights, and Jordan's West Bank.

Egypt and Syria attacked Israel on Oct. 6th 1973, this day being the major fast day of Yom Kippur, but were driven back by Israeli forces which crossed the Suez Canal.

Israel invaded Lebanon in 1978 after a Lebanese terrorist attack, withdrawing to be replaced by a 6,000 strong UN peace-keeping force.

In 1979, Israel and Egypt signed a formal peace treaty, ending 30 years of conflict.

In 1981 Israeli jets destroyed an Iraqi nuclear reactor near Baghdad, claiming it could have been used for nuclear weapons. In 1982 Israeli jets bombed PLO strongholds in Lebanon and invading Israeli forces encircled Beirut which was then evacuated after massive Israeli bombing of West Beirut.

During the Persian Gulf War of 1991 Iraq fired several scud missiles at Israel.

After decades of conflict peace talks with the PLO resulted in historic agreements but the conflict continues with talk by the US of a "two state solution" making no progress:

[1] Israel invaded Gaza in 2008.

[2] Hamas continued to fire rockets from Gaza into Israel, some landing close to Israel's central city of Tel Aviv in 2012.

[3] Israel continues to build housing in the West Bank, despite growing international opposition.

A 2015 UN report said that, after 3 wars in 3 years between Israel and the Palestinians, and with half a million people displaced in 2014, Gaza would be "uninhabitable" by 2020.

Conclusions

It is, perhaps, natural for people that live in a relatively small tribe to regard any outsiders as a threat should they trespass into the relatively small territory that the tribe regards as its own. In the case of primitive tribes such trespass is quite likely to be for the purpose of hunting and gathering foods that the local tribe believes it has a sole right to. Notably, by custom Tasmanian aborigine bands were able to deny outsiders right of access to their territory and, no doubt, those that broke such agreements risked sparking conflict.

Some cultures developed the habit of conflict and conquest and became more aggressive than others, so that acquisition of new territory as the population expanded became something of a habit, each new leader striving to live up to or exceed his predecessor's record of conquest.

Such behaviour undoubtedly relates to the alpha-male behaviour of several animal species, in the case of humans this exhibiting as type A personality.

Type A personality is a cluster of traits including ambition, impatience, competitiveness, and hostility. Only some type A's are abnormally hostile and it is this trait that is harmful to the health of all concerned, hostile people being more prone to CHD, whilst the health of the victims of their hostility is often imperilled also (Larsen & Buss, 2002).

From our early hunter-gatherer days humans have not ventured far without carrying tools and weapons for gathering and hunting. Other tribes on seeing strangers with weapons might, of course, fear conflict.

Once a history of conflict has been established, however, conflict seems to become something of a habit or 'practice' that tribes might use to gain new territory to house and feed rapidly expanding populations.

Chapter 6

IMPERIAL POSSESSION & CONFLICT

> *It has been a characteristic of collective human activity for centuries
> that one group attempts to dominate another. When the area of
> domination is large enough it may be called an 'empire'.
> The act of setting up an empire is called 'imperialism'.*
> Cowie HR, Collins MB, Ryan DB, *Imperialism, Racism and
> Re-Assessments*, Nelson, Melbourne (1994).
>
> *No body can be healthful without exercise,
> neither natural body or politic; and certainly to a kingdom
> or estate, a just and honourable war is the true exercise.*
> Sir Francis Bacon,
> "Of the True Greatness of Kingdoms and Estates", *Essays* (1625).

Introduction

Some of man's long history of Imperial possession and
conflict has already been described in Chapters 3 and 4,
including the exploits of Alexander the Great, the Roman
Empire, Ottoman Empire, the Spanish and Portuguese Empires,
the Dutch and French Empires, the Austro-Hungarian Empire,
Hitler's Third Reich, and the British Empire.

In the present chapter discussion will concentrate upon
European imperialism in the 'Age of Discovery' and subsequent
developments that still affect us today.

The Crusades and the Renaissance

Muslim invaders captured large areas of land at the eastern end of the Mediterranean Sea between the 8th and 15th centuries BC, including Jerusalem and the surrounding 'Holy Lands.' In 1095 the emperor of the Eastern Roman or Byzantine Empire appealed to the Pope for help to repel the Islamic threat. The result was a series of crusades over the next 200 years and these are discussed further in the following chapter.

The crusades, though launched for religious reasons, generated a lucrative trade in silks, spices, and elaborate carpets. The exchange of peoples, products and ideas that this trade generated encouraged a wider view of the world than the feudal way of life that had prevailed for a thousand years. Thus a new desire for knowledge emerged, one focus of it being the civilizations of ancient Greece and Rome, bringing Europe out of the Middle Ages and into the Renaissance (14th century to circa 1650).

Islamic control over the eastern Mediterranean greatly inhibited overland trade with Asia. Portugal and Spain and had gained little from this trade and in the period 1480-1530 their monarchs sponsored numerous expeditions seeking sea routes to India and China for the purposes of trade (Cowie et al., 1994).

The results changed history:
➢ In 1487 Bartholomew Diaz found and named the Cape of Good Hope at the 'bottom' of Africa.
➢ In 1492 Columbus sailed Westward across the Atlantic to discover the Americas for Spain.
➢ In 1498 Vasco da Gama sailed to India.
➢ In 1521 Magellan claimed the Philippines for Spain, naming it after his king, and then completed a circumnavigation of the globe in 1522.

In the 'Age of Discovery' that followed Europe rapidly discovered and colonized huge areas of the world.

Motives for European Imperialism

Motives for acquiring new colonies included importing silks, spices and Chinese porcelain to sell for profit, and obtaining new sources of raw materials and precious metals. Soon, however, overseas colonies became large markets for goods made in the 'home' nations.

European monarchs also 'claimed' to be ruled by 'divine right' and that their principal motives for colonization where to bring 'faith' to the 'heathen' peoples of the world:

Look at him well. This is a heathen; a being condemned to eternal flame unless you help him
Don't think we are merely going to destroy his people and lift their wealth. We are going to take from them what they don't value and give them instead the priceless mercy of heaven.
P. Shaffer, *The Royal Hunt of the Sun*, p. 5,
Hamish Hamilton, London (1964).

Imperialist expansion was also a demonstration of relative strength and thus status of rival nations and the kings of Spain and Portugal believed that their empires increased their prestige (Cowie et al, 1994).

Colonies also had many other important uses:

[1] As settlements for people from the crowded inner areas of major European cities.

[2] As plantation colonies for which purpose sometimes both the crop and the labour were imported from another area, an example being the sugar and tobacco plantations in the West Indies for which slaves were imported from Africa.

[3] As trading posts.

[4] As military bases from which a large surrounding area could be kept under control.

The British raj in India

After the arrival of Vasco da Gama in India in 1498, the Portuguese, and then the Dutch, French and British established trading bases there. After many years of rivalry between these powers the British established military and commercial supremacy and dominated India for almost 200 years (1757 – 1947).

The British East India Company, founded in 1600 and revived in 1702, gradually grew but was in competition with the Portuguese, French and Dutch.

British domination in India can be dated from 1757, when the British army seized the French settlements in Bengal and defeated the opposing army of the Nawab Suraj-ud-Daulah in the Battle of Plassey. By 1772 Bengal was under British control.

The British East India Company gradually expanded its influence, forcing the British Government to appoint a governor-general to take partial control over it.

Missionaries entered the region with government support, schools were opened, English was encouraged as the official language, and improved communications and irrigation were developed.

In 1857 Muslim and Hindu soldiers in the East India Company mutinied against the aloof and rigid discipline of English officers who ignored caste rules. This forced the British Government to take full control in 1858, but relations between the two peoples were irreparably damaged.

In 1885 the Indian National Congress was formed as a forum in which people could vent their grievances and suggest reforms. Subsequently, a more assertive branch of this movement was formed which demanded that Britain should "quit India" (Cowie, at al., 1994).

At the time of Queen Victoria's Diamond Jubilee celebrations in 1897 the British Empire was the world's largest, covering approximately a quarter of the globe, and a quarter of its people (Cowie et al., 1994).

India was an 'empire within an empire', being said to be over twice the size of the Roman Empire at its peak and having a population of 300 million.

In 1906 Indian Muslims formed the All India Muslim League, turning the religious division in India into a political one.

In 1909 educated Indians were allowed to elect representatives to advisory provincial councils, and Indian representatives were allowed to sit on executive councils in both the provinces and the capital. These reforms were widely interpreted as "window dressing" (Cowie et al, 1994).

During WW1 the Indian army grew to 1.2 million, more than half of that number serving overseas. Many British troops and officials left India during WW1, however, resulting in increased Indian participation in the civil service and strengthening claims for self-government.

In April 1919 a British general ordered his troops to fire at unarmed anti-British demonstrators in Amritsar in the Punjab province, killing 379 and wounding 1200.

In December 1919 the British Parliament passed the Government of India Act which introduced a system of government called a 'dyarchy' which gave control of such departments as education, health, agriculture and public works to Indian cabinet ministers. The central government, however, retained control of the key areas of law and order and finance.

Between 1919 and 1945 there were many conflicts and negotiations. In 1931 Gandhi represented the Indian Congress Party at a conference in London.

In 1935 the British Parliament passed the Government of India Act which gave self-government in the provinces but not full dominion status at federal level, defence and external affairs remaining under the control of the British-appointed viceroy.

In 1941 a small volunteer force called the Indian National Army was formed to help the Japanese drive the British out of India.

In 1942 Britain promised India self-government in return for co-operation in the war effort. The Indian Congress Party, however, claimed that the presence of British forces made Japanese invasion more likely and repeated 'quit India' demands. Anti-British riots broke out and 1000 Indians were killed, 1600 injured, and 14,000 people were imprisoned, including Gandhi and other Indian leaders.

Finally, in 1947 India was granted independence with Pakistan partitioned off as a separate and independent Islamic state. This caused a mass exodus of Hindus leaving Pakistan, and Muslims leaving India, and it is believed that at least 500,000 people died in the resulting riots and conflicts (Cowie et al., 1994).

Benefits of European Imperialism

Some Asian societies were unified by new European-generated activities, a common currency, a common language of commerce (for example English in India or French in Indo-China), and a coordinated railway system.

Some Asian countries, particularly Japan, saw a need to improve their economies using Western production and marketing methods. Japan grew in strength and, in part thanks to an alliance with England, had major naval victories over Tsarist Russia in 1904-5, thus gaining much additional territory.

Most colonized peoples resented European intrusion, and could not accept European customs and religious beliefs. Thus it was inevitable that they would eventually seek their own national identity and independence.

Many of the former Asian colonies of European powers that eventually obtained their independence have been able to function as separate nations because of their adoption of European technology and the European style of centralized administration that their nationalist leaders used to criticize.

India gained much from British rule, including unification of the country, a British form of government, and an efficient civil service. One of the world's largest railway networks had been built, along with many dams and irrigation works, transforming agriculture from a subsistence level to a commercial scale.

Having been largely tribal, few of the African civilizations were coordinated enough to resist Western colonization. After World War 2, however, the African colonies gradually gained independence peacefully but since then there have been many national and international conflicts in Africa, much of which is still considered to be part of the impoverished 'Third World'.

In the twentieth century the expansion of the USSR as a result of World War 2 was an imperialist act of major proportions and this and the decades of 'Cold War' that followed are discussed in Chapter 20.

Conclusions

Initially, at least, many of the peoples of colonized countries accepted their fate quietly, perhaps hoping for greater prosperity.

The greed and vanity of the imperialists, however, was excessive to the point of insanity (Panniker, 1959):

[An] ... aspect of British authority in India at this period was the conviction held by every European in India of enduring racial superiority. Seton Kerr, a Foreign Secretary of the Government, explained it was "the cherished conviction of every Englishman in India ... that he belongs to a race whom God has destined to govern and subdue".

The sheer arrogance and assertiveness of British rule was one reason for discontent in India, another, no doubt, the perception that the British were simply taking advantage of the country to increase their own power and wealth. The will of Indians to retain their own identity, culture and religion was also a motivating force, a tragic example of the latter being the great loss of life during the mass migrations after the partition of Pakistan.

With the dawn of the 20th century several countries began to strive for independence, encouraged perhaps by the final demise of the Spanish Empire in the Spanish-American War of 1898.

After India gained independence in 1947 a series of colonies in Africa gained independence in the 1950s and 1960s.

Thus, one by one the world's colonies have disappeared and only a few remain, and those largely small and in name only.

Now, indeed, the world's populations have intermingled to a significant extent, for example many native people from countries once colonized by Europe escaping from bad governments and conflict to live in Europe.

Hopefully, therefore, the multicultural societies that result will be stable ones and freer from internal and external conflict than in the past.

Chapter 7

RELIGIOUS CONFLICT

The Jews

Nomadic *Hebrew* tribes lived in the eastern Mediterranean area before 1300BC and circa 1020BC they conquered Canaan or ancient Palestine. They united under King Saul as a nation which included present-day Israel and parts of Jordan and Syria, but the nation was fraught with conflicts among its states.

After King Solomon's death in 922BC the nation was divided into the kingdoms of *Israel* (in the north, Samaria being founded in 870BC as its capital), and Judah (in the south and including Jerusalem). The kingdom of Israel was destroyed by the Assyrians in 734BC. In 721BC they annexed Judah but it retained nominal independence for the next 135 years.

The word Jew comes from the Hebrew *yehudhi,* meaning a member of the ancient Hebrew tribe of Judah, the ancient territory that became the Roman province of Judaea in AD6. The English word Jew is derived directly from the Latin *Judaeus,* meaning an inhabitant of Judea.

In 597BC Nebuchadnezzar II captured Jerusalem and Jewish nobles, warriors and artisans were deported to Babylon. Troubled by revolts in Babylonia (594BC) and Judah (588-587BC) Nebuchadnezzar destroyed Jerusalem and many more Israelites were deported to Babylonia in 586BC, many others fleeing to Egypt. Thus many Jews become part of the Diaspora, those Jews dispersed among nations outside Palestine

Persia conquered Babylonia in 539BC and, though the majority of the Jews living in Babylonia remained, many did return from exile to Palestine.

It was not until 168BC, however, that an independent Jewish kingdom was revived. Rome took control of this in the next century, suppressing Jewish revolts in AD70 and AD135.

In 1948 the modern state of Israel was established and the conflict-ridden history of this is outlined in Chapter 15.

Zoroastrianism

Zoroastrianism originated in Iran in the 6th century BC and was based on the teachings of Zoraster which accepted one supreme god, Ahura Mazda. This religion included an initiation ceremony, fire worship, rituals of purification to ward off evil spirits, and sacrifice of the sacred liquor haoma accompanied by recitation of large parts of the primary scripture, the Avesta.

The city of Rhagae (near Tehran) dates from the 3rd millennium BC and from the 3rd to 7th centuries AD it was a centre of Zoroastrianism. It was captured by the Muslims in 641 and followers of Zoroastrianism were persecuted in the 8th to 10th centuries, some migrating from Iran to India.

Islam

The Shiites were supporters of the 4th caliph Ali and when he was assassinated in 661 they claimed that only the descendants of Ali and his wife, Fatima, Muhammad's daughter, were entitled to rule the Muslim community.

During the early centuries of Islam, the Shiites, politically defeated and persecuted, became an underground movement. Shiites pay the tax called zakat (originally levied by Muhammad to help the poor and later levied by Muslim states) to their religious leaders rather than to state authorities. As a result, many Shiite leaders in Iran and Iraq have immense wealth and property.

During the 10th and 11th centuries, Shia Islam had a large following throughout the Middle East, but the spread of the popular mystical movement known as Sufism seems to have greatly diminished its strength.

At present Shiites are in the majority in Iran, and large numbers are found in Iraq, Syria, Lebanon, India, Pakistan, and parts of Central Asia, their total number exceeding 165 million.

The Sunnites constitute the vast majority of the world Islamic community. The doctrines and theology of the Sunnites were developed toward the end of the 9th century, and their theology was developed as a complete system during the 10th century.

Despite appeals from some Shiite leaders for rapprochement and solidarity with Sunni Islam, there has been considerable conflict between the two factions of Islam in recent decades, particularly in Iraq where it is ongoing on an almost daily basis.

Islamic Jihad has always been heavily focussed against Christianity. In the first century of Islam, 3,200 churches were destroyed or converted into mosques (Hammond, 2010).

In recent decades there has also been a spate of terrorist attacks against the West committed by Muslim extremist groups.

Regional Italian conflicts

Alboin became chief of the Lombards in 565, when the tribe lived in the region between the Danube River and the head of the Adriatic Sea. Three years later, with the assistance of the Avars, Alboin defeated the Germanic people known as the Gepidae. Then Alboin led the Lombards and 20,000 Saxons across the Alps into northern Italy and established the kingdom of Lombardy in the valley of the Po River, with Pavia as its capital.

When Albroin died in 572 separate bands united under regional leaders called 'duces'. The Lombards, like the Goths, followed the heretical creed Arianism which held that Christ was fully human and not divine, and were thus always in conflict with the native Italians.

The Lombard king Agiluf (r. 590-615) converted to orthodox Christianity which reduced conflict. Then the Lombards, seeking to increase their power, began to threaten Rome. In 754 Pope Stephen II sought help from the Franks and in 774 Charlemagne defeated the Lombards and deposed their last king. In 800 he was crowned emperor of the West by Pope Leo III.

When the Saracens took Sicily and threatened Rome in the 9th century Charlemagne's great-grandson, King Louis II, held them back. After Louis died Muslims overran southern Italy, forcing the popes to pay tribute.

The Crusades

The First Crusade was proclaimed by Pope Urban II in 1095 to assist the Byzantine emperor deal with territorial threats by the Turks. It defeated the Turks at Dorylaeum in 1097, established a foothold in northern Syria at Antioch in 1098, and liberated Jerusalem from Muslim control in 1099 (Chambers, 1993).

The Second Crusade was proclaimed by Pope Eugenius III in 1147 in response to the capture of Edessa in 1144 by the Turks but was a failure.

The Third Crusade was proclaimed by Pope Gregory VIII in 1189 after Saladin had captured Jerusalem in 1187. It was led by Frederick I of the Holy Roman Empire, Phillip II of France, and Richard I, 'the Lionheart'. It failed to regain Jerusalem but Richard negotiated a compromise allowing pilgrimage to the Holy Places.

The Fourth Crusade was proclaimed by Innocent IV in 1202 but was directed by Venetian interests to take Dalmatia and then Constantinople, and its original objectives were ignored.

Later Crusades were directed mostly at Egypt and North Africa. The 5th captured Damietta in 1219, and the 7th captured it again in 1249, but both crusades stalled in the Nile Delta. The 8th Crusade (1270-2) succeeded only in establishing treaties with the Mamluks in Egypt, and with Tunis. The 6th Crusade gained control of Jerusalem from 1229 until 1244, when the Latin forces were defeated by a joint Egyptian and Khwarizmian army, Latin forces finally being driven out of the Holy Land in 1291 (Chambers, 1993).

The Spanish Inquisition

The Spanish Inquisition was ordered by papal bull in 1478 to force Jewish and Muslim minorities to accept the Catholic faith. Between 1500 and 1526 fourteen permanent tribunals were established, two more being established in 1574 and 1640.

In the first 10 years 2,000 people were burnt and 15,000 others punished.

A further papal bull in 1547 saw the inquisition extended to Portugal, and then Brazil.

The Spanish Inquisition was established in Peru in 1570 and in Mexico in 1571. It was finally abolished in 1834.

The Reformation

The Protestant Reformation of Europe in the 16th century swept Europe, the seeds of discontent that led to it having been sown much earlier. The 14th-century English reformer John Wycliffe attacked the papacy itself, objecting to the sale of indulgences and questioning the moral and intellectual standards of ordained priests.

His teachings found an advocate in the religious reformer John Huss in Bohemia. The execution of Huss as a heretic in 1415 sparked the Hussite Wars, a violent expression of Bohemian nationalism, a precursor to religious civil war in Germany in Luther's time.

In France in 1516 a concordat between the king and the pope placed the French church substantially under royal authority. Earlier concordats with other national monarchies also prepared the way for the rise of autonomous national churches.

The Protestant revolution was initiated in Germany when Luther published 95 theses challenging the practice of indulgences in 1517. After publicly burning a papal decree ordering him to recant Luther went into hiding for a year but continued circulating pamphlets and translated the New Testament into German.

When Luther re-emerged he became a revolutionary leader able to exploit the religious and economic divide that had developed in Germany. The Peasant's War, inspired by Luther's teachings, began in 1524. Luther disapproved of the violence and the peasants were defeated in 1525.

A number of attempts at reconciling the Catholic and opposing views were made. When the Lutherans protested against the Catholics revoking an agreement the term 'Protestant' came into usage.

In 1530 the German religious reformer Melanchthon drew up a conciliatory statement of the Lutheran tenets, known as the Augsburg Confession, which was submitted to Emperor Charles V and to the Roman Catholic faction.

Although the Augsburg Confession failed to reconcile the differences between Roman Catholics and Lutherans, it remained the basis of the new Lutheran church and creed.

In 1546 the German emperor, in alliance with the pope and the Duke of Saxony, made war against the Schmalkaldic League, an association of Protestant princes. The Roman Catholic forces were successful at first but eventually the emperor had to end the religious civil war with the Peace of Augsburg in 1555.

Its terms allowed the rulers of the 300 German states to choose between Roman Catholicism and Lutheranism and enforce the chosen faith upon the ruler's subjects.

Lutheranism, by then the religion of about half the population of Germany, had spread to Scandinavia and became the state religion of Sweden in 1529, whilst in 1536 Denmark abolished Roman Catholic authority throughout its territories, then including Norway and Iceland.

In Switzerland Huldrich Zwingli became known in 1518 for denouncing the sale of indulgences. Like Luther, he considered the Bible the sole source of moral authority and strove to eliminate everything in the Roman Catholic system not in accordance with the Scriptures. In Zurich from 1523 to 1525 Zwingli lead people in burning religious relics.

As in Germany, the government was unable to prevent civil war and two short-lived conflicts broke out between Protestant and Roman Catholic regions in 1529 and 1531, Zwingli being killed in the second of these. Peace was restored when each region was allowed to choose its own religion, Roman Catholicism prevailing in the mountain regions and Protestantism in the valleys and cities, much the same situation persevering to this day.

In the generation after Luther and Zwingli French-born Calvin was even stricter in his beliefs and under his regime in Switzerland nonconformists were persecuted and even executed. He established a University in Geneva and his influence extended to France, the Spanish Netherlands, and Scotland.

The Reformation in France was led by Lefèvre d'Étaples who in 1523 translated the New Testament into French but he was soon regarded by the authorities as a radical and he and his followers were persecuted, many fleeing to Switzerland. By 1567 more than 120 pastors trained in Geneva by Calvin had returned to France to establish Protestant churches whose members were known as Huguenots.

The division of France into Protestant and Roman Catholic factions led to a series local conflicts and civil wars which were ended by the Edict of Nantes (1598). As over 90% of the French population remained Catholic, however, Protestant influence in France remained limited.

Most of the Dutch embraced Calvinism, which served as a potent bond in their nationalistic struggle against their Spanish Roman Catholic overlords. They revolted in 1568 and warfare continued until 1648, when Spain relinquished its claim to the country and the former Spanish Netherlands then became an independent Protestant nation.

In 1560 John Knox persuaded the Scottish Parliament to adopt a confession of faith and book of discipline modelled on those in use at Geneva. The Parliament subsequently created the Scottish Presbyterian church. The Roman Catholic Mary, Queen of Scots, attempted to overthrow the new Protestant church, but after a 7-year struggle, she was forced to leave the country.

In England Henry VIII was in dispute with the pope over his refusal to annul his first marriage to the childless Catherine. He sought opinions on the dispute from major European universities, eight of which supported his views.

Henry married Anne Boleyn in 1533 and two months later had the Archbishop of Canterbury declare his marriage to Catherine void. He was then excommunicated by the pope but retaliated by having Parliament pass an act appointing he and his successors head of the Church of England. Between 1536 and 1539 the monasteries were suppressed and their property seized.

Subsequently many Lutherans were burned as heretics and Roman Catholics who refused to recognize the king's leadership of the church were executed. Eventually, however, the Anglican Church adopted Protestant views.

Later Mary I attempted to restore Roman Catholicism as the state religion, and during her reign many Protestants were burned at the stake. A settlement was reached under Queen Elizabeth I in 1563 and Protestantism was restored, and Roman Catholics were often persecuted.

Europe's 30-year war (1618-1648)

The religious hatreds that flared into the Thirty Years' War had smouldered for more than half a century, in part because of the weaknesses of the 1555 Peace of Augsburg agreement between the Holy Roman emperor and the Lutheran princes of Germany. The result was a struggle between the Hapsburg-controlled Holy Roman Empire and the Protestant municipalities which spread to involve most of Western Europe. The war, one of the most destructive conflicts in European history, had four main phases:

1618-25: The Palatine-Bohemian conflict in which Protestant forces initially had the upper hand. Then, in part because of dissention amongst the Protestant forces, the pro-Catholic forces were ultimately victorious.

1625-29: The king of Denmark and Norway came to the aid of the German Protestants, in part wishing to end Hapsburg control of the Danish duchy of Holstein, Germany. Again the Protestants were defeated and Denmark had to give up small landholdings in Germany.

1630-35: Having earlier been asked for support by the North-German Protestants, the Swedish king, encouraged by a promise of French support, landed a well-trained army on the coast of Pomerania in 1630. While he was waiting for support from Brandenburg, Pomerania and Saxony to materialize, however, pro-Catholic forces captured and sacked the city of Magdeburg in 1631, after which Protestant inhabitants were massacred.

The Swedes then defeated the Catholic forces in three successive battles and moved into southern Germany for the winter. In 1632 they captured Munich. Further battles followed but ultimately the Protestant coalition abandoned its struggle and the Peace of Prague ended the third phase of the 30-year war.

1635-48: In 1635 France declared war against Spain, the chief Habsburg dominion aside from Austria, and allied with Sweden and German Protestant leaders, defeated a combined force of Saxons and Austrians at Wittstock, 93km northwest of Berlin, in 1636. The Habsburg position in Germany was further weakened by a defeat inflicted at Rheinfelden on the Swiss-German border in 1638.

After these setbacks the imperial armies were forced to surrender their European strongholds one after another. Between 1642 and 1645 the Swedes had numerous triumphs, overrunning Denmark, which had become allied with the empire, and ravaging large sections of western Germany and Austria.

In the west the French routed a Spanish army at Rocroi, France, in 1643. They were then defeated at Tuttlingen, Germany, but thereafter the French gained the upper hand, routing a Bavarian army at Freiburg in 1644, and an Austro-Bavarian army near Nördlingen in 1645. After central Bavaria was invaded, however, Bavaria agreed to a truce with Sweden and France in 1647.

Despite this, fighting continued in Germany, Luxembourg, the Low Countries, Italy, and Spain throughout the remainder of 1647. After further defeats, the Holy Roman Emperor signed the Peace of Westphalia agreement on Oct. 14, 1648. This established Switzerland and the Dutch Republic (the Netherlands) as independent states, gravely weakened the Holy Roman Empire and the Habsburgs, ensured the emergence of France as the chief power on the Continent, and disastrously retarded the political unification of Germany, the population of which had fallen by 20%.

Conclusions

It is clear that the greed, vanity and incompetence of religious leaders is often as great as that of political leaders. Thus they too have also sought wider influence and thus greater power, often resulting in conflict

All too often, however, the brainwashed masses believe in their propaganda and lies and follow their misguided policies blindly and enjoin in conflicts that arise from them.

Large, advanced societies, of course, require control and thence leaders, and from man's tribal days religious leaders have had great influence.

Throughout history many of them, like political leaders, have also indulged in ambitious and driven type A personality behaviours in seeking wider influence and thus greater power, all too often resulting in conflict, sometimes on a grand scale. Such people are undoubtedly psychopathic, the pathology of their condition including aggression, lying and cheating.

Religion has always been seen as a major difference between people, even when they only belong to different sects of the same religion. This was particularly true in the past when religious rites and prayer simply helped pass time, but is less true in modern societies where radio, TV, fast travel, phones, the Internet etcetera leave much less time for religion, if any, for most people in the West.

Religions insist their creed is 'right' and to break its rules is evil. Thus 'non-believers' can be regarded as evil, encouraging religious prejudice and conflict. Religious leaders too can be ambitious type A personality people and thus throughout history have often encouraged conflict.

7. Religious Conflict

Chapter 8

ETHNIC CONFLICT

Introduction

Ethnic discrimination, exploitation, and conflict have occurred throughout history. As noted in earlier chapters, there were centuries of exploitation of the peoples in the many Western colonies throughout much of the world, and ethnic conflict inevitably occurred frequently as a result.

As for more recent times, one study identified 58 ethnic civil wars between 1945 and 1999, these being 51% of the total number of civil wars (Caselli & Coleman, 2012).

Encyclopaedia Britannica Ready Reference 2003 defines *ethnic group* as: *Social group or category of the population that in a larger society is set apart and bound together by common ties of race, language, nationality, or culture.*

Macquarie dictionary's (1991) entry for *ethnocentrism* is: *the belief in the inherent superiority of one's own group and culture accompanied by a feeling of contempt for other groups and cultures.*

The third edition of the Shorter Oxford Dictionary defines *ethnomaniac* as: *one who is crazy about racial autonomy.*

The seventh edition of the Concise Oxford Dictionary defines *ethnic cleansing* as: *the mass expulsion or extermination of people from opposing ethnic or religious groups within a certain area.*

In the present chapter, therefore, discussion of ethnic conflict includes 'racial conflict'.

The Boer War

Throughout the 19th century ill feeling mounted between the Boers, Dutch-descended Afrikaners, and British settlers, resulting in the Afrikaner migration called the Great Trek (1835-1843) and the establishment of the Afrikaner republics Orange Free State and Transvaal (which became 'The South African Republic').

The discovery of gold in southern Transvaal in 1884 lured thousands of British prospectors to the area. The Afrikaners resented the newcomers or Uitlanders (foreigners) and taxed them heavily and denied them voting rights. The resentment on both sides grew, ultimately leading to a failed British-supported revolt by the Uitlanders against the Afrikaner government in 1885.

When the British refused to remove troops from border regions in 1889 the Orange Free State declared war and the Boers invaded Natal and Cape Colony, winning three battles in December. The British recovered and won a major victory in The Battle of Spion Kop and annexed the Orange Free State and then Transvaal in September 1990.

Refusing to surrender, the Boers continued a guerrilla campaign in the conquered territories. The British responded by establishing concentration camps, burning farms, and executing Boer irregulars.

In 1902 The Peace of Vereeniging promised the Boers self-government if they became British subjects.

In 1906 the British granted responsible government to the Transvaal and Orange Free State, and in 1910 the Union of South Africa was formed to unite them with Cape Colony and Natal (Natkeil, 1982).

Anti-Semitism

Scattered communities of Jews were always a minority that was easily identifiable. During the Middle Ages they had to exist outside the feudal system based on land and many engaged in trade and commerce.

In the early days of capitalism the Church forbade profit and money-lending with interest and most Christians left this activity to Jews. The growing wealth of Jews, however, led to resentment and anti-Jewish sentiment in Europe and in the 19th century thousands fled to the USA to escape it.

In his down-and-out days in Vienna Adolph Hitler wrote:

Was there any shady undertaking, any form of foulness, especially in cultural life, in which at least one Jew did not participate? On putting the probing knife carefully to that kind of abscess, one immediately discovered, like a maggot in a putrescent body, a little Jew who was often blinded by the sudden light. Adolf Hitler, *Mein Kampf,* q. in *Hitler: A Study in Tyranny*, A. Bullock, Penguin, Harmondsworth (1962).

It is believed that the brutal ethnic cleansing of Hitler's 'Final Solution' during World War II killed circa 6 million Jews. Notably, however, IBM's German subsidiary Demohag collected the detailed data on Germany's Jewish population whilst Du Pont made the Zyklon B gas used to kill them (Aarons & Loftus, 1999; Black, 2001)

The Ustashi

There can have been no more barbarous group that the Catholic, right-wing Croatian Ustashi. Formed in the 1930s, with the help of the Macedonian Internal Revolutionary Organization they assassinated King Alexander I of Yugoslavia in Marseille in 1934.

After the German invasion during WW2 a nominally independent Croatian State existed and the fascist Ustashi government set up concentration camps in which thousands of Jews, Gypsies and Orthodox Serbs were murdered in conditions of the utmost barbarity.

Towards the end of WW2 the invading Soviet Army saw an end to Croatian independence but the legacy of hatred between the Croats and Serbs lived on.

Death camps were again set up during the bitter conflict in the former Yugoslavia during the early 1990s.

The break-up of Yugoslavia

After the break-up of the Soviet Union in 1991 there was political and ethnic conflict in some former member states, particularly Yugoslavia where Slobodan Milosevic was one of the key figures. He had become president of Serbia in 1989. In 1990 he was re-elected, his Socialist Party of Serbia winning 194 of the 250 seats.

There was civil war in Croatia in 1991, and in Bosnia and Herzegovina in 1992, both of which have large Serb minorities. With support from the Yugoslav army, Serbian forces seized large parts of Croatia and Bosnia and Herzegovina. In April 1992 Serbia and Montenegro proclaimed themselves the successor state to Yugoslavia, taking the name Federal Republic of Yugoslavia (FRY).

Milosevic was widely blamed for providing financial and military backing to nationalist Serbs fighting in Croatia and Bosnia and received international criticism for the brutal atrocities that were committed by Serbs in those conflicts.

In February 1998 Milosevic ordered Yugoslav military forces into Kosovo to join Serbian police in suppressing growing unrest among the region's Albanian population. The Serbian forces killed more than 150 ethnic Albanians, including women and children, over a three-month period.

Conflict in the former Yugoslavia in the 1990s was widespread and tens of thousands of people were killed and hundreds of thousands displaced. Some of the conflict was religious and directed at the substantial Bosnian Muslim community.

Today the term Yugoslavia is still used to describe today's independent components of Bosnia & Herzegovina, Croatia, Macedonia, Serbia & Montenegro, and Slovenia.

Azerbaijan

Once part of the Roman and then Ottoman Empires, Azerbaijan joined the USSR in 1922. In 1992 fighting between mostly Muslim Azerbaijan and mostly Christian Armenia broke out over claims to Nagorno-Karabakh, an enclave in Azerbaijan mostly populated by Armenians. In 1994 a ceasefire was negotiated, leaving Armenian forces in control of the enclave.

Georgia

Georgia, having been annexed by Russia in 1801, became part of the USSR in 1922. It became an independent state in 1991. During 1991 rebellion forced the president to flee and he was replaced by a former USSR foreign minister.

In Abkhazia ethnic Abkhazis, reportedly aided by Russia, launched a bloody military campaign which by late 1993 had gained control over much of the region. In May 1994 a cease-fire agreement was reached and was supported by Russian peacekeepers.

Moldova

Moldova left the USSR and became an independent state in late 1991. In March 1992 fighting erupted in the Dnestr region between Moldovan forces and Slavic separatists, ethnic Russians and ethnic Ukrainians, who feared Moldova would merge with neighbouring Romania.

A peace accord with the separatists was signed in Moscow on May 8, 1997.

The American Negroes

Racial discrimination against Negroes in the USA was originally severe, of course, as they were imported as slaves. Slavery was abolished more than a century ago in the USA but Negroes continued to be discriminated against and live in relative poverty compared to whites.

In 1962, before the Civil Rights movement had had much impact the average black was in an occupation that ranked 24 points below the national average on the 96 point Duncan Scale (Jencks et al., 1975).

Gradually campaigns for a better 'deal' for Negroes made progress, but not without considerable conflict and violence, particularly in the 1960s.

Nevertheless, in the 1970s studies found that the average white child scored about 15 points better on standard tests than the average black child. Much of this difference can be attributed to environment, an American study of 19 pairs of identical twins reared apart finding that 4 of the pairs had IQ scores that differed by 15 points or more (Jencks et al., 1975).

In 1970, white men who worked full-time earned an average of $200/week, whereas black men averaged only $130/week, black women averaging only $90/week.

Since then, of course, the situation for blacks has improved considerably and, of course, the USA now has a black President for the first time.

Cyprus

The British colony of Cyprus was granted independence in 1959 after the murder of many British servicemen and colonial officials by the Greek terrorist organization EOKA which supported the Enosis movement for union with Greece. Thirty percent of key positions were reserved for Turks who were 18% of the population.

In 1974 a coup organized by Enosis and EOKA installed a local Greek Cypriot as president. In response Turkey invaded and took control of the northern third of the island before a ceasefire was declared. This zone was declared a separate Turkish Cypriot federated state in 1975 and 200,000 Greeks were expelled and replaced by thousands of Turks from the mainland.

South Africa's apartheid regime

The British colonies of Cape Colony, Transvaal, Natal and Orange River were unified to form the Union of South Africa in 1910. The priority of South African politics was maintaining white supremacy over the black majority.

In 1948 South Africa formally instituted its apartheid policy that enforced racial segregation. There was much protest against this, most famously in 1960 at Sharpeville, a suburb of Vereeniging, when 20,000 Africans gathered to demonstrate near a police station.

After the protesters began stoning police and their armoured cars, the police opened fire with submachine guns and 69 Africans were killed and 186 wounded, 48 women and children being among the victims. A state of emergency was declared in South Africa, and nearly 2,000 persons were detained. Reports of this incident helped focus international criticism on the apartheid policy which ended in 1989 (Encyclopaedia Britannica CD 1999).

The Rwandan genocide

The culmination of longstanding ethnic competition and tension between the Tutsi and Hutu peoples, over 500,000 people were killed in about 100 days in 1994. Estimates of the death toll have ranged as high as one million or 20% of the country's population. Organized Hutu militias, supported by many Hutu civilians, carried out the killings.

In response the rebel Tutsi Rwandan Patriotic Front defeated the army and seized control of the country.

The Australian Aborigines

The colonizing of Australia exacted a great toll on the aborigines, for example the Myall Creek massacre, The Black War in Tasmania, and the long battle between blacks and whites in the Hawkesbury region of New South Wales (Bell & Hall, 1991).

Numerous North American studies found that status attainment for blacks was not the same as for whites and that even when blacks were as well educated they were unable to achieve the same occupational and economic rewards. The same situation applies in Australia and may also result from discrimination (Broom et al., 1980).

In part because the aborigines are only a small minority, ethnic conflict between blacks and whites in Australia has only been on a small scale. Riots by aborigines in poor western suburbs of Sydney a few years ago were, however, of significant proportions.

Conclusions

The attitudes of ethnic groups typically relate to their history of living in a particular region. When that region is overtaken by others, of course, this is certain to cause great resentment, ultimately leading to rebellion. Sooner or later, successive conflicts wear down the foreign rulers and the region regains its independence, a story repeated dozens of times in the last two centuries.

Majority or more powerful ethnic groups who gain control of a region usually discriminate against and exploit weaker groups, in part for reasons of ethnic bias, but in part because of man's usual and 'animalistic' greed as seen in the rampant capitalism in much of the decadent West and comparable to the greed and ferocity with which some animal species feed and fight off other animals while doing so. In the human situation, of course, police forces and armies are used to quell dissidence, throughout history often with a great toll on human life.

Ethnic conflict involves disputes between human groupings which differ in race, nationality, language and culture. It is usually the result of different ethnic groups living in the same region of a country, perhaps as a result of migration of one of the groups to that region relatively recently in history. Then competition for 'space' and resources, prejudice over their differences, and jealousy over greater power and/or wealth of one group, are amongst the factors that may lead to conflict.

As in other areas of human conflict, conflict on any scale requires leaders and often these are people of importance in the ethnic community such as politicians or religious leaders. These leaders take up the 'cause' of the ethnic group and whip up prejudice and anger and eventually conflict.

Chapter 9

URBAN CONFLICT

Introduction

Human societies are more crime-ridden than ever before in history. Now 'white collar' crime is rife, guns are widely available, the illegal drugs industry is now one of the world's two largest, and crowded modern cities like Mexico City and Chicago encourage high crime rates.

In the USA more and more people feel forced to keep at least one gun at home to protect themselves. According to Thomas (2007):

➤ 1,135 companies in 98 countries make small arms.
➤ There are 640 million small arms at large in the world.
➤ 8 million new small arms are bought each year and 60% of these end up in the hands of criminals and civilians.
➤ 1 person is killed every minute with small arms.

Increasingly our cultures seem to celebrate bestiality and violence, whether in sports like boxing and martial arts, movies filled with scenes of sex and violence, or video games involving constant shooting and killing. Then, of course, constant media reports of violence seem to encourage 'copy cat' killings.

Mass shootings

In the USA, in particular, mass shootings have become increasingly frequent, in part because assault rifles with 50 round magazines can be purchased by ordinary citizens.

At the time of writing, there have been 186 mass killings in the USA since 2006, this including 146 mass shootings.

The FBI defines a 'mass shooting' as an incident in which four or more people are killed and nearly half of such incidents involve killing family members. Some of the major mass shootings in the USA since the Columbine High School shooting in 1999 have included:

➤ In early October 2015, a 26-year old student at a college in Umpqua killed nine. He reportedly demanded that victims tell him what their religion was, replying when told Christian: "Good, because you're a Christian, you're going to see God in just about one second." Only days later two people were killed in shootings at University campuses in the USA.

➤ 14/12/2012. 27 killed, including 18 children at an elementary school in Newtown CT.

➤ 20/7/2012. 12 killed and 58 wounded in a movie theatre in Auroro CO.

➤ 8/1/2011. A woman killed 6 and wounded 13 in a supermarket in Tucson AZ.

➤ 5/11/2009. 13 killed and 29 wounded at Fort Hood army base in Texas by an Army psychiatrist reportedly yelling "Allahu Akbar!"

➤ 3/4/2009. 13 killed and 4 wounded at an immigration centre in Binghampton NY.

➤ 5/12/2007. 10 killed & 4 wounded in a department store in Omaha NE. The 19-year old gunman killed himself.

➤ 16/4/2007. 32 killed and 24 wounded at Virginia Tech by student Seung-Hui Choi.

➤ 21/3/2005. A teenager killed two relatives, then 9 at Red Lake Senior High School, then killing himself.

➤ 12/3/2005. A church member killed 9 at a church meeting in Brookfield WI, and then killed himself.

➢ 29/7/1999. An Atlanta man killed his wife and 2 children with a hammer, then shooting 9 people before killing himself.

➢ 20/4/1999. Two teenagers killed 13 & wounded 21 at Columbine High School in Littleton CO, then killing themselves.

Mass shootings happen elsewhere in the world, of course, an example being the mass shooting in Australia at the Port Arthur prison colony site in Tasmania where 35 people were killed and 23 wounded in April 1996.

An analysis of 56 mass shootings in the USA in the period 2009 to 2012 found that 57% of cases involved domestic violence. In 60% of mass public shootings in the last century in the USA, officials found signs of mental illness. According to USA today, North-eastern University criminologist Alan Fox said: "Mass murderers don't take you up on treatment. They tend to externalize and blame other people for their problems. They blame the spouse, the co-workers, immigrants. They feel persecuted."

An epidemic of gun-related homicides

934 people died in mass shootings in the USA during the period 2006 – 2012. This number is less than 1% of all gun-related homicides and 33 Americans are killed every day, most of them by handguns, and often by a family member or intimate partner. Many other homicides involve acquaintances, neighbours, and co-workers.

Each time a major mass shooting such as that at an elementary school in Newtown in December 2012 occurs, there is a public outcry and calls for limiting gun sales and banning the sale of powerful assault rifles.

The National Rifle Association of America remains recalcitrant, however, claiming that it is every American's right to carry a gun in case of need. In addition, there are a great many gun shop owners who protest that their businesses would be harmed by stricter gun control laws. No doubt the huge arms industry also provides financial support for campaigning against stricter gun laws.

International murder rates

Murder rates vary considerably around the world, examples of the rates per year, per 100,000 people being:

- ➢ Africa 17.0.
- ➢ Americas 15.4.
- ➢ Asia 3.1.
- ➢ Europe 3.5.
- ➢ Oceania 2.9.
- ➢ World 6.9.

Examples of the full range of rates in different countries are:

- ➢ Australia 1.0.
- ➢ Colombia 31.8.
- ➢ Congo 30.8.
- ➢ Ivory Coast 56.9.
- ➢ Papua New Guinea 13.0.
- ➢ Russia 10.2.
- ➢ South Africa 31.8.
- ➢ UK 1.2.
- ➢ US 4.8.
- ➢ Venezuela 45.1.

Whilst murder rates and the gun law issue in the US command a lot of attention in the press in this country (Australia), however, murder rates in many other countries are higher, in some cases far higher, though admittedly those countries with the highest rates have epidemics of crime and civil unrest, a few being in a state of civil war involving large numbers of displaced people.

Other crime

There is plenty of other violence in society, with or without guns, for example:

➢ Random street violence and theft.
➢ Violence in and outside pubs and clubs.
➢ Violence and theft on trains and train stations.
➢ Robbery of shops, often late at night, and often with real or fake guns.
➢ Sexual assault and rape, usually with some violence.
➢ Domestic violence which contributes to a high proportion of shootings and mass killings.

Conclusions

The general public, of course, abhors crime and, indeed, lives in increasing fear of it.

Criminals on the other hand, are tough and uncompromising and, whether for reasons of profit or grievance, they feel entitled to carry out crimes.

Often, however, ordinary people who 'would not dream' of committing any sort of crime lose control under the stress of marital arguments, sudden loss of a job, or financial problems. Lawyers often defend such crimes as being so-called 'crimes of passion' involving some degree of temporary insanity.

Many crimes, especially serial crimes or mass shootings, are committed by social outcasts, people who feel alienated or wronged by society.

Domestic violence, of course, usually involves a long history of contact during which grudges and bad feeling have developed, often culminating in a 'scene' involving heated verbal exchanges which then provoke immediate violence, or a subsequent plan for perhaps violent revenge.

Society is 'conditioned' to some extent to accept violence by a culture of:

➢ Violent sports such as boxing and martial arts.
➢ Bruising contact sports frequently involving on-field violence such as rugby.
➢ Movies rife with sex scenes and extreme violence.

➢ Video games filled with violence and constant shooting.

Nevertheless, society at large does not condone crime and the media constantly reinforces a negative attitude to crime, often calling for greater police numbers to keep crime in check.

As the figures for small arms sales given at the start of the chapter show, small arms are far too widely available in modern society and greater restrictions are needed.

In response to the Port Arthur shooting in Australia the government instituted a successful gun 'buy back' scheme that took thousands of handguns and rifles off the streets.

In response to public concern, in Melbourne the government has recruited a special force to police suburban rail stations at night. Such measures, along with higher penalties for crimes of violence, may help reduce them in number.

50% divorce rates are now common in the West and there is a need to reduce this by providing more counselling services for married couples. Often their problems are financial, however, and more needs to be done to decrease the widening gap between rich and poor in capitalist societies.

Chapter 10

POLITICAL CONFLICT

> *It is politics that begets war.*
> *Politics represents the intelligence, war its instrument,*
> *not the other way around. The only possible course in war*
> *is to subordinate the military viewpoint to the political.*
> Karl Marie von Clausewitz, *On War* (1883).

Introduction

The first of four definitions that WordWeb 6 gives for politics is: *Social relations involving intrigue to gain authority or power.* It's first of two definitions for intrigue is: *A crafty and involved plot to achieve your (usually sinister) ends.*

All too often the people do, indeed, find that their political rulers are 'crafty' and corrupt and seek to overthrow them, resulting in political conflict. Just as often, ambitious people competing for power are the cause of political conflict, often resulting in civil wars. There have been countless examples of political conflict throughout history and a few of these are briefly described in the following chapter.

The Revolt of Ciompi

This was a popular rebellion in Florence in 1378 which was still recovering from the losses of the Black Death, a bubonic plague that killed almost half the population of Western Europe.

The rebellion was led by workers who were not allowed guild membership and were thus disenfranchised. The merchant oligarchy was briefly overthrown and replaced by a popular government but a counter-coup returned it to power.

The English Civil Wars

These were England's greatest internal conflict and were between supporters of Charles I (the Cavaliers) and supporters of parliament (the Roundheads) who were in opposition to growing royal power. The king left London and raised his standard two months later in Nottingham. After an inconclusive initial battle at Edgehill in October 1642 royalist forces abandoned an advance on London when confronted by a parliamentary force at Turnham Green, the king withdrawing to Oxford to make his military headquarters there.

The Royalists won control of most of Yorkshire at Adwalton Moor on June 30th 1643, and they were victorious at Lansdown and Broadway Down (July), while Charles's nephew Prince Rupert captured Bristol. Parliament was victorious at Winceby (Oct. 11th 1643) and took Lincoln.

After the inconclusive first Battle of Newbury (September 1643), both sides sought allies. Parliament negotiated Scottish military aid and the king made peace with the Irish (who had been in rebellion since 1641), thereby freeing troops for deployment in Britain.

Despite the Parliamentary victory at Marston Moor (July 2), the Royalist operations of 1644 were generally more successful but a second Battle of Newbury (September 20) was again inconclusive.

In 1645 parliament's New Model Army had an overwhelming victory at Naseby (June 14) and the last Royalist army was beaten at Langport (July 10).

In Scotland the marquess of Montrose was defeated at Philiphaugh (September 13) and the Scots swept through the North of England while Parliamentary forces swept through the Southwest.

In 1646 the Royalist troops disbanded and Oxford surrendered. In May 1646 Charles surrendered to the Scots who in June 1647 handed him over to Parliament.

Charles escaped and, having made a deal with a Scottish group to establish Presbyterianism in England, there were a series of royalist rebellions and a Scottish invasion in July 1648. All were defeated and Charles was finally tried and executed in January 1649.

Fighting next broke out in Ireland where Oliver Cromwell suppressed a major uprising of Roman Catholics and Royalists (1649-50). A Scottish rebellion under Montrose was also crushed in April 1650.

Charles II then made terms with the Presbyterian Covenanters but Cromwell defeated them at Dunbar (Sept. 3, 1650) but then allowed Charles, recently crowned in Scotland, to march deep into England. The utter rout of the Royalists at Worcester (Sept. 3, 1651), and Charles II's subsequent flight abroad, effectively ended the civil wars.

As many as 100,000 men, or 10% of the male population, were killed in these wars.

The American Civil War

The 1860 election of Abraham Lincoln, who opposed the extension of slavery to new territories, precipitated the conflict. South Carolina succeeded from the Union and 10 other states soon followed, the 11 states forming the Confederacy early in 1861.

War broke out on 12th April 1861 when Southern forces took Fort Sumter in South Carolina. Most of the battles were in the South and the Confederacy won early victories.

The North won at Antietam in 1862, soon after which Lincoln signed the Emancipation Proclamation freeing all slaves in the Confederacy. This reduced available manpower in the South so that the North, with much greater manpower and industrial resources, began to prevail with major victories at Vicksburg and Gettysburg in 1863.

Union forces had overrun Atlanta and Georgia by 1864 and the war ended on 9th April 1945, having cost a great many lives.

Angola

In the 1950s and 1960s three organizations fought for independence from Portugal. These were the MPLA (The Popular Movement) which was Marxist, the FNLA (The National Front) which defended the interests of the northern tribes, and the UNITA (The National Union for Total Independence of Angola).

The cities mainly supported MPLA but FNLA and UNITA received support through Zaire. In 1975 South African forces moved into southern Angola, strengthening the UNITA movement.

The MPLA secured control of the capital Luanda in July 1975 and, with the help of military supplies from eastern Europe, gained control of 12 of the 16 Angolan districts.

FNLA and UNITA, helped by South African forces fought back with some success but, with the help of troops sent from Cuba, the MPLA regained control and proclaimed Angola independent in February 1976.

Namibia

Explored by the Portuguese in the late 15th century, Namibia was annexed by Germany in 1885 as German Southwest Africa. It was captured in World War I by South Africa which received it as a UN mandate in 1918 which it refused to give up after World War II.

Founded in 1960, the South-West Africa People's Organization (SWAPO) tried to achieve independence from South Africa diplomatically and in 1966 the UN passed a resolution ending South Africa's mandate but South Africa challenged the decision.

SWAPO turned to armed struggle with the support of the Angolan ruling party and the Soviet Union, using Angola as a base for launching guerrilla attacks. From 1978 South Africa made retaliatory strikes in Angola.

The same year the UN recognized SWAPO as the Namibian people's sole representative. In 1988 the UN passed a resolution that South Africa should withdraw its troops from Namibia and that free elections should be held.

South Africa accepted this resolution and Namibia finally achieved independence in 1990.

Mozambique

Mozambique became an overseas province of Portugal in 1951 and an independence movement became active in the 1960s. After years of war the country was granted independence in 1975. Run by the Marxist Front for the Liberation of Mozambique (Frelimo) the country was wracked by civil war in the 1970s and 1980s.

In 1990 a new constitution introduced a multiparty government and a market economy. A peace treaty was signed with rebel groups in 1992.

The Congo

In 1960 the Belgian Congo gained its independence but an army mutiny led to disorder during which a tribal leader, aided by Belgian residents and Anglo-Belgian companies, declared the mineral-rich province of Katanga to be an independent state. In 1961 and 1962 mercenary forces defended Katanga from UN forces but in 1963 the secession of Katanga ended peacefully.

In 1964 communist-supported rebels gained strength in the East and established the Stanleyville 'People's Republic' which was suppressed with Western help.

Political unrest continued until 1965 when a coup installed General Mobutu as president. He survived an attempt by mercenaries to oust him and in 1971 the country was renamed Zaire. Mobutu held power for over three decades, amassing vast wealth while his country collapsed. When he was overthrown in 1997 the country was renamed The Democratic Republic of the Congo.

Argentina

The Spaniards arrived in 1515-16 and by the late 19th century nearly all the native Indians had been killed. There was large-scale Italian, German, and Spanish immigration in the decades after 1880. Social reforms were enacted in the 1920s but military juntas ruled from 1930 to 1946 when General Juan Peron was elected president.

Peron allowed labour reforms but suppressed free speech and ran the country into debt. He was exiled after a 1955 coup which was followed by a series of military and civilian governments. Peron returned in 1973 and was elected president but died soon afterwards and was succeeded by his wife Eva Duarte. She was ousted by a military junta which was then under siege from leftist guerrillas. The junta killed 5,000 people and jailed and tortured many others.

On April 2nd 1982 Argentine troops seized the British-held Falkland Islands. The British navy and air force blockaded the area, British forces invading and forcing the Argentinean troops to surrender on June 14.

The 1983 Argentinean elections restored democratic government but by 1989 Argentina had severe economic problems and hyperinflation sparked rioting and looting in several cities. In the 1990s harsh economic measures were taken to stabilize the economy and reduce foreign debt.

The Korean and Vietnam Wars

Korea having been portioned at the end of World War 2, the communist North invaded the South in 1950. With the USA supporting the South war continued until 1953.

In the 1960s a similar problem arose in Vietnam, and again the USA supported the South, leading to a long and bloody war.

Both these conflicts are discussed in Chapter 14.

The Cold War

Hitler's ambitions of overtaking much of Europe during World War 2 vanished with his demise and the defeat of Germany by the allies. Perhaps with the help of double agents such as British double agent Kim Philby, Russia was able to stave off German invasion, greatly weakening Germany's forces in the process.

Then Russia stole a march on the West and occupied much of Europe, leading Churchill to coin the term "iron curtain." Thus Russia had, in effect, won World War 2, whereas, as it turned out, the other allies had simply helped Russia in doing so.

This launched the Cold War, a long period of tension between the USSR and the West, particularly the USA. When Russia developed nuclear weapons in the 1950s this heightened tensions greatly, and it was not until Michael Gorbachev's leadership of the USSR that the Cold War largely ended.

The Cold War is discussed further in Chapter 14.

Conclusions

Political conflict is, of course, about power and, as all history proves, power corrupts. Given power, it seems that many people become addicted to it. The same seems to apply to money, of course, and many a crooked politician has amassed great wealth. Such politicians, of course, are those that hang onto power until the populace is obliged to forcefully remove them from office.

Politicians made leaders being, of course, good liars but having a good 'front', people's attitude to them is usually tolerant at first. As their incompetence and/or corruption becomes more evident, however, the attitudes of the people change for the worse, often resulting in some form of conflict, be that political or physical.

Politicking, of course, involves a 'plot' to achieve the ambitions of groups and the individuals within them. Often throughout history, of course, both fair means and foul have been used, no better example of foul means being the 'night of the long knives' when Hitler had several hundred suspected political opponents killed.

Such behaviour, of course, is more than an exhibition of ambitious type A personality. It is more than the aggression of a psychopath, it is psychotic behaviour.

It is such ambitious, impatient, competitive, domineering and hostile behaviour that characterizes the politicians who instigate hostility directly, or indirectly, because others react to their excessive greed and corruption and rebel against it.

Such rebellion may exhibit first as strikes, protest marches, demonstrations outside government buildings, and sometimes riots. When these measures are seen by leaders to be a threat armed conflict may ensue.

Politicians and leaders speak from 'on high' and thus communication with the people is almost entirely a one-way affair via official media channels, and then usually only via members of their political organization or government.

The only peaceful way of the people venting their grievances is such means as letters to the newspapers and there is little chance of much notice being taken of these.

The only peaceful means of changing a government is by voting for an alternative one and, all too often in history, that has not been possible, often resulting in growing frustration and eventual conflict.

Chapter 11

REVOLUTION

> *Revolution is not a bed of roses,*
> *it is a struggle to death between the future and the past.*
> Fidel Castro, Second Anniversary of the Cuban Revolution,
> Speech in Havana, January 1961.

Introduction

There have been many revolutions in history, one of the earliest being the Gladiator's War or Third Servile War (72 – 71BC) led by Spartacus. One with a comparable cause was the Peasants Revolt of June 1381 in England which was precipitated by oppressive taxes and other grievances.

The English Civil Wars, sometimes referred to as 'The English Revolution' or 'The Puritan Revolution', were summarized in Chapter 20.

In the last century almost all the European colonies around the world have all gained independence, some of these by revolutionary means. Similarly, the so-called Revolution of 1989, which began with demolition of part of the Berlin Wall by civilians in November 1989, freed East Germany from the USSR and began the dismantlement of the USSR.

The American Revolution

A prelude to this was the Boston Massacre of 5th March 1770 when British troops killed five people after firing upon a crowd protesting against British regulations and troop presence.

Another was the Boston Tea Party in 1773 when, as a protest over British taxation, 342 chests of dutiable tea were destroyed by workers disguised as Indians. Britain's parliament responded by passing the Intolerable Acts bill in 1774 to punish Massachusetts, leading to the establishment of the First Continental Congress (1774).

In April 1775 fighting broke out between colonial militia, known as the Minutemen, and British troops at the Battles of Lexington and Concord in Massachusetts.

Colonial forces captured Fort Ticonderoga in May 1775 but lost the battle of Bunker Hill.

In June 1775 The Second Continental Congress elected George Washington to command the Continental Army and in July the congress issued the Declaration of Independence.

The British evacuated Boston in May 1776 but defeated Washington's troops in several skirmishes in the New York area.

Washington's surprise attacks at Trenton (25th Dec. 1776) and Princeton (Jan. 1977) were small victories but they gave encouragement to his cause. He won the Battle of Saratoga in upstate New York in June 1977, this battle convincing the French to join his cause, bringing much needed financial and military support, including a fleet.

In September 1777 the British won the Battle of Brandywine in Pennsylvania. In 1778 British forces invaded South Carolina and moved north but were forced to surrender to the colonial and French forces in Virginia in 1781. After two years of negotiation the Treaty of Paris was signed in September 1783.

The French Revolution

Causes included a large underfed population, loss of support for the feudal system, an expanding bourgeoisie excluded from political power, and a fiscal crisis deepened by participation in the American Revolution.

The revolution began with the storming of the Bastille on July 14th 1789, resulting in a reformation of the government and wide-ranging political, social and economic measures, including the abolition of feudal, aristocratic, and clerical privileges, and confiscation of Church property to pay off public debt.

The Constitution of 1791 established a short-lived constitutional government and the king tried to flee the country but was apprehended at Varennes.

In April 1792, unjustified fears of invasion by Austria having been raised, France declared war on Austria and Prussia, beginning the French Revolutionary Wars. A succession of defeats of the French army followed.

After an insurrection on August 10th 1792 France was declared a republic. The following month the September Massacres occurred when rioting crowds in Paris, panicked by advancing armies, broke into prisons and massacred thousands of people.

Louis XVI and his queen were executed in January 1793. Then the ruling party, the republican Girondins, was overthrown by the radical Jacobins led by Robespierre, beginning the dictatorial Reign of Terror.

Robespierre was executed in 1794 and, with military force used to suppress opposition, the government of the Directory was formed in 1795. This was overthrown by Napoleon Bonaparte in the Brumaire Coup in 1799, leading to the First Empire (1804 – 1815) which spread the Revolution's ideas of 'Liberty, Equality, Fraternity' and popular sovereignty.

The Fenian movement

The Fenian movement began in 1858 and was named after the Fianna, a legendary band of Irish warriors in the 2nd and 3rd centuries. The movement was a secret oath-bound society which planned a revolution to achieve independence for Ireland.

The movement grew in Ireland as the Irish Republican Brotherhood, and amongst Irish Nationalists in the United States as Fenian Brotherhood.

The Fenian movement also had branches in England, the British dominions, and several other countries.

The US branch smuggled money and arms to the Irish branch, though informers caused much of this to be intercepted, and many of the Fenian leaders in Ireland were arrested.

Hoping to pressure England into granting Ireland independence, the US Fenians attempted to invade Canada in 1866, most of the invasion force being stopped by US authorities, but a small force did cross the border near Buffalo in June, but was repelled by Canadian volunteers and forced to surrender to an American gunboat in the Niagara River. The Fenians made two other failed attempts to invade Canada in 1870 and 1871.

In 1866 and 1867 the Fenians attacked police stations in Ireland, and set off bombs in England, but the rebellion was put down and hundreds of suspected rebels were imprisoned.

The Fenians ceased to exist circa 1885 but their ideals were adopted by Sinn Fein in the early 20th century.

The Russian Revolutions

The Revolution of 1905 was a series of nationwide strikes, demonstrations and mutinies. 'Bloody Sunday' (9th Jan.), a massacre of demonstrating workers by soldiers, heightened the tensions and Tsar Nicholas II was forced to legalize political parties and allow elections.

In the Bolshevik-led October Revolution of 1917 armed workers (Red Guards) arrested members of the Provisional Government and they were replaced by the Soviet of People's Commissars, chaired by Lenin who had exploited the crisis situation in Russia resulting from war with Germany to foment revolution.

The Russian Civil War (1918 – 1922) followed in which Anti-Bolshevik forces (Whites) were supported by Britain, France, the USA, and Japan. The Red Army eventually prevailed and, though Poland, Finland and the Baltic states were given independence, Armenia, the Ukraine and Georgia remained under Soviet control.

The Revolution of 1918

In the wake of defeat in WW1 Germany's monarchy fell because of growing social disorder. On November 9th the leader of the Social Democratic Party of Germany (SPD) formed a socialist government which met in Weimar on 19th January 1919 to draft a constitution.

The SPD had relied upon monarchist and right-radical military forces to restrain the radical left, however, restricting major socio-economic and administrative changes, some feel opening the way for the subsequent rise of the Nazi Party which had been formed in 1919.

The Chinese Revolution

This broke out on October 10th 1911 in central China when an anti-monarchist army unit mutinied. Dissent spread and by the start of 1912 delegates from 16 provinces had elected a provisional president of a Chinese republic. Fearing foreign intervention to protect their economic interests, he offered the presidency to the commander of the royal army who became President of a unified republic after the abdication of the young emperor.

The revolution, however, brought little social change.

The Chinese Civil War

Immediately after Japan surrendered in August 1945 communist challenges for supremacy of China re-emerged. The US brokered a treaty on 14th January 1946 but soon hostilities resumed, by July 1946 stopping US supplies to the nationalist forces.

The still better equipped nationalist forces took the communist capital, Yan'an, on 19th March 1947. Gradually the communists moved from rural-based guerrilla campaigns to full-scale battles, recapturing the city a year later.

In a decisive series of battles in late 1948 and early 1949 the nationalist forces lost 500,000 men. The communists then captured Beijing and Tianjin (Jan.), Nanjing (April), and Shanghai and Canton (Oct.).

The People's Republic of China was formally proclaimed by Mao Zedong on 1st October 1949, the nationalists withdrawing to Taiwan on the 7th of December.

The Cuban Revolution

Cuba revolted against Spanish rule in the Ten Years' War (1868-78), and again in 1895. The US took control after the Spanish-American Wars of 1898, when the entire Spanish fleet was destroyed near the seaport of Santiago de Cuba, but granted Cuba independence in 1902.

The US invested heavily in the sugar, tourism and gambling industries until circa 1950 but inequalities in the distribution of wealth festered popular discontent.

Fidel Castro was the son of a prosperous sugar planter. He became a lawyer, worked on behalf of Havana's poor, and was a candidate for Cuba's legislature when General Fulgencio Batista overthrew the government in 1952.

Castro led a failed rebellion against Batista in 1953 and was captured and sent to prison. He then went to Mexico where, with Che Guevara and others, he continued plans to overthrow Batista.

Castro led an armed expedition back to Cuba in 1956 where most of his men were killed, a dozen survivors hiding in the mountains from where they organized guerrilla groups throughout the island.

On January 1st 1959 Batista fled the country and Castro nationalized commerce and industry and expropriated US-owned land and businesses.

Under Castro all opposition was ruthlessly suppressed but health services and literacy were greatly increased.

The US made many attempts to assassinate him and the failed Bay of Pigs invasion led to the Cuban Missile Crisis which raised the threat of imminent nuclear war between the US and Russia.

For three decades Cuba received considerable economic support from the USSR, in return sending troops to prop up Soviet client states in Angola and Ethiopia.

With the disintegration of the USSR circa 1990, Cuba's economy suffered considerably, resulting in relaxation of controls over business activity.

Conclusions

Revolutions may result when governments are seen to be incompetent, corrupt and oppressive. They have a 'democratic' basis and are more likely to succeed when the majority of the people are in support of it.

Civil unrest initially exhibits itself as protest marches and demonstrations outside government buildings.

When such demonstrations are disallowed, or when people are killed by police or troops during such protests, an escalating cycle of violence often results.

When, over a number of years, civil discontent grows and governments are seen to refuse to meet civil demands, if not suppress them, perhaps with violence, then a growing number of people become increasingly frustrated.

When the 'contact history' becomes too negative tensions and pressures in society may reach a breaking point and revolution ensues.

Most revolutions have been the result of excessive differences in society, with a favoured few being seen to get richer and richer while most of the population suffers increasing levels of poverty.

It is particularly when oppressive regimes are seen to take an unsympathetic attitude to the complaints of the people that the peoples' attitude towards those regimes worsens and their resolve to replace them increases.

All that is needed is for a small group of revolutionary leaders to emerge who, with promises of improvement, persuasively seek supporters and organize protests which are sufficiently alarming to the authorities to consider reforming the government and allowing free elections that may result in some of the changes the populace desires.

Revolutions usually occur in times of economic difficulty which, of course, most affect common working people. When large numbers of them lose their jobs, of course, that can only make revolution still more likely.

Then dissident groups will quickly proliferate and grow if persuasive activists with an attractive message and goal lead the 'cause'. Marxism, for example, was a goal that inspired a number of revolutions in the 20th century.

Chapter 12

THE WORLD WARS

> *War is nothing but a continuation of politics*
> *with the admixture of other means.*
> Karl Marie von Clausewitz, *On War* (1883).
>
> *War is one of the constants of history,*
> *and has not diminished with civilization or democracy.*
> Will Durant, *The Lessons of History*
> (co-written with Ariel Durant, 1968).

Introduction

Until 1914, in man's long and seemingly endless history of warfare, wars were usually 'one step at a time' affairs in which a group or nation fought only one other group. When empires were being built, of course, there would be a prolonged sequence of successive conflicts as each new territory was added to the empire.

Sometimes, of course, two parties would enjoin to tackle another, but generally that was as complex as wars needed to be.

World War 1 changed all that and two groups of nations spanning most of the globe became involved in what was later called 'The Great War.'

Then came World War 2 which exceeded it in ferocity and resulted in massive loss of human life. It ended with the use of nuclear bombing of two Japanese cities and we can only hope, therefore, that there will never be a third world war.

World War 1

The 'Great War' was sparked by the assassination of Archduke Ferdinand and his wife by a Serbian nationalist at Sarajevo in Bosnia on 28th June 1914.[1] Encouraged by Germany, Austria declared war on Serbia on the 28th of July. Russia mobilized in support of Serbia (28-30 July) and Germany declared war on Russia on August 1st.

Germany invaded Belgium on the 4th of August, bringing Britain into the war to support the French. Under the terms of an agreement with Britain (1902, 1911) Japan joined the Allies, Italy following in May 1915.

Turkey allied with Germany in November 1914, Bulgaria also doing so in October 1915.

The French army prevented the Germans from invading France via Belgium and then, with the help of the British, prevented them from reaching the Channel ports.

The Central Powers occupied Russian Poland and most of Lithuania. They then overcame strong resistance to take control of Serbia, Albania and Romania.

In April 1915 the Allies began the Gallipoli Campaign aimed at re-supplying Russia and defeating Turkey but it ended in failure. They also fought Turkey in Mesopotamia and a campaign in Macedonia lasted three years.

In 1916 the Germans attacked France but they were held back by the Battle of Verdun (Feb. – July) which was one of the bloodiest of the war. The Allies began the first battle of the Somme (July – Nov.), causing the Germans to abandon the Verdun offensive on July 16th.

---

[1] The authors are inclined to think that Germany's leaders (the top couple in the hierarchy) might have had ideas of expansion prior to this event and then found it an OK excuse to launch a war in which to make a march to gain more territory. WW1 also had a lot to do with ill-feeling between the royal cousins Edward 7, a notorious philanderer, and Kaiser Wilhelm (SBS1 7:30PM 14/4/2015). E7, of course, might have listened once too often to Edward Elgar's *Land of Hope and Glory*, a British 'hymn' still sung by many with vigour.

In January 1917 the Germans began unrestricted submarine warfare to stop shipments of arms to Britain from the USA. That same month Germany's Foreign Secretary, Arthur Zimmerman, sent a telegram to the German minister in Mexico containing the terms of an alliance between Mexico and Germany by which Mexico was to attack the USA with German assistance in return for the US states of New Mexico, Texas and Arizona.

The 'Zimmerman telegram' and US shipping losses motivated the USA to declare war on Germany on 6th April.

The British began the Battle of Cambrai (Nov. 20 – Dec. 3) with 400 tanks, an unprecedented number, but the battle ended in stalemate.

In March 1917 the Russian Revolution began and on December 15th Russia signed an armistice with Germany.

In the spring of 1918 the Germans launched a major attack in the west which was ultimately repelled after several months of success, thanks to rapidly increasing numbers of US troops taking part. The German army was in full retreat by September.

After military losses in Palestine and Mesopotamia, Turkey agreed to an armistice on 31st October 1918.

Italian victories and advancing French and British forces ended the resistance of Bulgaria and Austria-Hungary.

When an armistice with Germany was signed in November the Allies had recaptured western Belgium and nearly all of France.

At its end The Great War had cost the lives of 8.5 million troops whilst 10 million civilians were killed or wounded. Troop casualty rates (killed and wounded) were very high, circa 75% for Russia and France, 90% for Austria and Hungary, and 65% for Germany.

World War 2

In the late 1930s Germany sought approval from Britain for its expansionist ideas, Hitler having had such ideas, and built up Germany's armed forces for the purpose, for some time (Time-Life, 1988, 1999). Such approval was not forthcoming and Germany invaded Bohemia-Moravia in March 1939.

Britain, France and Russia responded by forming a pact promising mutual assistance against Germany.

To open Germany's path to Poland the German and Soviet foreign ministers signed the Hitler-Stalin pact on 23rd August 1939. This renounced the use of force against each other, promised extensive economic cooperation, and effectively partitioned Eastern Europe between them.

Germany invaded Poland on 1st September, overrunning it in four weeks, prompting Britain and France to declare war on 3rd September.

Six months of relative peace followed until Germany occupied Norway and Denmark in April 1940. Belgium and Holland were invaded on 10th May and invasion of France immediately followed. Holland surrendered in 4 days, Belgium in 3 weeks, and France in 7 weeks.

Having declared alliance with Germany in 1936, Italy declared war on Britain and France in June 1940.

In the Battle of Britain Germany failed to achieve supremacy over England in the air. Germany then began U-boat attacks against British supply routes.

In April 1941 Germany invaded Yugoslavia, then moving on to invade Greece.

British efforts were concentrated against Italy in the Mediterranean and North Africa.

Rommel was sent to reinforce the Italians in Africa and a fierce campaign continued for three years until the Allies were finally victorious in mid-1943.

Allied forces then invaded Sicily and Italy, forcing Italy to make peace on 3rd September 1943.

In June 1941 Germany broke the Hitler-Stalin pact and invaded Russia on a 2,000 mile front, German armies advancing rapidly on three fronts to the outskirts of Leningrad in the north, towards Moscow in the centre, and to the Volga River in the south.

Increasing Soviet resistance and heavy winter snows halted the German advance and from November 1942 they were in retreat, suffering defeats at Stalingrad (winter 1942-43) and Kursk (May 1943).

Leningrad remained under siege for almost 2.5 years (until Jan. 1944), about half its population dying from starvation and disease, but the Germans were finally driven out of the USSR in August 1944.

In June 1944 the Allies launched a second front against Germany by invading Normandy and then liberating Paris on the 25th of August. The Allies advanced into Germany in February 1945, linking with the Russians at the River Elbe on the 28th of April. Germany finally surrendered on the 7th of May 1945.

On the 7th of December 1941 Japan attacked Pearl Harbour and other US and British bases, the USA declaring war the next day (Young, 1992). Germany and Italy declared war on the USA on the 11th December. After four months Japan controlled South-East Asia and Burma.

In June 1942 Allied naval victories in the Pacific stopped the Japanese advance. Bitter fighting continued until 1945 when the USA dropped atomic bombs on Hiroshima (6th August) and Nagasaki (9th August), forcing Japan to surrender on the 14th of August.

On August 20, 1945, the Kremlin created a special committee involving captains of wartime industry to build atomic weapons. Two further rearmament projects soon followed, the first for building missiles, the second for antiaircraft defence (Zubok, 2007).

The human cost of the war was enormous. The Allied military and civilian losses were 44 million and those of the Axis, 11 million. Military deaths on both sides were 19 million in Europe and 6 million in the war against Japan.

The highest numbers of deaths, military and civilian, were: USSR 13M/7M; China 3M/10M; Germany 3.5M/3.8M; Poland 120k/5.3M; Japan 1.7M/380k; Yugoslavia 300k/1.3M; Romania 200k/465k; France 250k/360k; British Empire & Commonwealth 452k/60k; Italy 330k/80k; Hungary 120k/280k; and Czechoslovakia 10k/ 330k. The US had 292k battle deaths and 115k deaths from other causes but had no significant civilian losses.

The foregoing numbers may not include all of the estimated 6 million Jews murdered in German extermination and labour camps.

Spies and military intelligence

Nations have had military spies and information or intelligence gatherers since Roman times, if not before. The 'spook' business is not as glamorous as in the movies and can be sordid and messy (Doyle, 2000).

Referred to earlier, in WW1 the 'Zimmerman letter' was intercepted by allied military intelligence and influenced the USA's decision to enter the war.

Before WW2 an English peer is believed to have given Japan information on aircraft carrier design, the defences of Singapore, and intelligence which may have helped plan the attack on Pearl Harbour.

The 'Cambridge four' of Philby, Blunt, Maclean and Burgess was recruited by the KGB in the early 1930s. No doubt they helped Stalin win World War 2 hands down (Philby et al., 2000).

Stalin was also helped by a group of Soviet Jews code-named MAX which fed the Germans the lie that, around the time of the battle of Stalingrad, the Russians were weakening. Nothing could be further from the truth and the Russians dropped powdered tularemia bacillus on the unsuspecting Panzer divisions in Stalingrad, an act that may have been the turning point in the war (Alibek, 1999).

One of the greatest intelligence blunders of all time was the FBI in the USA ignoring several intercepted signals during 1941 that suggested the Japanese might attack Pearl Harbour (Hughes-Wilson, 1999). Still recovering from the Great Depression which nearly destroyed the Union, the USA had no 'overseas' intelligence organization at that time.

At the end of WW2 Philby's information emboldened Stalin prior to the crucial Yalta conference. After WW2 he also helped thwart a number of covert CIA-MI6 Cold War operations against the USSR, for example that in Armenia in 1949.

Three key WW2 conferences

The first inter-allied conference of WW2 was the Tehran Conference of 28 November to 1 December 1943, attended by Stalin, Roosevelt and Churchill. They discussed coordination of Allied landings in France with the Soviet offensive against Germany, Russian involvement in the war against Japan, and the establishment of a post-war international organization. Failure to agree on the future government of Poland is said to have foreshadowed the Cold War.

These same leaders met at the Yalta Conference of 4-11 February 1945, agreeing on the disarmament and partitioning of Germany, the establishment of the UN, and the composition of the Polish government. It was also secretly agreed that Russia would declare war on Japan when war with German ended.

The Yalta conference was seen by many as a triumph for Stalin and after it Roosevelt was outraged by Soviet occupation methods in Eastern Europe but died suddenly on April 12, 1945. As a result, the Truman administration abruptly terminated Lend-Lease deliveries to the USSR in late April 1945, but after protests from Moscow they were soon resumed.

The last of the great WW2 strategic conferences was the Potsdam Conference of 17 July – 2 August 1945. During this Churchill (and later Clement Atlee), Stalin and Truman discussed post-war settlement in Europe. Soviet power in Eastern Europe was informally recognized, Poland's border with Russia was established along the Oder-Neisse Line, and it was decided to divide Germany into four zones of occupation.

Conclusions

Before World War I a number of nations including Germany, Russia and Austria-Hungary had increasingly aggressive foreign policies (Chambers, 1993).

The assassination of two people was a poor excuse for starting what became WW1 when, of course, the Serbian nationalist movement should have been dealt with directly by the Austro-Hungarian government, perhaps by negotiations in the first instance. Once war had been declared on Serbia, however, Germany seemed all too keen to join in and this was what led to a world war.

The history of the preceding century also set the scene for the war, involving as it did increasing political and economic rivalry and the establishment of increasing large military forces.

Before World War II Hitler's plans for expansion into Europe were hatching, grievances remained from Japan's history of struggle against China, and there was a conflict of interests in the Pacific between Japan and the USA.

Hitler's celebrated 'night of the long knives' foreshadowed what was to come, perhaps, his ruthless ambition being the cause of World War II. His extermination of 6 million Jews was convincing proof that he was severely psychotic.

That Hitler was a bit cranky was witnessed on one occasion by the famous pioneer of thoracic surgery Ferdinand Saerbruch. He had been summoned by Hitler so that he could be sent to attend to the Turkish Minister for Foreign Affairs who was seriously ill (Sauerbruch, 1953).

Having earlier been warned about Hitler's temper, Sauerbruch was taken to a large room to wait for Hitler who arrived preceded by an enormous dog which bounded towards Sauerbruch. Used to dogs, Sauerbruch stood stock still and spoke soothingly to the dog.

Because of the dog's lack of aggression Hitler threw a tantrum which lasted several minutes. He raved that how could he win when those supposed to protect him behaved like this. Hitler threatened to have Sauerbruch arrested but Sauerbruch, as he had done with the dog, managed to calm Hitler down.

Hitler had a manic belief in the superiority of the Aryan races, whereas the Jews were defiled, and this was a major reason for his insane belief that Germany should dominate Europe, if not the world.

Hitler had a well-oiled propaganda machine led by Joseph Goebbels, head of the Ministry of Public Enlightenment and Propaganda, and German public followed blindly, if not enthusiastically:

> *The broad mass of a nation . . . will more easily fall victim to a big lie than a small one.*
> Adolph Hitler, *Mein Kampf* (1933), ch. 10.

Bottom line

The bottom line on both world wars and most others is:

All wars are planned by old men in council rooms apart.
Grantland Rice, *Two Sides of War* (1955).

Besides Hitler, there have been countless other despotic leaders throughout history, to the point at which one is reminded not only that 'power corrupts', but also that those who crave power the most are likely to be psychopaths (Time-Life, 1989).

12. THE WORLD WARS

Chapter 13

THE COLD WAR

> *An iron curtain has descended across the Continent.*
> Winston Churchill, *Address to Westminster College,*
> Fulton, USA (March 3, 1946).

Introduction

Hitler's ambitions of overtaking much of Europe during World War 2 vanished with his demise and the defeat of Germany by the allies. Perhaps with the help of double agents such as British double agent Kim Philby, Russia was able to stave off German invasion, greatly weakening Germany's forces in the process (Philby et al, 2000).

Then Russia stole a march on the West and occupied much of Europe, leading Churchill to coin the term "iron curtain" in a speech in March 1946. Thus Russia had, in effect, won World War 2, whereas, as it turned out, the other allies had simply helped Russia in doing so.

This launched the Cold War, a long period of tension between the USSR and the West, particularly the USA. When Russia developed nuclear weapons soon after the USA this heightened tensions greatly, and it was not until Michael Gorbachev's leadership of the USSR in the late 1980s that the Cold War began to wind down (Chambers, 1993).

The Bikini tests

On July 24, 1946, the US government exploded two nuclear bombs in the Bikini Lagoon, 2,500 miles west of Honolulu. The first was similar to that used on Nagasaki the previous year and the second, the 'Baker shot', more powerful. The two explosions destroyed most of the 85 surplus and mostly aging US ships anchored in the lagoon.

The following year an article in *Life* magazine concluded that, if a bomb similar to the Baker bomb were to explode off the tip of Manhattan in a strong southerly wind, two million people would die immediately or as a result of intense radioactive fallout (Whittell, 2012).

The Soviet Union could not help but notice and exploded its first nuclear weapon just three years and one month after the Bikini blasts, increasing the tensions of the Cold War.

The Berlin Airlift

In June 1948, Soviet Spies discovered that the Western Allies planned to unify as much as Germany as possible, especially Berlin. Joseph Stalin reacted to this information by blockading the roads, railways and canals that went into West Berlin. To defeat the blockade American and British planes flew in daily supplies until Stalin ended the blockade in May 1949.

The Cold War

The term Cold War was first used by Bernard Baruch during a congressional debate in 1947. It was the open but restricted rivalry that developed after the Soviet Union seized control of Eastern Europe towards the end of World War II, the US and Britain then fearing further expansion of Soviet power in Western Europe and elsewhere.

The Cold War was waged principally on political, economic, and propaganda fronts. It was at its peak in 1948-53 with the Berlin blockage and airlift, the formation of NATO, the victory of the communists in the Chinese civil war, and the Korean War (Encyclopaedia Britannica 99).

One of the seeds of the Cold War was Robert H. Goddard's patenting a rocket propulsion apparatus in the USA in 1914 (Ikenson, 2004). After Germany began firing rockets at London early in World War 2, Goddard played a major role in developing rocket launching systems for the USA.

With the advent of nuclear bombs rockets became the principal mode of delivery and the USSR and USA built up massive stockpiles of nuclear missiles ready to be launched at the touch of a button, contributing greatly to the tensions of the Cold War.

In 1957 Russia launched Sputnik, the world's first orbital satellite, launching an era of spy satellites that continues to this day.

The Cuban missile crisis of 1962 was a highlight when the US blockaded Cuba to prevent completion of construction of Soviet nuclear missile bases in Cuba. The result was an intense round of threats, counter-threats, and negotiations for several days, at the end of which the USSR finally agreed to dismantle the bases.

There was a period of détente from 1967 to 1979 during which there was increased trade and cooperation and the SALT treaties were signed. Relations cooled again when the USSR invaded Afghanistan.

Soviet Cold War spies

The 'Cambridge four' of Philby, Blunt, Maclean and Burgess was recruited by the KGB in the early 1930s and they were of considerable assistance in helping Stalin win World War 2 (Philby et al., 2000).

At the end of WW2 Philby's information emboldened Stalin prior to the crucial Yalta conference. After WW2 he also helped thwart a number of covert CIA-MI6 Cold War operations against the USSR, for example a planned invasion of Armenia in 1949.

In 1951, Burgess and Maclean defected to the Soviet Union to avoid arrest for treason, Philby doing likewise several years later.

Klaus Fuchs left Germany at the start of WW2 to work in the UK. He began spying for the Soviet Union in 1941 and in 1943 he moved to the USA to work on the Manhattan Project.

In 1946 he returned to the UK and continued to spy for the USSR. In December 1949 an MI5 agent told Klaus Fuchs he was suspected of espionage and a few weeks later he confessed and was imprisoned for nine years, returning to East Germany at the end of his sentence (Burgan, 2005).

Julius Rosenberg also worked on the Manhattan project and spied for the USSR with the help of his wife Ethel. They were arrested in 1953 and executed for spying.

Another top undercover Soviet spy was William Fisher who was planted in the US in 1948 under the name Emil Goldfus. He helped rebuild the Soviet spy network in America, resulting in a flow of nuclear information from Los Alamos and the top secret fuel enrichment laboratory at Oak Ridge, Tennessee. Such information helped Russia catch up with US, exploding its first atomic bomb in August 1949, and its first H-bomb in August 1953, only 9 months after the first US H-bomb test at Bikini Atoll.

Such events led to the formation of a US committee led by Senator Joseph McCarthy to hunt for Communist spies. McCarthy claimed that there were many spies in the US armed forces. He also accused several prominent Americans, including Lauren Bacall, Danny Kaye and Humphrey Bogart, of being Communists, leading to the term 'McCarthyism'.

George Blake, a British diplomat in South Korea who spied for MI6, was imprisoned when North Korea invaded South Korea in 1950. While in prison Blake, perhaps as a result of 'brainwashing', became supportive of communism and when released in April 1953 he became a double agent for the Soviet Union.

In October 1953, Blake learned about plans to build a tunnel under East Berlin by MI6 and the CIA to tap Soviet telephone lines. The tunnel was completed in 1955 and, in part to protect Blake's position, the Soviets then used it to feed them a mixture of real and false information for several months.

In April 1956, however, the Soviets demolished the spy tunnel.

In 1961 the British finally learned that Blake was a double agent and arrested him. He escaped, however, and went to Moscow to live.

Gunter Guillaume was one of many spies for the Stasi, the East German intelligence service, who sent him to West Germany in 1956. There he met the West German leader Willy Brandt from whom he gained information useful to the Soviets. He was caught in 1974 and later swapped for two West German spies held in East Germany.

Western Cold War spies

Since the Russian Revolution of 1917 the US, UK and their allies had feared and spied on Russia and it reciprocated. Since World War 2 the CIA played a major role in overturning foreign governments not to its liking, for example replacing Muhammad Musaddiq, the Ruler of Iran in 1953 because the Americans thought he was too friendly with the Soviet Union.

In 1954, the CIA helped force the Guatemalan president, Jacobo Arbenz, out of power because he supported the Russians and had bought weapons from them.

In following decades the CIA played a role in bringing down several governments not to its liking in South America, Africa and the Middle East.

In 1976 CIA agent Antonio Mendez went to Moscow where he created a disguise for a US agent working with a Soviet double agent called TRINITY. He gave the US agent a brown wig, a fake moustache, and used putty to make his nose look wider. Then, over his normal clothes, the agent wore those of a typical Soviet worker.

In 1977, however, TRINITY was arrested by the KGB, when he bit a pen containing poison to kill himself and avoid interrogation and torture.

Ryszard Kuklinski, a Polish colonel, was a 'mole' for the USA for almost ten years. In 1981 he moved to the United States to avoid capture by Soviet agents.

The Soviet Union sent Dimitri Polyakov to New York in 1951 where he began spying on the USA while working for the UN. Having become disillusioned by what he felt was a harsh Soviet government he became a double agent for the USA in 1961, revealing the names of many Soviet spies around the world.

Polyakov also gave the Soviets false information about US chemical and biological weapons while giving the US important information about the weapons being developed by Soviet scientists.

In 1985 a double agent working for the Soviet Union told the Russians that Polyakov was spying for the Americans but by this time he had returned to Russia where he was executed for treason.

The Berlin Wall

After the division of Germany, in the years 1949 to 1961 circa 2.5 million East Germans fled to West Germany to escape Communism, often by crossing from East Berlin to the western half of the city.

To prevent this, in 1961 the East German authorities built a wall between East and West Berlin. The 4m high and 45km long Berlin Wall came to symbolize the Cold War. Construction of the wall began on the night of August 12-13, 1961, and it developed into a system of concrete walls, barbed wire, watchtowers, gun emplacements, and mines.

Thereafter many East Germans trying to cross it were shot and the Berlin Wall became the outstanding symbol of the Cold War.

Despite many protests against it, the Berlin Wall remained for three decades.

The Hungarian rebellion

The Soviet Union kept tight control over the Warsaw Pact members Albania, Czechoslovakia, Bulgaria, East Germany, Hungary, Poland, Romania and Russia. To ensure control over their governments Russian and East German spies were placed throughout these countries.

In October 1956 some Hungarians began protests against one-party Communist government, demanding greater freedom of speech and writing. After several riots involving fighting between protesters and police, Soviet troops marched into Hungary, but the protests continued and thousands of people were killed or wounded during the rebellion.

The Soviets installed a new leader, Imre Nagy, but it transpired that he too wanted to reduce Soviet control of Hungary. So the Soviets sent KGB leader Ivan Serov to the Hungarian capital, Budapest.

On 3 November 1956, Serov and his men burst into a meeting of Hungary's leaders and arrested them. Nagy was killed and a new leader, Maryas Rakosi installed.

The U2 spy plane

On May 1 1960, an American U2 spy plane flown by Francis Gary Powers was downed by a Russian missile while taking spy photographs of Russian military facilities.

Powers parachuted to safety and, having declined to take lethal poison provided to avoid capture, he was imprisoned by the KGB.

In 1962 Russia agreed to exchange Powers for a Soviet agent, Rudolf Abel, imprisoned by the Americans.

Powers died in a helicopter crash in 1977 but the U2 incident was a highlight of the Cold War.

The Bay of Pigs invasion

In April 1961 the US sponsored an invasion of Cuba led by anti-Castro Cuban exiles. The invasion force of 1,500 men landed at Bahia de Cochinos (Bay of Pigs) on the southern coast, but failed to win local support and was rapidly overwhelmed by Cuban troops, the failed invasion proving a considerable embarrassment to the US administration of John F. Kennedy.

The Cuban missile crisis

In October 1962 a U2 spy plane took pictures showing Soviet nuclear missiles in Cuba. President John F. Kennedy demanded that the Russians remove the missiles but the Soviet leader, Nikita Khrushchev, refused and a tense standoff ensued for a couple of days.

While their military top brass prepared for nuclear war the two leaders held secret talks by phone while several US ships sailed towards Cuba and placed themselves in the path of Soviet ships heading towards Cuba.

At what seemed like the last minute Khrushchev finally agreed to remove Russia's missiles from Cuba, and turned back the fleet of Soviet ships heading Cuba, and in return the US agreed not to invade Cuba

The Cold War winds down

After the Suez crisis of 1956, the Berlin crisis of 1958-61, and Cuban missile crisis of 1962, Nikita Khrushchev fell into disfavour because of his bluffing and gambling, and particularly for his 'brinkmanship' during the Cuban crisis

He was replaced as General-Secretary of the Communist Party of the Soviet Union by Leonid Brezhnev in October 1964. Brezhnev had been a political commissar in the Red Army in WW2, after which he became a party official in the Ukraine and Moldavia, and then Chairman of the Presidium of the Soviet Union from 1960 to 1964. He then became first to hold the position of General-Secretary (1964-82) and President of the Soviet Union (1977-82).

Brezhnev maintained strict control internally, involving military intervention in other socialist states such as Czechoslovakia (1968), combined with peaceful existence and détente abroad. Some believe he was largely responsible for a massive military and ailing economy that was a precursor to the disintegration of the Soviet Union.

In 1985 Michael Gorbachev became President of the USSR. Realizing that the USSR could not afford to keep up with the USA in the nuclear and biochemical 'arms race' he met with the US president Ronald Reagan to discuss arms control.

In 1987 the USSR and USA agreed to remove many nuclear weapons from Europe.

In the summer of 1989 Hungary was allowed open elections and began to allow East Germans passage to Austria and West Germany.

By autumn the East German regime was on the verge of collapse and on November the 9th people began demolishing sections of the Berlin Wall without government interference, and the government soon participated in the demolition. In 1990 East and West Germany were reunited, heralding the dismantling of the Soviet Union and, it is said, the end of the Cold War.

The Soviet Union had contained fifteen 'republics' and in 1991 the USSR was dismantled and these became the independent nations of:

- Armenia
- Azerbaijan
- Belarus
- Estonia
- Georgia
- Kazakhstan
- Kyrgyzstan
- Latvia
- Lithuania
- Moldova
- Russia
- Tajikistan
- Turkmenistan
- Ukraine
- Uzbekistan

In the 1990s, several countries released information about their spying activities during the Cold War. The USA arrested several Americans who had helped the Soviet Union, including FBI agent Robert Hanssen who was arrested for spying during the Cold War and charged with treason (Burgan, 2005).

Tensions still remain between Russia and the West, particularly the USA, however, so that to some extent remnants of the Cold War remain.

In addition, the rise of communist China has if anything widened the scope of these Cold War remnants. Memories of failed Western attempts to suppress communist movements in Korea in the 1950s, and in Vietnam in the 1970s, also contribute to these tensions.

Thus spying is a global activity indulged in by nearly all governments, but particularly the more powerful countries such as America, Russia and China. Spying is now very high-tech, involving satellites, drones and cyber activity.

Chapter 14

MALAYA, KOREA, VIETNAM & CAMBODIA

In revealing the workings of the government that led to the Vietnam War, the newspapers nobly did precisely that which the Founders hoped and trusted they would.
Hugo La Fayette Black, American judge,
re. publication of the Pentagon Papers in 1971.

The Malaysian Emergency

In 1948 the Malaysian Communist Party (MCP) began a campaign against British rule, much of its support coming from the Chinese rural population. After growing MCP violence, including the murder of European estate managers, on 16 June 1948 the British administration declared a state of emergency throughout Malaya.

In the early years of the insurrection the MCP achieved a number of notable successes, including assassination of the High Commissioner, Sir Henry Gurney, in October 1951.

By the mid-1950s, however, by means of a combination of fierce military measures, substantial resettlement of the Chinese rural population, and the introduction of political initiatives that clearly would soon bring independence to Malaysia, the insurrection was ended, though officially it did not end until 31 July 1960.

The Korean War

Korea was a united kingdom under the Silla Dynasty circa AD 668 and was sometimes associated with the Chinese empire. Korea achieved complete independence after the Sino-Japanese war of 1894-95 but was annexed by Japan in 1910 as the province of Chosun.

After Japan's defeat in World War 2 Korea was partitioned at the 38th parallel at the Potsdam conference in July 1945, Russian troops moving in on August 10th, and American troops on September 8th.

After a series of border clashes, the communist North invaded the South in June 1950. The UN asked the United States and other countries to send troops to defend South Korea. The Western allies forced the invaders back to the Chinese frontier but China then entered the war and, together with the North Koreans, occupied Seoul. The UN forces counter-attacked, retaking all territory south of the 38th parallel, and an armistice was signed in 1953.

French control in Vietnam ends

Communist insurrection in Vietnam began with the formation of the Indochinese communist party in 1929, followed by abortive revolts in the 1930s. Leaders of the party such as Ho Chi Minh and Vo Nguyen Giap established bases in caves in the northern Vietnamese mountains and began to build networks throughout Vietnam. In 1941 they created a united front group, the Viet Minh (*Viet Nam Doc Lap Dong Minh Hoi*) which downplayed its communist basis and emphasized the struggle for independence (*doc lap*) from France.

French troops began unsuccessful military operations against the Viet Minh in 1943. On December 22, 1944, the Viet Minh under Vo Nguyan Giap formed the Vietnam People's Army.

At the height of World War 2 Vietnam, Cambodia and Laos, collectively known as French Indochina, were occupied by Japan but America's attention was firmly focussed on defeating Germany.

The only battles that took place, therefore, were between the French and Japanese, or between the French and the Viet Minh.

Early in 1945, however, an American aircraft carrier fleet, Task Force 38, entered the South China Sea to make air raids against Japanese naval and air forces in Indochina. The Office of Strategic Services, forerunner of the CIA, ran an escape network in Indochina to rescue Allied airmen downed in southern China (Prados, 2009).

News of atomic bombs dropped on Japan on August 6 and 9, 1945, galvanized the Viet Minh and on August 12 they staged a general uprising in Vietnam and on August 16 Ho Chi Minh declared himself president of a provisional government of an independent Vietnam, which became the Democratic Republic of Vietnam (DRV).

Japan's surrender on August 15 made it necessary to disarm Japanese garrisons throughout China, Southeast Asia, and the Pacific. The Allied plan for this was temporary occupation by Nationalist Chinese of the north, and British forces in the south. This began a chain of events that led from the August Revolution to a Vietnamese war of Independence against France.

Britain's 20th Indian Division began arriving in Saigon in September. Initially faced by riots, the British used 4,000 Japanese troops to help establish order. Then they rearmed 1,400 French colonial troops that had been imprisoned by the Japanese. At the end of September French navy ships arrived carrying substantial forces, and on October 9 the British handed over power to the French.

On March 6, 1946, the French signed an agreement with the DRV reorganizing Vietnam as a "Free State" that would be part of the Indochinese Federation and the French Union, with the north and south to be reunited according to "decisions taken by the populations consulted by referendum."

Three successive sets of further talks failed, followed by an incident in which shelling by French warships at Haiphong killed thousands of Vietnamese. In retaliation, on December 19, 1946, the Viet Minh attacked the French in Hanoi and elsewhere, beginning a war that lasted until 1954.

With the Cold War having increased America's fear of communism, the US began to give substantial aid to the French forces in Vietnam and by the time Dwight D. Eisenhower became US president in January 1953 the US was paying 40% of the cost of the French war.

On March 13, 1954, Viet Minh artillery guns laboriously emplaced at Dien Bien Phu opened fire on a French military base whose airstrip was soon rendered useless. Over the next few days the Vietnamese captured parts of the base and the French appealed to the US for help, who in turn tried to enlist British involvement by citing the "domino theory."

Dien Bien Phu fell to the Vietnamese on May 7, leading to the end of French control in Vietnam. The Geneva Conference followed, leaving North Vietnam under the rule of Ho Chi Minh, with the South ruled by Emperor Bao Dai, and then by Ngo Dingh Diem. Elections were planned to choose a single government for all Vietnam but when they failed to take place conflict was renewed.

The Indo-China War between France and the Viet Minh lasted from 1946 until 1954 and ended with the French defeated, leaving the North and South with separate governments, the North being communist and supported by the Soviet Union and China, the south being supported by the USA.

The Vietnam War

In the late 1950s Communist guerrillas in South Vietnam called the 'Viet Cong' began trying to overthrow the government. North Vietnam supplied their weapons, and later sent soldiers as well.

In December 1960 the National Liberation Front (NLF) was formed, its military arm being the People's Liberation Armed Forces (PLAF).

Fearing the spread of communism, from 1961 the USA increased its aid to the South and sent "military advisors" to help establish and train the Army of the Republic of Vietnam (ARVN) for conventional war.

In 1962 president John F. Kennedy approved a 20,000-man increase in the ARVN, doubled the US military contingent to 1,200, and increased military aid greatly.

In 1964 the North Vietnamese attacked US ships and US president Lyndon Johnson ordered retaliatory bombing of North Vietnam. Although war was never declared officially, the US Congress passed the Gulf of Tonkin Resolution which authorized US forces in South-East Asia to repel any armed attack and to prevent further aggression.

US bombing of North Vietnam continued and in 1965 the US began increasing its troop commitment so that by 1968 more than 500,000 US soldiers were fighting in Vietnam. Conflict against the elusive communist guerrilla forces dragged on without an end in sight and opposition to the war in the USA grew.

Under the Nixon administration US fighter-bomber sorties against targets in South Vietnam increased from 400 in March 1972 to 10,526 in April. This year also saw the first use of laser-guided bombs by the US.

To avoid large-scale US bombing the Vietnamese built hundreds of kilometres of cramped underground earth tunnels from which they were able to launch small scale attacks and then quickly disappear. In response American and Australian forces used 'tunnel rats' to investigate and help destroy these tunnels, and this proved to one of the most daunting tasks in military history.

When US planes bombed Haiphong harbour, damaging Soviet merchant ships and killing five Russian seamen, Russia responded by sending a destroyer and a submarine armed with nuclear missiles to the area, later sending two more submarines to monitor US activity.

The American bombing campaigns made extensive use of 'Agent Orange' to defoliate much of the landscape and thus make it safer for incursions by their land forces. Because of the highly toxic nature of Agent Orange, and thus fears of long-term environmental deterioration, there was widespread opposition against its use around the world.

Cambodia and Laos were also caught up in the Vietnam War and pressure to end it grew in the USA. There were many large antiwar protests, particularly a march on the Pentagon in the autumn of 1967, and veterans groups which lobbied for American withdrawal from Vietnam were formed.

Peace negotiations were begun in Paris in 1968 and in 1973 a ceasefire agreement was signed. Despite this the North Vietnamese advance continued until Saigon was captured two years later, ending the war. Vietnam was officially reunited on July 2, 1976.

Spying in Vietnam

During the Vietnam War US intelligence agents worked closely with the Vietnamese. The CIA also recruited Laotian soldiers to help quell North Vietnamese incursions into Laos.

One of the most notorious spies for the communists was US sailor John Walker who worked in the radio room at a key naval office. In 1967 he met Soviet diplomats who agreed to pay him for secret US codes which revealed the locations of many US ships used to bombard Viet Cong positions near the coast. This information allowed the Viet Cong to move soldiers and supplies before they could be hit.

KGB agent Oleg Kalugin, who worked with Walker, recalled:

"He would drop these big brown bags filled with top secret, classified information, and it took some time for us to convince him that this was not right, that he should use . . . cameras and other gadgets" (Burgan, 2005).

Walker was paid up to $4,000 a month for his spy activities. After several years as a spy, Walker asked his brother and a friend to also spy for the Soviet Union and they agreed. Later he also added his son to this spy ring.

US authorities did not learn about this spy ring until 1985, by which time it had helped the Soviets read more than a million US messages. According to Burgan (2005):

"The KGB later said that Walker was its most important spy during the Cold War."

Cambodia

Peripheral areas of Cambodia were invaded by the Siamese and Vietnamese during the 19th century. France established a protectorate in 1863 and granted independence in 1953.

Relations with the US were broken in 1965 when South Vietnamese planes attacked Vietcong forces in Cambodia. They were restored in 1969 after the Cambodian leaders accused Viet communists with arming Cambodian insurgents.

In 1970 pro-US Premier Lon Noi seized power, abolishing the monarchy and demanding removal of 40,000 Vietnamese troops. Former leader Prince Norodom Sihanouk formed a government-in-exile in Beijing, and war began between the new government and Communist Khmer Rouge guerrillas, the US providing economic and military aid.

On April 17, 1975, Khmer Rouge revolutionary forces led by Pol Pot captured Phnom Penh. In only four years the Pol Pot regime executed over a million people (some estimates put it as high as 3 million) and evacuated all cities and towns, sending almost the entire population to open country.

Severe border fighting with Vietnam broke out in 1978 and the Vietnamese invaded and captured Phnom Penh on January 7, 1979, forming a Vietnamese-backed government the next day. Thousands of refugees fled to Thailand and widespread starvation was reported.

Pol Pot fled to the jungles of southwest Cambodia and he and remnants of the Khmer Rouge held power until 1997 in the region of the border between Cambodia and Thailand with UN recognition as the rightful government of Cambodia.

Pol Pot died in 1998 and conjecture remains that he was poisoned or committed suicide.

On January 10, 1983, Vietnamese forces launched an offensive against rebel forces in the west. They overran a refugee camp on January 31, forcing 30,000 refugees to flee to Thailand.

Vietnam then launched a major offensive against camps on the Cambodian-Thailand border, engaged Khmer Rouge guerrillas, and crossed the border and clashed with Thai troops. Vietnam withdrew nearly all its troops by September 1989.

Following UN-sponsored elections in Cambodia that ended on May 28, 1993, the two leading parties agreed to share power in an interim government and a new constitution was adopted. On September 21, a constitution re-establishing a monarchy was adopted by the National Assembly. This took effect on September 24 with Sihanouk as king.

The Khmer Rouge, which had boycotted the elections, opposed the new government, and armed violence continued in the mid-1990s. In August 1996, Ieng Sary, a Khmer Rouge leader, broke with the guerrillas and formed a rival group which supported the monarchy and Khmer Rouge strength rapidly diminished.

On July 5, 1997, co-prime minister Hun Sen staged a coup, ousting Prince Norodom Ranariddh. Pol Pot, the Khmer Rouge leader who had held power during the late 1970s was denounced by his former comrades at a show trial on July 25 and sentenced to lifetime house arrest.

Conclusion

Just as Russia took control of much of Europe after World War 2, it also played a role in the partitioning of Korea, and communist influence and conflict occurred throughout much of Asia, much of it supported by China.

In Vietnam the death toll of troops and civilians was at least a million, but the Vietnamese government estimates two million.

The US-sponsored invasion of Cambodia resulted in perhaps another two million deaths in its "killing fields."

Chapter 15

TERRORISM

> *Fighting terrorism is like being a goalkeeper.*
> *You can make a hundred brilliant saves but the only shot*
> *that people remember is the one that gets past you.*
> Paul Wilkinson (b. 1937), British scholar & author on terrorism.
> *Daily Telegraph*, London, 1 Sept. 1992.

A brief history of terrorism

Terrorism has a long history, for example:

➤ Secret societies in some ancient tribal cultures sometimes maintained their status through terror.

➤ A Shiite Muslim sect carried out terrorist campaigns against Sunni Muslims in the 12th century.

➤ In the 19th century the aftermath of the French Revolution saw occasional outbreaks of terrorist activity in support of revolution, culminating in the successful Russian Revolution of 1917.

➤ In the 20th century organizations in several countries including Croatia, Ireland, Macedonia, and Palestine often carried out terrorist activities in other countries. Sometimes these were government supported, as in the assassination of Archduke Francis Ferdinand of Austria in Sarajevo in 1914 which sparked World War I.

Northern Ireland

There has been conflict between Catholics and Protestants in Northern Ireland for centuries. The roots of the problem go back to the province of Ulster where the Roman Catholic earls of Tyrone rebelled against English rule circa 1600. They were forced to flee and most of the land was confiscated by King James I who gave it to Protestant Scotch, Welsh and English settlers.

Ulster was further colonized by Cromwell in the mid-17th century and in the early 20th century its opposition to Irish Home Rule led to the formation of Northern Ireland.

Since then there has often been conflict between Catholics and Protestants, this reaching a peak in the 1960s and 1970s when the Irish Republican Army (IRA) used terror tactics against Ulster Protestants and British military forces which resulted in 3000 people being killed before the 1994 cease-fire. Sinn Fein, the political branch of the IRA, was founded in 1902 and dominated the 1918 election. Its power diminished after 1926 but it participated in the peace talks on Northern Ireland in the 1980s and 1990s.

The Rev. Ian Paisley became the extreme voice of Protestant opinion in the sectarian strife of Northern Ireland, leading many demonstrations and repeatedly being imprisoned for unlawful assembly. He was elected to the House of Commons in 1970, was cofounder of the Democratic Unionist Party in 1971, and also organized the Third Force, a paramilitary group of Protestant fighters.

South Africa and the ANC

Nelson Mandela was one of the founders of the African National Congress which campaigned for democracy and thus equality for the black people of South Africa during the 1950s. Eventually the ANC abandoned its policy of non-violence and established a military wing with Mandela being made its leader in December 1961. He was arrested in August 1962 and imprisoned.

South Africa had a large biochemical warfare (BW) research program at that time, building up an arsenal of anthrax, botulinum, Ebola, Marburg and HIV virus. In fact, certain people in South Africa testified that many people in the antiapartheid movement were poisoned using BW material.

Latin America

Latin America has a long-standing tradition of political violence. So-called urban guerrilla movements were a new development, as terrorist activities shifted from country areas to the cities. One such group was Shining Path, a Peruvian Maoist terrorist group which used extremely brutal and indiscriminate tactics to destabilize the government, in turn provoking strong countermeasures.

In Colombia from 1948 to 1956 'La Violencia', a wave of urban and rural violence cost 200,000 lives.

In the 1990's members of Colombia's cocaine cartel used terrorist tactics to force the government to reduce enforcement of anti-drug-trafficking laws.

During the 1990 election campaign 3 presidential candidates were assassinated. In August 1996 left wing rebels of the Revolutionary Armed Forces of Colombia (FARC) killed 80 soldiers and police in ten separate incidents.

In March 1998 FARC forces ambushed elite government troops in a remote southern jungle region, killing about 70 soldiers in the worst government defeat in the 35 years since guerrilla hostilities began. Government sources estimated that more than 41,000 Colombians, mostly poor farmers, fled their homes to escape the growing violence between guerrillas and paramilitary units.

Japan

In 1995 the religious cult Aum Shinrikyo released deadly sarin nerve gas in the Tokyo subway (Lifton, 1999), killing 12 people and injuring 5,500.

This small group isolated its converts and brainwashed them for long periods and had ambitious plans which included obtaining nuclear weapons (Lifton, 1999).

Socialist revolutionary terrorism

Throughout history people have risen up against oppressive monarchies, governments and occupation by foreign powers. The long-running Third Servile War or Gladiator's revolt led by Spartacus against the Romans just before the time of Christ is a well-known example.

Modern systematic terrorism evolved with the growth of revolutionary ideologies in the wake of the French Revolution, and proponents and opponents of revolutionary values engaged in terrorism after the Napoleonic Wars.

The Russian revolutionary movement before World War I had a strong terrorist element and Leon Trotsky employed terrorism as a principal instrument of policy. The political instability of the 1920s and 1930s which followed the Russian Revolution also included prevalent terrorist activity.

In West Germany the so-called Red Army Faction, better known as the Baader-Meinhof Gang, robbed several banks and raided US military installations. This group frequently cooperated with Palestinian terrorists, notably in the murder of Israeli athletes at the Olympic Games in Munich in 1972.

The Japanese Red Army terrorist group also cooperated with Palestinian terrorists.

The Italian Red Brigades carried out numerous acts of terror, in particular kidnapping and murdering former Prime Minister Aldo Moro in 1978.

To this day socialist terrorism occurs in parts of Africa, Asia, Europe, and South America, for example Maoists using terrorism in Nepal.

Right-wing terrorism

Japan was ruled by the militarist shogun almost continuously from 1192 up to 1867, when pro-imperial terrorism helped restore imperial government in Japan in 1868.

The political instability in some countries in the 1920s and 1930s which followed the Russian Revolution was often accompanied by terrorist activity from both extremes of the political spectrum.

More recently right-wing terrorism in support of authoritarian rule was responsible for the 1980 bombing of the Bologna railway station in Italy. In 1993 the historic Uffizi Gallery in Florence was one of the targets of a series of terrorist bombings attributed to the Mafia.

State sponsored terrorism

After the Russian Revolution the British secret service provided considerable covert support to the White Russian army resisting the revolution. When that failed they began counter terrorist activities against the new Russia, for example Lieutenant Agar's sinking of the Red Fleet cruiser Oleg in Kronstadt harbour in 1919 (Brook-Shepherd, 1998).

Fidel Castro was of such concern to the US that no less than 30 attempts were made on his life during the 1960s.

During the Vietnam War, North Vietnam backed a Communist campaign of terrorism and subversion in South Vietnam.

North Korea has carried out several terrorist attacks against South Korea, including a bombing in Rangoon in 1983 in which 17 people were killed, and the bombing of a Korean Air Lines passenger airliner in 1987 by North Korean agents.

Bombing of the Greenpeace ship Rainbow Warrior in Auckland harbour in 1985 by French secret service agents was also an example of state-supported terror.

Cult groups

There are many 'cult groups' around the world, some of which have caused conflict.

In 1995 the religious cult Aum Shinrikyo released sarin nerve gas in the Tokyo subway, killing 12 people and injuring 5,500 (Lifton, 1999).

In the US there are several sectarian and religious militia groups such as the Klu Klux Klan, Aryan Nation, Posse Comitatus, The Order, The Texas Militia and many others (Dees, 1996; Jones & Israel, 1998; Snow, 1999).

The 1995 Oklahoma City bombing, in which 168 people were killed, was the most spectacular act of terrorism on US soil before the September 11 attacks. It was in revenge for the mass deaths in 1993 of most of the members of the Branch Davidian movement at Waco after a 51-day siege by federal agents.

The FBI charged Timothy McVeigh and Terry Nichols with the bombing but only McVeigh was convicted.

McVeigh's chief defence counsellor, however, found that McVeigh and Nichols had had contacts with Aryan Nation, other people with neo-Nazi sympathies and, most interesting of all, Nicholls had been to the Philippines several times where he had been in contact with Ramzi Yousef who in turn had had contact with al-Qa'ida and Osama Bin Laden (Jones & Israel, 1998) and been responsible for the 1993 bombing of the World Trade Centre, and for the plot to destroy Philippines Airlines Flight 434 in 1994.

Another supposedly lone bomber in the USA was Theodore Kaczynski, known as the Unabomber.

Not only must the US expect further attacks from external organizations like al-Qa'ida, there is also the possibility of attacks organized by one of its militia groups:

> *I suspect Americans will begin engaging in terrorism*
> *on a scale the world has never known.*
> William Pearce, author of *The Turner Diaries* (1978)
> and leader of the National Alliance, a US neo-Nazi group.

Israeli and Palestinian terrorism

Jewish radicals such as the Stern Gang and the Irgun Zvai Leumi resorted to terrorism against Arab communities and other groups during their struggle for an independent Israel in the late 1940s.

The greatest Islamic grievance is the Israel issue. That much of Palestine was given by the UN to the Jews in 1948 was bad enough, but the territories occupied by Israel after the 1967 war, including Jerusalem, compounded this grievance greatly.

Thus in the 1960s Israel's adversaries began to use terrorism much more systematically. In the 1970s the Black September group, so-named after the expulsion of Palestinian guerrillas from Jordan in September 1970, carried out many attacks.

The Palestine Liberation Organization (PLO) has conducted commando and terrorist operations both within Israel and in other countries right up until the present day.

In response Israel has carried out actions against PLO and other targets which can be considered as terrorism.

Islamic terrorism

Revolution in Iran in 1978 and the rise of Islamic fundamentalism saw terrorism spread globally thanks to new groups such as al-Qa'ida, some examples being:

➢ The 1976 hijacking of an Air France airplane at Entebbe by the Black September Group (an offshoot of the PLO).
➢ The 1980 attack on a synagogue in the Rue de Copernic in Paris.
➢ The 1981 assassination of the French ambassador in Lebanon.
➢ The 1982 assassination of the Israeli diplomat Yacob Barsimentov by the Lebanese Revolutionary Army.
➢ The 1982 attack on the Goldenberg Restaurant in the Rue des Rosiers in Paris by Abu Nidal (an offshoot of the PLO).
➢ The 1983 attack on Orly by the Secret Army for the Liberation of Armenia (SAALA).
➢ The 1983 suicide truck bombing of the American HQ in Lebanon, killing 241 marines, and on the French HQ, killing 58 paratroopers.
➢ The 1985 hijacking of the Italian ship the Achille Lauro by the PLF (Palestine Liberation Front).
➢ The 1985 simultaneous hijacking of El Al Airline counters in Vienna and Rome (Abu Nidal).
➢ The 1986 wave of public explosions in public places in Paris (5 in September alone) by the CSAPP (Committee for the Support of Arab Political Prisoners).

➤ In 1988 a bomb destroyed a Pan American Flight over Lockerbie, Scotland, killing all 259 people on board and 11 on the ground. Subsequently two Libyan agents were charged with the crime and one of them convicted.
➤ The 1989 mid-air explosion of a UTA plane, killing 171.
➤ Fundamentalist terrorism directed against the socialist government of Algeria led to virtual civil war in the 1990s.
➤ Bombing of New York's World Trade Centre in 1993.*
➤ Bombing of US embassies in Kenya and Tanzania in 1998 with the loss of 224 lives.*
➤ Bombing of the USS Cole in 2000.*
➤ Attacks on the US by three hijacked planes on September 11, 2001 which cost almost 3,000 lives.*
➤ A car bomb attack in Bali on a bar popular with Westerners that killed almost 200 people in 2002.
➤ The Nov. 2003 Istanbul truck bomb attacks.*
➤ Chechen 'hostaging' 800 people in a Moscow theatre. Russian troops gassed the building, resulting in 200 deaths.
➤ The 2004 Khobar massacre.*
➤ Attacks on trains and buses in Spain and England in 2004 and 2005.*
➤ June 2008 car bombing of Danish embassy in Pakistan.*
➤ Sept. 2008 truck bombing of Marriot Hotel in Pakistan.*
➤ The 2009 Khost CIA bombing killed 8 agents.*
➤ 2003-present: many bombings in Iraq.*
➤ April 2015: The Somalia-based terrorist group Al Shabaab captured and killed 140 Kenyan University students, separating Christians to do so.
➤ 2010-present: much of Iraq and Syria overtaken by Islamic State (IS) with many atrocities (public beheadings etc.), high casualty rates, abductions of large numbers of women, with millions displaced from their homes.

* = known or believed to be due to al-Qa'ida.

Besides the globally active al-Qa'ida and IS, there are many other terrorist organizations around the world besides those mentioned above, most of them Muslim, including:

➢ Gaza and the West Bank: Hamas and the PLO.

➢ Israel: Kahane Chai (Kach).

➢ Lebanon: Hezbollah.

➢ Iraq: QJBR (al-Qa'ida in Iraq).

➢ Afghanistan: the Taliban

➢ Turkey: Revolutionary People's Liberation Party/Front.

➢ Iraq and Syria: Islamic State (IS or ISIL, ISIS).

➢ Bangladesh: Harkat-ul-Jihad al-Islami (HUJI-B)

➢ Sri Lanka: Liberation Tigers of Tamil Eelam (LTTE).

➢ India: Indian Mujahideen (IM).

➢ Japan: Aum Shinrikyo.

➢ Pakistan: Harakat ul-Mujahadin (HUM).

➢ South-East Asia: al-Jama'a al-Islamiya (JI).

➢ Uzbekistan: Islamic Jihad Union (IJU).

➢ Somalia: Al-Shabaab

➢ Uganda: Lord's Resistance Army.

➢ UK & Ireland: Continuity IRA (CIRA), Real IRA (RIRA).

➢ Greece: Revolutionary Organization 11 November.

➢ Spain: Euskadi Ta Askatasuna (ETA).

➢ Colombia: FARC & the National Liberation Army (ELN).

➢ Peru: Shining Path (SL).

Al-Qa'ida

Osama Bin Laden, of course, had been on the side of the Americans in helping the Taliban fight the occupying Russian forces in Afghanistan in the 1980s (Nojumi, 2002).

In the 1990s, enraged at the presence of US troops in Saudi Arabia during the Persian Gulf War, he and his associates in al-Qa'ida turned their attention to the Americans with the bombing of several US embassies in the Middle East and Africa, culminating in the spectacular plane attacks of September 11, 2001.

An article in *The Australian* newspaper on 3 November 2004 reported that Bin Laden had vowed in one of his regularly released videotapes to send the US broke. He claimed that every dollar spent by al-Qa'ida on terrorist strikes had cost the US $1 million in economic damage. He estimated the US deficit at more than $US 1 trillion.

Al-Qa'ida's attacks often involve simultaneous suicide attacks on neighbouring targets. Its aim is removal of all foreign influences in Muslim countries and creation of a world-wide Islamic caliphate. As Salafist jihadists they oppose man-made laws yet ignore any religious scripture which might forbid the murder of civilians and bloody conflict.

Al-Qa'ida is intolerant of non-Sunnis and regards liberal Muslims as heretics and has carried out numerous sectarian attacks, for example the Sadr City bombings and the April 2007 Baghdad bombings, and such activities continue to this day.

Al-Qa'ida operates through unregulated banks and the 9/11 Commission report estimated that it needed $30M/year for its operations which include military training, finance, operations management, and a media division.

Al-Jama'a al-Islamiya

Established circa 1969, this militant Islamist terrorist organization is dedicated to establishing an Islamic caliphate in Southeast Asia. JI has cells in Thailand, Singapore, Malaysia, the Phillipines, Irian Jaya and Australia, and has connections with al-Qa'ida and the Moro Islamic Liberation Front.

JI was responsible for the 2000 bombing of the Jakarta Stock Exchange, the 2002 Bali bombing, the 2003 JW Marriott hotel bombing in Jakarta, the 2004 Australian embassy bombing in Jakarta, the 2005 Bali bombing, and the 2009 JW Marriott and Ritz-Carlton hotel bombings in Jakarta. JI was also responsible for dozens of bombings in the southern Philippines, usually with the help of the Abu Sayyaf Group (ASG).

Several JI leaders have been captured in the last decade.

Al-Shabaab

Al Shabaab (Harakat al-Shabaab al-Mujahideen, HSM), is a jihadist terrorist group based in Somalia. In 2012, it pledged allegiance to the militant Islamist organization Al-Qaeda but some of the group's leaders quarrelled with Al-Qaeda over the union, and quickly lost ground.

Al-Shabaab's troop strength was estimated at 7,000 to 9,000 militants in 2014. As of 2015, the group has retreated from the major cities, controlling a few rural areas.

Al-Shabaab is an off-shoot of the Islamic Courts Union (ICU), which splintered into several smaller factions after its defeat in 2006 by Somalia's Transitional Federal Government (TFG) and the TFG's Ethiopian military allies. The group describes itself as waging jihad against "enemies of Islam", and is engaged in combat against the Federal Government of Somalia and the African Union Mission to Somalia (AMISOM).

Al-Shabaab has been designated as a terrorist organization by Australia, Canada, the United Arab Emirates, the United Kingdom and the United States. As of June 2012, the US State Department has open bounties on several of the group's senior commanders.

In early August 2011, the Transitional Federal Government's troops and their AMISOM allies managed to capture all of Mogadishu from the Al-Shabaab militants.

An ideological rift within the group's leadership also emerged, and several of the organization's senior commanders were assassinated.

Due to its Wahhabi roots, Al Shabaab is hostile to Sufi traditions, and has often clashed with the militant Sufi group Ahlu Sunna Waliama'a. The group has also been suspected of having links with Al-Qaeda in Islamic Maghreb and Boko Haram.

In August 2014, the Somali government-led Operation Indian Ocean was launched to remove remaining insurgent-held pockets in the countryside. On 1 September 2014, a US drone strike carried out as part of the broader mission killed Al-Shabaab's leader and optimistic political analysts suggested that the insurgent commander's death might lead to Al-Shabaab's fragmentation and eventual dissolution.

Boko Haram

Boko Haram, meaning "Western education is forbidden", is a jihadist group based in north-east Nigeria but also active in Chad, Niger and Cameroon. Estimates of the group's membership vary from 7,000 to 10,000 fighters.

The group initially had links to al-Qaeda, but in 2014 it expressed support for the Islamic State of Iraq and the Levant before pledging formal allegiance to it in March 2015.

After its founding in 2002, Boko Haram's increasing radicalization led to a violent uprising in July 2009 in which its leader was executed. Its unexpected resurgence, following a mass prison break in September 2010, was accompanied by increasingly sophisticated attacks, initially against soft targets, and progressing in 2011 to include suicide bombings of police buildings and the United Nations office in Abuja.

The government's establishment of a state of emergency at the beginning of 2012, extended in the following year to cover the entire northeast of Nigeria, resulted in a marked increase in both security force abuses and militant attacks. Boko Haram killed more than 13,000 civilians between 2009 and 2015, including around 10,000 in 2014, in attacks occurring mainly in northeast Nigeria.

More than 1.5 million people have been displaced in the violence. Corruption in the security services, and human rights abuses committed by them, have hindered efforts to counter the unrest.

Since 2009 Boko Haram have abducted more than 500 men, women and children, including the kidnapping of 276 schoolgirls from Chibok in April 2014.

650,000 people had fled the conflict zone by August 2014, an increase of 200,000 since May, and by the end of the year 1.5 million had fled.

The Nigerian military initially proved ineffective in countering the insurgency, hampered by an entrenched culture of official corruption. Since mid-2014, the militants have been in control of swathes of territory in and around their home state of Borno, estimated at 50,000 square kilometres (20,000 sq mi) in January 2015, but have not captured the capital of Borno state, where the group was originally based.

As a result of joint military operations by the Nigerian, Chadian and Cameroonian armies, local vigilante groups, local hunters and local fishermen, Boko Haram lost its capital Gwoza and most of its occupied territories but it still controls southern parts of Borno State.

The Taliban

This fundamentalist Islamic political movement spread into Afghanistan where it formed government in 1996 but gained diplomatic recognition only from Pakistan, Saudi Arabia and the United Arab Emirates.

The Taliban strictly interpret sharia law, limiting the rights of women. The top leadership group is the Quetta Shura based since circa 2001 in the city of Quetta in the Balochistan province of Pakistan.

Members of Pakistan's Inter-Services Intelligence (ISI) are believed to have attended meetings of the Quetta Shurah and supported the Taliban. In 2009 the Pakistani government acknowledged the existence of Quetta Shurah for the first time and since that time several of its members have been detained at various locations in Pakistan.

Islamic State

The Sunni terrorist organization Islamic State (IS), also known as Islamic State in Levant (ISIL), have been the major revolutionary terrorist group in recent years, having overtaken much of Iraq and Syria a few years ago.

IS has committed countless atrocities, beheading and burning people alive, and making propaganda videos of such actions. Such propaganda has succeeded in recruiting young Muslim men and women globally, the women being used for suicide bombings or as wives and household and sexual slaves.

Despite many Saudi Arabian bombing raids in Syria, and US drone attacks in Iraq and elsewhere, IS continues to control major areas in Iraq and Syria.

Thanks to Russian involvement in Syria in recent years, however, IS controls much less territory there but IS-inspired terror attacks continue around the world.

Conclusions

The term fundamentalism is used to describe conservative trends in various religious denominations, notably Islam, Judaism, and Hinduism.

Fundamentalists oppose governments they consider too liberal, or try to win political office in order to represent fundamentalist views. In Israel, for example, the Likud party has a strong power base amongst Jewish fundamentalists who believe the Jewish scriptures justify Israel's possession of land claimed by the Palestinians.

Fundamentalist and radical leaders are, of course, at pains to differentiate themselves from mainstream society. Those who do not follow their extreme dictates they denigrate, often with long speeches that seem nonsensical to all but their 'disciples' who, all too often, are used to carry out acts of terrorism aimed at eventually empowering the leaders politically by weakening any political opposition.

All too many Muslim fundamentalists, however, hold impractically extreme views not in keeping with the modern technological world.

Terrorism is to be abhorred at all times but yet Islamic terrorism continues around the world to the point at which most non-Muslims regard Muslim fundamentalists as primitive, unpleasant, and dangerous, and have little better regard for Muslims in general.

In non-Muslin countries, many journalists and politicians have linked Islamic fundamentalism to violence and terrorism. In fact, Islam preaches tolerance, but also requires its followers to protest against what they see as political and moral abuses of their societies. Unfortunately, all too often such protest has been of the violent kind and, most culpable of all, there is all too little complaint from other Muslim leaders or the general Muslim community.

Bottom line

Islamic terrorism remains a major and costly problem in the world today. In the countries from which it originates it is bad for business, especially tourism, of course. Elsewhere it considerably increases government military and police expenditures, also increasing costs in many industries such as the airline industry.

Worldwide there were 11,604 terrorist attacks in 2010, 5% more than the year before. There are still hundreds of people active in al-Qa'ida and it still exerts much influence, particularly in Afghanistan, Iraq, Pakistan, and Yemen.

A former leader of the CIA bin Laden team during the 1990s said in 2011 that, far from winning the war against terrorism, the West was losing and did not understand the conflict (article in *The Times* by Tom Coghlan in May 2011).

He concluded:

It is support for Israel, support for the Saudi police state, it's our presence in the Arab peninsula, it's support for the Russians in the Islamic Caucasus. There is no more effective recruiter for al-Qa'ida than the status quo of American foreign policy.

The first three points are those which Bin Laden made when he openly declared war on the US in 1998.

That there has been no resolution of the 'Palestine question' after so long is shameful and firm UN resolutions are needed to force an ever-intransigent Israel to more equally share the area that was Palestine for most of the last two thousand years and right up to 1948. If Israel chose to ignore such resolutions then the West should withdraw all support for Israel, no matter what the consequences.

Conversely, since Korea was divided in 1945 it has remained a problem and, perhaps, the country should be reunited in some way.

On terrorism, civil war etc., the bottom line on such problems is that they are often caused by the stirrings of a few radical outcastes with nothing better to do, Bin Laden perhaps having been an example. That they sometimes have such influence on the gullible, in turn resulting in enormous loss of life, is tragic and the human race has to wise up to the propaganda and lies it has been fed from pulpits, lecterns, soap boxes, and by the media for millennia.

A recent example of this was the bombing of the 2013 Boston marathon by two young Muslim men who had been influenced by the ravings of radical Muslim clerics, little Hitlers that this world needs to rid itself of as soon as possible. As it is, however, is it likely that the Muslim religion will come to be regarded as somewhat evil for the rest of human history in the same way as the Nazis will be.

PART 2
WORLDWIDE CONFLICT

Chapter 16

THE MIDDLE EAST

*People do not want words – they want the sound of battle
. . . the battle of destiny.* Gamal Abdel Nasser,
speech to National Assembly, Jan. 20, 1969.

*We don't thrive on military acts. We do them because
we have to, and thank God we are efficient.*
Golda Meir, *Vogue*, July 1969.

The Sunni/Shi'a split

When the Prophet Mohammad died in Medina in 632 no successor had been chosen and his father-in-law assumed the role of caliph, supreme leader of the Islamic community.

In 644 a Christian slave from Persia stabbed the caliph. As he slowly died he chose a six-man council of generals to organize the election of his successor.

The new caliph was Uthman ibn Affan of the Umayyad clan, a wealthy merchant who had been a close companion of the prophet. He built public works, an Islamic navy, and compiled the first authoritative version of the prophet's teaching. He also appointed many members of his family to rule Islamic lands.

On Friday 17 June 656, Egyptian rebels killed the caliph and debate over who should replace him ensued. Some thought a member of the Umayyad clan should be chosen, but Mohammad's son-in-law Ali assumed control, refusing to have the Egyptian rebels executed for Uthman's murder.

A civil war followed until Ali was murdered in 661 and Uthman's tribe claimed control over the Islamic world. They were opposed by Ali's son Hussein, but he too was killed in October 680.

The 'Partisans of Ali', in Arabic *Shi'at Ali* or *Shi'a* for short, believe only the descendants of Ali should be caliph, whereas the Sunni majority believes the first four caliphs were the legitimate successors to Mohammad. The Shi'as are the stricter sect, whereas the Sunnis are fragmented in similar manner to the many Protestant denominations.

In the Afghan civil war of the 1990s, Iran supported the embattled Shi'a in the north, and Pakistan and the US supported the Sunni-backed Pathan Taliban movement.

Today there are about 800 million Sunnis and 120 million Shi'as, most of the latter being in Iran and Iraq, and conflict between the two sects continues with almost daily bombings in those and other countries.

The Shi'as, which are about 15% of all Muslims, have several sects, the principle divisions being (Massoulié, 2003):

Islamites: including the Druze in Lebanon, Syria, Israel and Jordan; the Nizarites (from the Assassins) or Contemporary Islamites in Syria, Lebanon, Oman, Turkistan, Afghanistan and Pakistan.

Nusayrites or 'Alaouties: Syria, Lebanon and Alevia in Turkey.

Zaydites: North Yemen

Duodecimains or 'Imamites (90% of Shi'ites): Iran, Iraq, Bahrain and the Gulf, Lebanon, Syria, India, Afghanistan, Pakistan and the former USSR.

The Crusades

After the Islamic conquest of Jerusalem in 638, Christian pilgrims were harassed and massacred. During the Muslim invasion of Syria in 634 thousands of Christians were massacred. From 635-643 many more were slain as Mesopotamia and then Egypt were conquered.

In the 8th century a Muslim ruler banned all displays of the Cross in Jerusalem, increased the penalty tax (Jizya), and forbade Christians to engage in religious instruction, even of their own children.

In 772, the Calipha al Mansur ordered the hands of all Christians and Jews branded. In 789, Muslims beheaded a monk in Bethlehem, plundering the monastery and slaughtering many more Christians.

In the tenth century Muslim rulers began a new wave of destruction of churches. On Palm Sunday in 937, Muslims went on a rampage in Jerusalem, plundering and destroying the Church of Calvary and the Church of the Resurrection.

In 1004 the Fatimid Calipha Abu Ali al-Mansur al-Hakim launched a wave of church bombing and destruction, confiscation of Christian property, and slaughter of Christians and Jews. In the next 10 years 30,000 churches were destroyed and countless Christians killed.

In 1009, Al-Hakim ordered the destruction of all Christian places of worship in Jerusalem and Christians and Jews were persecuted even more severely than previously under Muslim rule. Humiliating and burdensome decrees were heaped upon them, Christians being forced to wear heavy crosses around their necks, and Jews being forced to wear blocks of wood in the shape of a calf around their necks (Hammond, 2010).

In 1065, thousands of Christian pilgrims were attacked by Muslims in violation of earlier agreements of safe passage.

The Christian Byzantine Empire had conquered much of Syria and Palestine, including Antioch in 969. Then the Seljuk Turks invaded and conquered Christian Armenia and most of Asia Minor. They took Jerusalem in 1070 AD, defeated the Greeks at Mantzikert in 1071 AD, conquered Antioch in 1084, and by 1092 all the Christian parishes in Asia were under Muslim control so that the Byzantines appealed to the West for help.

On 27 November, 1095, the pope called upon the knights of Europe to retake the Holy Land and rescue the Holy Sepulchre and by May 1097 the armies of the first crusade were assembled (Hammond, 2010).

On July 1, 1097 AD, the Crusaders defeated the Turks at the battle of Dorylaeum. On 20 October 1097 they laid siege to the fortified city of Antioch, invading and capturing it on 3 June 1098.

After a period of recuperation and re-supply the Crusaders marched towards Jerusalem in April 1099. On July 15, 1099, they defeated and slew the Muslim forces occupying Jerusalem.

In 1112, aided by Norwegian troops and the Genoese, Pisan and Venetian fleets the Crusaders began to conquer the ports of Syria, completing their task with the fall of Tyre in 1124, so that they now controlled the Kingdom of Jerusalem, the principalities of Antioch, Tripoli and Edessa.

In 1144 the Muslims counter-attacked and regained the principality of Edessa. Damascus fell in 1169.

In 1169 the Kurdish prince Saladin succeeded his uncle as grand Vizier of Egypt and in 1171 he helped overthrow the Shi'ite Fatimid dynasty.

In 1187 Saladin's army conquered Jerusalem.

Europe responded with the Third Crusade led by Emperor Frederik Barbarossa of Germany, King Phillip of France, and Richard the Lionhearted, King of England. Acre surrendered to Richard on 13 July 1191, and after numerous battles against Saladin a treaty guaranteeing Christians safe access to Jerusalem and other holy places was secured.

After Saladin's death, the Crusaders again conquered Jerusalem in 1229, but it was retaken by the Muslims in 1244. Then Caesarea surrendered on condition that its 2,000 knights were spared, but once the Muslims had taken control they were all murdered. When the Muslims overtook Antioch they executed 16,000 Christians and sold 100,000 people into slavery. By the end of the 13th century, the last Crusader remnants in Palestine and Syria had been wiped out (Hammond, 2010).

The Ottoman Empire

The first Caliphs had ruled from Mecca. By 711 Islam had spread to North Africa and Spain, spreading to Southern France by 718.

The Ummayad dynasty ruled from Damascus for about 90 years until 749 and the Abbasid dynasty ruled from 750 until 1258 AD, Baghdad becoming the new capital of Islam. Its empire was destroyed by Genghis Khan in the 13th Century.

The Ottoman Empire was founded by Emir Osman I in 1301 and Sunni Turks began to build a new Islamic empire which eventually encompassed the whole of North Africa, the near East, India, the Balkans of South-Eastern Europe.

The only exception was Persia (now known as Iran) which embraced Shi'ism (Massoulié, 2003).

From 1350, for 300 years Turkish Muslims invaded Christian villages to exact an annual 'blood levy' in which one in five Christian boys were forced into the Sultan's armies, an additional burden to the crippling Jizya tribute tax.

On 29 May 1453 the Turks conquered Constantinople, slaughtering tens of thousands of civilians, Turkish soldiers fighting over boys and young women. By 1529 the Turks were besieging the gates of Vienna.

The tide turns in the Mediterranean

Cyprus fell to the Turks in 1571 and, after incurring heavy losses, they inflicted unspeakable cruelties and mutilations on Christian prisoners.

Turkish expansionism was halted at the Battle of Lepanto on 7 October 1571 when a Christian fleet of 208 warships organized by the pope defeated a Turkish fleet of 230 warships, killing 15,000 Turks and taking 15,000 prisoners. When the Turks were later defeated outside the gates of Vienna the overt threat to Europe was ended.

The Ottoman Empire began to decline and when Sultan Murab III died in 1595 his son had his 19 brothers murdered to protect his throne. Then he had seven of his father's concubines sown into sacks and thrown into the river.

After an orgy Sultan Ibrahim had all 300 women of his harem put into sacks and thrown into the Bosphorus and only one survived by being picked up by a ship bound for France.

When Ibrahim was finally assassinated the Ottoman Empire was riddled with corruption (Hammond, 2010).

The end of the Ottoman Empire

In the early 19th century the Ottoman Empire suffered defeats at the hands of Russia and Austria, whilst the Greeks and Serbs mounted successful wars of liberation.

The last century of Ottoman rule, however, saw the most complete destruction of Christian communities throughout the Middle East, Asia Minor, the Caucasus, and the Balkans,

In 1822, the entire populations of the Island of Chios, tens of thousands of people, were massacred or enslaved. In 1823, the Turks slaughtered 8750 Christians at Missolonghi.

In 1850 thousands of Christians were murdered in the province of Mosul. In 1860 more than 12,000 Christians were slaughtered in Lebanon. In 1876, 14,700 Bulgarians were murdered by the Turks.

The Turks slaughtered over 200,000 Armenian Christians in Bayazid (1877), Alashgurd (1879), Sassun (1894), Constantinople (1896), Adana (1909) and Armenia (1895-1896). In 1915 the Turks massacred more than 1.5 million Armenian Christians, and 100,000 Maronite Christians in Lebanon and Syria.

In 1922 the Turks destroyed Smyrna and massacred its Christian population of 300,000. On 9 September 1922, a mob organized by the Turkish army attacked a Greek Orthodox priest, ripping his eyes out and dragging him bleeding through the streets. When he raised his right hand and repeated: "Father, forgive them," they cut it off and he was hacked to pieces. The burning of Smyrna began on 13 September and many of its inhabitants were incinerated.

Iran

In 1941, Allied forces deposed the Iranian leader, Reza Shad, thinking he was supportive of Hitler, allowing transport of weapons to the Soviet Union.

In 1951, Prime Minister Ali Razmara, who was sympathetic to the West, was assassinated and succeeded by Mohammed Mossadegh who took control of Iran's oil assets.

This upset the British who had acquired special rights to extract and sell oil from Iran's southern oil fields in 1901.

With the Cold War well under way the US suspected Mossadegh of links with Iranian communists, also feeling that Iran would be a good place for US military bases because it was neighbour to the USSR. On April 4, 1953, CIA director Allen Dulles approved US$1 million to be used "in any way that would bring about the fall of Mossadegh."

The resulting overthrow of the Iranian government in 1953 was the first secret operation by the CIA outside of the Cold War and one of its most successful.

According to Suter (2008), "the coup planted the seeds for widespread Iranian hatred of the US. The US's role in overthrowing Mossadegh's moderate constitutional government was not forgotten. This hatred eventually erupted in 1979 when the shah was overthrown."

On 16 January 1979 the shah fled the country, and on 1 February the Islamic leader Ayatollah Khomeini returned from exile in Paris, inheriting defence forces which had more British-made tanks than the British Army could afford.

Khomeini established a constitution in which all major decisions would have to be in accordance with conservative Shi'a religious thinking, pronouncing (Hammond, 2010):

We shall export our revolution, to the whole world. Until the cry 'Allah Akbar' resounds over the whole world. There will be struggle. There will be Jihad ... Islam is the religion of militant individuals ... Islam will be victorious in all the countries of the world, and Islam and the teachings of the Quran will prevail all over the world ... This is the duty that all Muslims must fulfil.

In October 1979 President Carter US allowed the exiled and ailing Shah to enter the US for cancer treatment. Remembering the CIA coup of 1953, and fearing further US interference, on 4 November 1979 Iranian students occupied the US embassy in Tehran, taking the US diplomats as hostages.

In April 1980 Operation Eagle Claw began and 8 helicopters were launched from US Navy ships to rescue the diplomats. When three of them crashed in severe desert winds the mission was aborted. Finally, with other Arab countries acting as intermediaries, negotiations saw the release of the hostages in January 1981.

After 10 months of conflict with Iraq over the disputed Shatt al-Arab waterway that divides the two countries, Iran and Iraq began open warfare on September 22, 1980. The war lasted for 8 years, killed millions and brought both countries to the verge of bankruptcy (Suter, 2008).

There was further conflict with Iraq over Kuwait in 1991, many Kurdish refugees from northern Iraq fleeing to Iran.

In recent years there has been growing international concern about Iran's nuclear research program. UN inspectors have sometimes been allowed to inspect Iran's nuclear research facilities, but there are growing fears amongst the US and its allies that Iran could develop a nuclear weapon within a year.

According to Suter (2008):

"There is a risk that if the Americans were to carry out a surprise attack on Iranian nuclear installations, the Iranian-born Grand Ayatollah Ali al-Sistani, the supreme Shi'a religious leader in Iraq, could authorize an attack on the US in Iraq."

With sectarian conflict in Iraq continuing, and Islamic State forces having overtaken large areas of the country, Iraq is now in crisis. Thousands of coalition troops acting as military advisors and trainers seems to have done little to help, perhaps because many members of the Iraqi Army are not prepared to kill fellow Iraqis because of religious or political differences.

Iraq

The Tigris-Euphrates valley, formerly called Mesopotamia, was the site of one of the earliest civilizations in the world. The Sumerian city-states of 3,000 BC originated the culture of the Semitic Akkadians, Babylonians, and Assyrians.

Mesopotamia was overtaken by the Persians, Greeks, and Arabs, the latter founding Baghdad from where the caliph ruled a vast empire in the 8th and 9th centuries. Mongol and Turkish conquests led to a general decline in the region, including a decline in population.

In 1919 the partition that was the origin of the border that separates Syria and Iraq was made (Massoulié, 2003).

Britain obtained a League of Nations mandate over Iraq after WW1. An independent monarchy was established in 1932. A left-wing pan-Arab revolution established a republic with links to the USSR in 1958.

A local faction of the Baath Arab Socialist Party ruled by decree from 1968. The USSR and Iraq signed an aid pact in 1972 that provided arms and several thousand advisers. In 1978, execution of 21 communists and a shift of trade to the West indicated a more neutral policy which strained relations with the USSR.

During the 1973 Arab-Israeli war Iraq sent forces to Syria. Within a month of taking power, Saddam Hussein began a bloody purge in the wake of a reported coup attempt against his new regime. After years of conflict, which included Iraqi bombing of Kurdish villages in Iran, the Kurdish minority were defeated in 1975 when Iran withdrew support.

After 10 months of conflict with Iran over the disputed Shatt al-Arab waterway that divides the two countries, Iraq and Iran began open warfare on September 22, 1980.

On June 7, 1981, Israeli airplanes destroyed a nuclear reactor near Baghdad, claiming it could be used to produce nuclear weapons.

The Iraq-Iran war spread to the Persian Gulf in April 1984 with missile attacks on oil tankers. On May 17, 1987, an Iraqi warplane launched a missile attack on the USS Stark, a US Navy frigate on patrol in the Persian Gulf, killing 37 US soldiers. Iraq claimed the attack was a mistake. The war ended in August 1988 when Iraq accepted a UN cease-fire resolution.

Over a million people were killed during the Iran-Iraq war (Massoulié, 2003).

Iraq attacked and overran Kuwait on August 2, 1990, using chemical weapons to kill thousands of Kurds, and beginning an international crisis.

According to Massoulié, (2003):

Sadam Hussein - - then attacked Kuwait on August 2, 1990. In order to eliminate the Iranian front from the international coalition, the Iraqi president recognized the 1975 Algiers Accords on August 15, the very Accords that had begun eight years of war. One million dead for no reason.

On August 6, the UN imposed a ban on all trade with Iraq and called on member countries to protect the assets of the legitimate government of Iraq. In response Iraq declared Kuwait to be its 19th province on August 28.

A US-led coalition "Operation Desert Storm" began air and missile attacks on Iraq on January 16, 1991, after the expiry of a UN deadline for Iraq to withdraw its forces from Kuwait. Iraq retaliated by firing scud missiles at Saudi Arabia and Israel.

On February 23 the coalition began a ground offensive to free Kuwait, soundly defeating the Iraqi forces in only 4 days. 175,000 Iraqi troops were taken prisoner and casualties were, according to some estimates, about 85,000, but according to others 200,000 dead (Massoulié, 2003).

The cease-fire agreement required Iraq to scrap all its poison gas and germ warfare weapons and allow UN inspectors to check the sites. UN sanctions were to remain until Iraq complied but Iraqi cooperation with UN inspectors was intermittent.

After the war there were revolts against Saddam Hussein throughout Iraq. In February 1992 Iraqi troops drove Kurdish insurgents and civilians to the Iranian and Turkish borders, beginning a refugee crisis.

On June 6, 1993, US missiles attacked Iraq's intelligence HQ in Baghdad, citing as grounds an Iraqi plot to kill President George Bush during his visit to Kuwait in April 1993.

In August 1995, two of Saddam Hussein's sons-in-law defected to Jordan; both were killed after returning to Iraq in February 1996. Saddam was found and executed in 2006.

After fighting in the protected zone of northern Iraq between a Kurdish faction allied with Iraq, and another allied with Iran, Baghdad sent troops into Arbil on August 31, 1996. The US responded with missile strikes against air defence sites on the south.

On December 9, 1996, the UN allowed Iraq to sell limited amounts of oil for food and medicine. On December 12, Saddam's son Odai was seriously wounded in an assassination attempt in Baghdad.

Following the September 11, 2001, terrorist attacks on New York's World Trade Centre, on September 12, 2001, President George W. Bush called on the UN to force Iraq to destroy its chemical and biological 'weapons of mass destruction' or WMDs (Suter, 2008).

On May 1, 2003, the US, supported by Britain and Australia, invaded Iraq and within a few months had total control of the country. Saddam Hussein was finally found and killed in 2006 and coalition forces gradually withdrew until all had left the country by 2011, leaving behind limited numbers of military advisors and trainers for the rebuilt Iraqi army. This US-led invasion of Iraq resulted in a disputed number of civilian casualties, perhaps a million.

The Sunni minority government was replaced by an elected government dominated by the majority Shi'ite sect and this led to continuing sectarian conflict that continues to this day, as it does throughout most of the Middle East.

In late May 2015 Islamic State (IS) forces, having captured much of northern Iraq, including several important towns, seemed to be gaining the upper hand over Iraq's army, despite the years of arms supply and training it had received from the West, raising the possibility once again of direct Western military intervention in Iraq.

Israel

Efforts by Jews to establish a national state in Palestine began in the late 19th century with the formation of the Zionist movement by Moses Hess (1812-1875), Leon Pinsker (1821-1891), and Theodor Herzl (1860-1904).

Britain supported Zionism, and in 1923 assumed political responsibility for what was Palestine, in part because of its interests in protecting its oil interests in the Middle East (Massoulié, 2003).

Migration of Jews there during Nazi persecution led to deteriorating relations with Arabs.

In 1947 the UN partitioned the region into separate Jewish and Arab states, a decision opposed by neighbouring Arab countries. The State of Israel was proclaimed in on 14 May 1948 in Tel Aviv, a few hours after the announcement of the end of the British mandate (Massoulié, 2003).

Egypt, Jordan, Syria, Lebanon, and Iraq immediately declared war on it, but Israel managed to hold out.

At this point, according to Massoulié (2003):

The problem of the Palestinian refugees became increasingly apparent: 750,000 people among the 1.5 million Arabs of which Palestine consisted, left Israeli territory. "Driven from their country" according to the Arabs; "encouraged to leave by their leaders" according to the Israelis, their flight is still a source of debate. Whatever the cause, this massive departure was a godsend for the Israeli government, for it ensured that the new state would be Jewish. From 1950 onwards Israel had more than a million Jewish citizens and only 60,000 Palestinian Arabs.

Then in the 1967 Six-Day War Israel claimed the West Bank from Jordan and the Gaza Strip from Egypt.

Another war with Israel's Arab neighbours followed in 1973, but the Camp David Accords led to the signing of a peace treaty between Israel and Egypt in 1979.

Israel invaded Lebanon to quell the Palestine Liberation Organization (PLO) in 1982, and in the late 1980s a Palestinian resistance movement arose in the occupied territories.

Peace negotiations between Israel and the Arab states and Palestinians began in 1992. Israel and the PLO agreed in 1993 upon a five-year extension of self-government to the Palestinians of the West Bank and the Gaza Strip. Israel signed a full peace treaty with Jordan in 1994.

Israeli soldiers and Lebanon's Hezbollah forces clashed in 1997. Following numerous contentious talks between Israel and Lebanon, Israeli troops abruptly withdrew from Lebanon in 2000.

In the last decade the UN has failed to broker a "two state solution" and conflict between Israel and Palestine continues.

Jordan

Jordan shares much of its history with Israel, since both once occupied the area known historically as Palestine. Much of present-day eastern Jordan was incorporated into Israel under David and Solomon c. 1000 BC. It fell to the Seleucids in 330 BC and to Muslim Arabs in the 7th century AD.

The Crusaders extended the kingdom of Jerusalem east of the Jordan River in 1099. Jordan submitted to Ottoman Turkish rule during the 16th century.

In 1920 the area comprising Jordan (then known as the Transjordan) was established within the British mandate of Palestine. Transjordan became an independent state in 1927, although the British mandate did not end until 1948.

After hostilities with the new state of Israel ceased in 1949, Jordan annexed the West Bank of the Jordan River, administering the territory until Israel gained control of it in the Six-Day War of 1967.

In 1970-71 Jordan was wracked by fighting between the government and guerrillas of the Palestine Liberation Organization (PLO), a struggle that ended in the expulsion of the PLO from Jordan. In 1988 King Hussein renounced all Jordanian claims to the West Bank in favour of the PLO.

In 1994 Jordan and Israel signed a full peace agreement.

Lebanon

Much of present-day Lebanon corresponds to ancient Phoenicia, which was settled c. 3000 BC. In the 6th century AD, Christians fleeing Syrian persecution settled in northern Lebanon and founded the Maronite Church.

Arab tribesmen settled in southern Lebanon and by the 11th century had founded the Druze faith. Part of the medieval crusader states, Lebanon was later ruled by the Mamluks.

In 1516 the Ottoman Turks seized control and they ended the local rule of the Druze Shihab princes in 1842.

Poor relations between religious groups resulted in the massacre of Maronites by Druze in 1860. France intervened, forcing the Ottomans to form an autonomous province for the Christian area known as Mount Lebanon.

Following World War I, Lebanon was administered by the French military, but by 1946 it was fully independent.

After the Arab-Israeli War of 1948-49, over 200,000 Palestinian refugees settled in southern Lebanon.

In 1970 the Palestine Liberation Organization (PLO) moved its headquarters to Lebanon and began raids into northern Israel. The Christian-dominated Lebanese government tried to curb them, and in response the PLO sided with Lebanon's Muslims in their conflict with Christians, sparking a civil war by 1975. In 1976-82 Syrian and UN troops tried to maintain a cease-fire.

In 1982 Israeli forces invaded, trying to drive Palestinian forces out of southern Lebanon, but withdrew in 1985 with the conflict unresolved. Israeli troops returned, but a cease-fire was agreed to in 1996. It was broken when Israeli soldiers and Lebanon's Hezbollah forces clashed in 1997.

Following numerous contentious talks between Lebanon and Israel, Israeli troops abruptly withdrew from Lebanon in 2000 and there has been relatively little conflict between Israel and Lebanon since that point.

Palestine

Settled since early prehistoric times, mainly by Semitic groups, Palestine was occupied in biblical times by the kingdoms of Israel, Judah, and Judaea. It was subsequently held by virtually every power of the Middle East, including the Assyrians, Persians, Romans, Byzantines, Crusaders, and Ottoman Turks.

Palestine was governed by Britain under a UN mandate from the end of World War I until 1948, when the state of Israel was proclaimed. Armies from Egypt, Jordan, Syria, and Iraq attacked Israel the next day but were defeated by the Israeli army.

750,000 Palestinian refugees fled the conflict:

As for those who had fled the fighting or had refused to live under Israeli domination, they formed a miserable throng living in refugee camps of the UN administration (UNRWA) that had been set up to help them. In 1950 UNWRA had 957,000 people within its jurisdiction; even by the Israelis' lower estimate of 600,000, it was still almost half the population of Palestine that had been uprooted in this fashion (Massoulié, 2003).

Since that time conflict with Israel has continued to this day, the conflict drawing in other players such as Lebanon, Egypt, Jordan, and also the USSR and US as providers of weapons.

With Israel annexing much of Palestine during the Six Day War of 1967, Palestinian resentment and hostility was greatly increased, and to this day the Palestine Liberation Organization (PLO) conducts sporadic rocket attacks in Israel, and Israel responds with much greater force.

Saudi Arabia

Nejd, in central Arabia, had long been an independent state and centre for the Wahhabi sect. It fell under Turkish rule in the 18th century but in 1913 Ibn Saud, founder of the Saudi dynasty, captured the Turkish province of Hasa in East Arabia. By 1926 he had taken the Hejaz region in West Arabia and most of Asir in SW Arabia.

The discovery of abundant oil in the 1930s brought the country to the attention of the world's major oil companies and thence the governments of the UK and USA, with whom it forged strong links. Western support for Israel has often soured these relations, and Saudi Arabia fought against Israel in the 1948 and 1973 Arab-Israeli wars.

From the onset of the 1967 Arab-Israeli war Saudi Arabia provided financial support to Egypt, and later to Syria, Jordan and Palestinian groups.

When Iraq began the Persian Gulf War by attacking Kuwait in 1990, Saudi Arabia accepted the Kuwait royal family and 400,000 Kuwaiti refugees, and invited Western and Arab troops to deploy on its soil in support of its defence forces. In 1991 US soldiers were killed when an Iraqi missile hit their base in Dhaharn, and in 1995 and 1996 US soldiers were killed by truck bombs.

A US State Department report on Human Rights in the Kingdom of Saudi Arabia in 2000 AD said:

Freedom of religion does not exist. Islam is the official religion, and all citizens must be Muslims. Neither the government nor society in general accepts the concepts of the separation of religion and state, and such separation does not exist. Under sharia, conversion by a Muslim to another religion is considered apostasy. Public apostasy is a crime punishable by death if the accused does not recant. Islamic religious education is mandatory in public schools at all levels. All children receive religious instruction ... citizens do not have the right to change their government, ...there is legal and systematic discrimination based on sex and religion.

According to Hammond (2010), Saudi religious police routinely intimidate, abuse and detain citizens and foreigners. The authorities flog, amputate, and execute by beheading, stoning, and firing squad - in 2014 alone it was reported that 100 people were beheaded.

Trials are closed and based on sharia law, and a Saudi court even ordered that the eye of an Egyptian man be removed as punishment. Saudi Arabia has funded construction of more than a thousand mosques in the US, and several thousand in other parts of the world, but no churches or synagogues are permitted in Saudi Arabia.

Syria

From the 3rd millennium BC Syria was under the control variously of Sumerians, Akkadians, Amorites, Egyptians, Hittites, Assyrians, and Babylonians. In the 6th century BC it became part of the Persian Achaemenian dynasty, which fell to Alexander the Great in 330 BC.

Seleucid rulers governed it 301-164 BC and then Parthians and Nabataean Arabs divided the region.

Syria flourished as a Roman province (64 BC-AD 300) and as part of the Byzantine Empire (300-634), until Muslims invaded and established control.

It came under the Ottoman Empire in 1516, which held it, except for brief rules by Egypt, until the British invaded in World War I. After the war it became a French mandate, achieving independence in 1944. It united with Egypt in the United Arab Republic (1958-61).

During the Six-Day War (1967), it lost the Golan Heights to Israel, and Syrian troops frequently clashed with Israeli troops in Lebanon during the 1980s and '90s.

Hafiz al-Assad's long and harsh regime was marked also by antagonism toward Syria's neighbours Turkey and Iraq.

After much conflict, currently the Islamic State (IS) terrorist organization is in control of much of Syria. IS being a Sunni group, it has slaughtered many Shi'ites in Syria because they are "non-believers".

Turkey

Turkey's early history corresponds to that of Asia Minor, the Byzantine Empire, and the Ottoman Empire.

Byzantine rule emerged when Constantine the Great made Constantinople (now Istanbul) his capital. The Ottoman Empire, begun in the 12th century, dominated for more than 600 years, ending in 1918 after the Young Turk revolt precipitated its demise. Under the leadership of Mustafa Kemal Ataturk, a republic was proclaimed in 1923, and the caliphate abolished in 1924.

Turkey remained neutral throughout most of World War II, siding with the Allies in 1945. Since the war it has alternated between civil and military governments and has had several conflicts with Greece over Cyprus. The 1990s saw political and civic turmoil between Islamists and secularists, whilst conflict with a Kurdish minority continues to this day.

Currently Turkey is seen as less radical and less hostile to the West than most other countries in the Middle East.

Yemen

Yemen was the home of ancient Minaean, Sabaean, and Himyarite kingdoms. The Romans invaded the region in the 1st century AD. In the 6th century it was conquered by Ethiopians and Persians. Following conversion to Islam in the 7th century, it was ruled nominally under a caliphate. The Egyptian Ayyubid dynasty ruled there from 1173 to 1229, after which the region passed to the Rasulids.

From 1517 through 1918, the Ottoman Empire maintained varying degrees of control, especially in the north-western section.

A boundary agreement was reached in 1934 between the north-western imam-controlled territory, which subsequently became the Yemen Arab Republic (North Yemen), and the south-eastern British-controlled territory, which subsequently became the People's Democratic Republic of Yemen (South Yemen).

Relations between the two Yemenis remained tense and were marked by conflict throughout the 1970s and 1980s. They united as the Republic of Yemen in 1990 and the 1993 elections were the first free, multiparty general elections held in the Arabian Peninsula, and also the first in which women participated. In 1994, after a two-month civil war, a new constitution was approved.

Conclusion

Throughout the Middle East Islamic extremists seek by Jihad to ultimately take over the world, for 1,500 years having wrought untold destruction and slaughtered many millions of non-Muslims in this quest.

Sectarian Islamic feuds, mostly between Sunnis and Shi'ites, have also killed countless Muslims and continue to do so.

At present groups such as Islamic State, which now controls much of Iraq and Syria pose a great threat of increasing global conflict.

Concerns over Iran's nuclear program continue, some believing that Iran will soon have nuclear weapons.

Meanwhile the seemingly endless conflict between Israel and Palestine continues, creation of the state of Israel in 1948 having, in the authors' opinion, marked the beginning of 'World War 3'. Indeed, many of the boundaries set in the Middle-East by departing colonial powers, and later the UN, have been a major factor in subsequent conflict.

16. THE MIDDLE EAST

16. THE MIDDLE EAST

Chapter 17

AFRICA

> *Poverty has a home in Africa - like a quiet second skin.*
> *It may be the only place on earth*
> *where it is worn with unconscious dignity.*
> Bessie Head, *Tales of Tenderness and Power* (1989).

Muslim influence and control

Soon after Muhammad and his followers established the new religion, Muslim armies conquered all of North Africa

When Muslims captured Tripoli in 643, all the Jews and Christians were forced to surrender their women and children as slaves. When Carthage was captured it was burned to the ground and most of its population slaughtered (Hammond, 2010).

At a two-week conference of Muslim leaders from 80 countries hosted by Muammar Gaddafi in Tripoli in October 1995, strategies to transform Africa into an Islamic continent were discussed. Participants agreed that their goals were to make Arabic the primary language of Africa and Islam the official religion. One Saudi MP, Farouk Cassim said: "It will probably be the biggest revolution to sweep Africa."

The head of the Islamic Propagation Centre International (IPCI) declared that South Africa, which at present is less than 2% Muslim, was a primary goal of the Islamic offensive: "We are going to turn South Africa into a Muslim state. We have the money to do it" (Sunday Times 22/10/95).

The Congo

Prior to European colonization, several native kingdoms had emerged in the region, including the 16th-century Luba kingdom and the Kuba federation, which reached its peak in the 18th century.

European development began late in the 19th century when King Leopold II of Belgium financed Henry Morton Stanley's exploration of the Congo River. The 1884-85 Berlin West Africa Conference recognized the Congo Free State with Leopold as its sovereign.

The growing demand for rubber helped finance the exploitation of the Congo, but abuses against native peoples outraged Western nations and forced Leopold to grant the Free State a colonial charter as the Belgian Congo in 1908.

Independence was granted in 1960, and the country's name was changed to Zaire. The post-independence period was marked by unrest and mercenaries were recruited to deal with rebel forces, most famously the legendary 'Mad Mike Hoare's 5 Commando Group, the film *The Wild Geese* being loosely based on the exploits of this group (Smith, 2012).

Ultimately, however, the turmoil then in the Congo culminated in a military coup that brought Gen. Mobutu Sese Seko to power in 1965, military regimes ruling for most of the time since then.

Mismanagement, corruption, and increasing violence devastated the infrastructure and economy. Mobutu was deposed in 1997 by Laurent Kabila, who restored the country's name to Congo. Instability in neighbouring countries and desire for Congo's mineral wealth led to military involvement by numerous African countries. Kabila was assassinated in 2001 and succeeded by his son.

Egypt

Archaeological records of ancient Egyptian civilization date back to 4,000 BC. A united kingdom arose circa 3200 BC and extended into Nubia and Syria.

Imperial decline allowed invasion by Hyksos and Assyrians from Asia, the last native dynasty falling in 341 BC to the Persians. In following centuries Greeks, Romans, Byzantines and Arabs invaded.

The Mamluks, a military caste of Caucasian origin, ruled from 1250 until defeated by the Ottoman Turks in 1517.

Britain took control of the administration in 1882, though nominal allegiance to the Ottoman Empire continued until 1914. Egypt was a British protectorate from 1914 to 1922.

A 1936 treaty allowed Egyptian autonomy but Britain retained bases in Egypt and fought Germany and Italy from these in 1940-42. In 1951 Egypt abrogated the 1936 treaty and in 1956 the Sudan became independent.

When the state of Israel was proclaimed in 1948, Egypt joined other Arab nations invading Israel but was defeated.

An uprising on 23 July 1952 was led by the Society of Free Officers and forced King Farouk to abdicate. When the republic was proclaimed on 18 June 1953, Maj. Gen. Mohammed Naquib became president and premier. Lt. Col. Gamal Abel Nasser became premier in 1954 and was voted president in 1956. He took over the French-built Suez Canal from British control on 26 July 1956.

After terrorist raids across its border, Israel invaded Egypt's Sinai Peninsula on 29 October 1956. Egypt rejected a cease-fire demand by Britain and France and on October 31 the two nations bombed and invaded each other until accepting a UN cease-fire on November 7.

A UN Emergency Force guarded the 117-mile long border between Egypt and Israel until May 19, 1967, when it was withdrawn at Nasser's demand.

Egyptian troops entered the Gaza Strip and the heights of Sharm el Sheikh, 3 days later closing the Strait of Tiran to Israeli shipping. Full-scale war broke out on 5 June, ending with a UN cease-fire on 10 June, by which time Israel had captured the Gaza and Sinai Peninsula, controlled the each bank of the Suez Canal, and re-opened the gulf. Sporadic fighting continued until a new cease-fire was agreed on 7 August 1970.

In a surprise attack on 6 October 1973 Egyptian forces, aided by a Russian airlift, crossed the Suez Canal into the Sinai, while at the same time Syrian forces attacked the Israelis on the Golan Heights. The US responded with an airlift to Israel who counterattacked, crossing the canal and surrounding Suez City. A UN cease-fire took effect on 24 October.

A disengagement agreement was signed on 18 January 1974 and Israel withdrew from the canal's west bank. Under a 1975 accord Israel returned the Sinai oil fields. On 26 March 1979 Egypt and Israel signed a formal peace treaty, ending 30 years of war.

Israel returned control of the Sinai to Egypt in 1982.

In 1981 tension between Muslim fundamentalists and Christians led to street riots and on October 6 President Sadat was assassinated and succeeded by Hosni Mubarak.

Egypt supported the Allied invasions of Iraq in 1991 politically and militarily.

Islamic fundamentalist terrorism grew in the 1990s and Egyptian security forces raided Islamic militants, some of whom were executed for terrorism. On 14 October 1994, Nobel literature laureate Naquib Mahfouz was stabbed by Islamic militants and President Mubarak escaped assassination in Ethiopia on June 28 1995.

Liberia

Liberia was founded in 1822 by US black freedmen who settled at Monrovia with the aid of colonization societies, and it became a republic on July 26, 1847.

Claiming rampant corruption, an Army Redemption Council of enlisted men staged a bloody predawn coup on April 12, 1980. President Tolbert was killed and replaced by Sergeant Samuel Doe after a disputed election, Doe surviving a subsequent coup in 1985.

A civil war began in 1989 and rebel forces gained much territory and advanced on the capital in June 1990. Doe was captured and killed in September.

Peacekeeping forces came from several countries but factional fighting intensified and a series of ceasefires failed.

On 1 September 1995 a transitional Council of State was formed but factional fighting flared up again in April 1996, devastating Monrovia. On 3 September 1996 Ruth Perry became modern Africa's first female head of state, leading another transitional government, by which time the civil war had killed 150,000 and displaced half the population.

On 19 July 1997 former rebel leader Charles Taylor was elected president after Liberia's first national election for 12 years. Discontent with his regime gradually grew until he fled to Nigeria. He was arrested in March 2006 and tried for war crimes (Suter, 2008).

Libya

On 1 September 1969 Colonel Muammar Gaddafi and a group of young military officers overthrew the regime of 79 year-old King Idris while he was overseas. No-one was killed and the king died in exile.

Gaddafi abolished the monarchy and established the Libyan Arab Republic, closed down British and American bases that had stood since the end of WW2 when Libya was freed from Italian control. Gaddafi's closing of these bases made him popular throughout the Arab world.

Gaddafi nationalised the oil industry and in October 1970 he expelled the Italians who had occupied the country since 1911, giving their land to Libyans.

Gaddafi made Libya of the world's most notorious sponsors of terrorism throughout the 1970s and 1980s.

In May 1985 the US expelled all the employees of the Libyan embassy in Washington DC for suspicious activities. In March and April 1986 the US carried out military attacks on Libya to assert its right to fly and sail near the Libyan coast.

On 5 April 1985 a discotheque in West Berlin frequented by American serviceman was bombed, killing two US servicemen and a Turkish woman whilst wounding 229 others. America suspected Libya and retaliated with a bombing raid on Tripoli on 15 April which killed 37.

On 21 September 1988 a Pan Am Boeing 747 blew up over the Scottish village of Lockerbie killing 270 people, including 11 on the ground. In April 1990 British investigators announced finding an electronic component linking two Libyan agents to the explosion. The UN imposed sanctions on Libya to force it to hand over the two agents for international trial.

In March 1989 Libyan agents blew up a French UTA plane over Niger, killing 170 people, including the wife of the US ambassador to Chad.

Gaddafi disapproved of Islamic fundamentalism and was one of the first world leaders to warn about Osama Bin Laden and call for his arrest. In retaliation the Islamic Fighting Group, sponsored by Bin Laden, attempted to assassinate him in 1996.

In 1999 Gaddafi handed over the two Libyan terrorists wanted in connection with the Lockerbie bombing and paid compensation to the victims' next of kin and to those on the French UTA flight.

In December 2003 Gaddafi renounced attempts to acquire weapons of mass destruction, inviting checks by international inspectors. On 24 March 2004 British PM Tony Blair visited Libya, the first such visit since Churchill during WW2, signalling that Gaddafi had made peace with the West.

Nigeria

Like Sudan, Nigeria has a Muslim north and a Christian south, Christians being in the majority. It has the largest population in Africa: 120 million people in 490 ethnic groups, about 10% being Anglican.

According to Hammond (2010) twelve northern states in Nigeria have proclaimed Shari'a law and:

Christians have been severely persecuted in Nigeria's northern states. Literally hundreds of churches have been destroyed and thousands of Christians murdered in recent years.

The Muslim Brothers issued this statement which declared as the objective: "The establishment of the Shari'a of Allah and the destruction of the Kafir from the place of the earth .... it is this Kafir which gives these slaves (Christians) ....

It puts them on same level, it even raised the Christians higher than the Muslims ... it is also necessary that we rise and destroy oppressors and the Kafir system ... Ulamas should rise up and take the lead for the annihilation of Kafir ... oh we are tired of Kafir system of government, Jewish Laws and decrees, and --- Christianity ... all the Christians ... must be brought out to public and be shot. From now on, Thursdays and Fridays must be work-free days ... 'fight them until there remains no tumult (fitna) on the face of the earth and religion (way of life) becomes for Allah alone.' Quran.

In Ghoko, Muslims attacked the homes, farms and churches of Tiv people. When federal forces largely under Muslim control were sent in even more properties were burned. In Vaase they killed 1,200 civilians and in Taraba State up to 100 churches were destroyed by Muslim mobs.

According to Hammond (2010):

The conflict between the Cross and the Crescent in Nigeria is intensifying.

Indeed, after suffering a succession of Islamic dictators for 38 years, and although sharia law is enforced in the 12 northern states, in the first free elections in Nigerian history a Christian president was elected.

Sierra Leone

In the 1991 war the Revolutionary United Front (RUF) began fighting against corruption of the Sierra Leone government, but in the diamond-rich south-eastern territory controlled by the RUF corruption and violence were on a greater scale. There the rebels recruited men to dig up the diamonds to finance their military efforts, moving the UN to call them 'blood diamonds'.

Some 50,000 people were killed in the civil war, and about a third of the country's population were forced to relocate.

In February 1998 a Nigerian-led force overtook the Sierra Leone capital, Freetown, but not before five thousand people were killed. In a temporary ceasefire the rebels were included in a new government which soon disintegrated.

In October 1999, the UN sent the first of 17,500 peacekeeping troops. In May 2000 the RUF took hundreds of the peacekeepers hostage, and action which led to the capture of the RUF leader, Foday Sankoh, who died in detention in July 2003 after a stroke.

According to Suter (2008): "Sierra Leone's poverty-stricken population has a life expectancy of only about forty years. Only about 3 per cent of the population are aged over sixty-five and almost half is aged under fourteen. The damage the civil war did to the country will take generations to heal."

Somalia

Muslim Arabs and Persians first established trading posts along the coasts in the 7th-10th century. By the 10th century Somali nomads occupied the area inland from the Gulf of Aden, and the south and west were inhabited by various groups of pastoral Oromo peoples.

Intensive European exploration began after the British occupation of Aden in 1839, and in the late 19th century Britain and Italy set up protectorates in the region.

During World War II the Italians invaded British Somaliland (1940) but a year later British troops retook the area, and Britain administered the region until 1950, when Italian Somaliland became a UN trust territory.

In 1960 it was united with the former British Somaliland, and the two became the independent Republic of Somalia.

Since then it has suffered political and civil strife, including military dictatorship, civil wars, drought, and famine. In the 1990s no effective central government existed.

In 1991, a proclamation of a Republic of Somaliland, on territory corresponding to the former British Somaliland was issued by a breakaway group. Without international recognition it operated more smoothly than the area of traditional Somalia.

A UN peacekeeping force intervened in 1992 to secure food supplies, but fighting continued and the peacekeeping force left in 1995 and the country remained in turmoil.

Severe floods devastated the southern region in 1999.

Somalia is home to the militant terrorist group Al Shabaab, and as a consequence has suffered both internal conflict, and also been the base for terrorist activities in other countries, for example Al Shabaab's capture and killing of 140 Kenyan University students in early April 2015.

South Africa

Bushmen and Hottentot were the original inhabitants but Bantus, including Zulu, Xhosa, Swazi, and Sotho, occupied the area from northeast to South Africa before the 17th century.

The Dutch settled the Cape of Good Hope area in the 17th century. When Britain seized it in 1806, many Dutch trekked north to found the Transvaal and the Orange Free State.

Diamonds were discovered in 1867, and gold in 1886.

The Dutch Boers resented British encroachments and the Anglo-Boer War followed in 1899-1902.

Britain won and on 32 May 1910 created the Union of South Africa, incorporating the British colonies of the Cape and Natal, the Transvaal, and the Orange Free State. After a referendum it withdrew from the Commonwealth and became the Republic of South Africa on 31 May 1961.

Protests against the apartheid system, which had been officially recognized in 1948, were brutally suppressed. On 21 March 1960, 69 black protestors were killed in Sharpeville. During 1978 antiapartheid protests 800 people, mostly Bantus, were killed.

In 1981 South Africa launched military actions against guerrilla groups in Angola and Mozambique.

In 1983 a referendum led to greater freedoms for Coloured and Asian minorities, and laws against interracial sex and marriage were repealed in 1985.

In 1986 South African troops invaded Zimbabwe, Botswana and Zambia to attack black nationalist African Nationalist Congress (ANC) guerrilla strongholds.

In 1990 the government lifted its ban on the ANC, and on 11 February ANC leader Nelson Mandela was freed after more than 27 years in jail.

In 1993 a new constitution in which all races could vote was agreed upon. In this partially self-governing black territories or "homelands" were incorporated into a national system of 9 provinces.

In the 1994 elections the ANC won 62.7% of the vote, the National Party winning only 20.4%, and Mandela became president. The Inkatha Freedom Party won 10.5% and control of a mainly Zulu province, fighting between the ANC and Inkatha having killed 10,000 people in the Zulu region since the mid-1980s.

Since that time the lot of black people has improved considerably, but poverty is still rife amongst blacks, many of whom still live in shanty suburbs of the main cities.

Recently high unemployment has led to protests against foreign businesses and shops, and many foreign-owned shops have been attacked.

Sudan

Sudan is the largest country in Africa (2,503,890 sq. km) and like Nigeria, it has a Muslim north and a Christian south, with Muslims outnumbering Christians.

It was settled by Egyptians in antiquity and was converted to Coptic Christianity in the 6th century. Arab conquests brought Islam in the 15th century.

In the 1820s Egypt overtook Sudan but in the 1880s a revolution was led by Muhammad Ahmad, who called himself the Mahdi (leader of the faithful), and his followers, the dervishes.

In 1898 an Anglo-Egyptian force crushed the Mahdi's successors. In 1951 the Egyptian Parliament abrogated its 1899 and 1936 treaties with Great Britain and amended its constitution to provide for a separate Sudanese constitution. Sudan voted for complete independence as a parliamentary government effective January 1, 1956.

In 1969 a Revolutionary Council took power, but a civilian premier and cabinet were appointed and the government announced it would create a socialist state.

Sudan was plagued with economic problems, civil war, and influxes of refugees from neighbouring countries in the 1980s and 1990s. After 16 years in power, President Jaafar al-Nimelry was overthrown in a bloodless military coup on April 6, 1985.

In 1986 Sudan held its first democratic elections in 18 years, but the elected government was overthrown in a bloodless coup on June 30, 1989.

In the mid-1980s rebels in the south, which was populated largely by black Christians and followers of tribal religions, took up arms against government domination by the predominantly Arab-Muslim northern Sudan.

War and subsequent famine cost an circa 1.3 million lives and displaced nearly 3 million southerners by the mid-1990s.

In 1993 Amnesty International accused Sudan of practicing "ethnic cleansing" against the Nuba people in the South, and Sudan was cited for human rights violations by the UN Human Rights Commission on March 9, 1994. Egypt publicly blamed Sudan for an attempted assassination of Egyptian President Hosni Mubarak in Ethiopia on June 25, 1995.

In March 1996 elections were boycotted by opposition groups. Since then, the northern National Islamic Front Government of Sudan has signed a peace treaty granting autonomy to the South, exempting them from sharia Law and allowing them to elect a Christian president (Hammond, 2010).

Zambia

As Northern Rhodesia the country was administered by the South Africa Company from 1889 to 1924, when a legislature and office of governor was established. On 24 October 1964 it became an independent republic within the Commonwealth.

In 1970 the government took over 51% of two foreign-owned copper-mining companies, and in 1975 privately-held land and other enterprises were nationalized.

In the 1980s and 1990s low copper prices and severe drought resulted in famine, and food riots erupted in June 1990. The 1991 elections ended one-party rule, and the new government sought to sell state enterprises, including the copper industry.

Zimbabwe

Under Cecil Rhodes, the British South Africa Company had conquered the area by 1897. Britain granted self-government as Southern Rhodesia in 1924.

Under a 1961 constitution voting was restricted to keep whites in power. On 11 November 1965, Prime Minister Ian Smith declared the country independent but Britain demanded that voting rights be broadened to allow eventual rule by the black African majority.

Negotiations between the government and Black Nationalist groups failed to prevent increasing guerrilla warfare in the 1970s.

Elections in 1979 gave the United African National Council a slim majority in a black-dominated Parliament and a British cease-fire was accepted by all parties on 5 December. Independence was granted on 18 April 1980.

In 1992 President Robert Mugabe declared a drought a national disaster and appealed for foreign donations of food, money and medicine. An 'economic adjustment' program caused severe hardship but Mugabe was re-elected in 1996 when opposition candidates withdrew.

In the late 1990s it was estimated that about one million people in Zimbabwe had HIV infections.

Conclusions

Soon after the 'creation' of the Muslim religion Arabs conquered and raped much of North Africa. Then for hundreds of years Africa was 'carved up' by colonizing European nations. This left a legacy of conflict that continues to this day.

Racial conflict is still rife in Africa, and religious conflict more so, Muslims terrorist groups such as Al Shabaab inflicting many atrocities, killing thousands, and displacing millions from their homes in several African countries.

Most of Africa is still riddled with poverty, making continuing conflict on political and religious grounds certain.

Chapter 18

ASIA

> *China remains too important for America's national security to risk the relationship on the emotions of the moment . . . No government in the world would have tolerated having the main square of its capital occupied by tens of thousands of demonstrators.*
> Henry Kissinger, referring to the massacre in Tiananmen Square in June 1989, *New York* Times (Augyust 20, 1989).

Afghanistan

After World War 2 the Soviet Union supported the government in neighbouring Afghanistan. The Soviet government opposed all religion but most people in Afghanistan were Muslims, many of whom periodically fought against the Soviet-backed Afghan government so that Soviet troops were kept in Afghanistan to keep the peace.

In 1979, however, the KGB sent in special agents to kill the country's leader, Hafizullah Amin, because he wanted to improve relations with the West.

A decade of conflict followed during which Afghan fighters would periodically attack Soviet troops and then retreat into their mountain strongholds.

Pakistanis who worked with the CIA trained Osama bin Laden to help fight the Soviets.

In 1989, the cash-strapped and soon to be disbanded Soviet Union could no longer afford to continue fighting in Afghanistan and withdrew its troops.

During the 1990s the fundamentalist Taliban took power in Afghanistan. The Taliban supported Osama Bin Laden who, working from a base in the mountains in southern Afghanistan, led the al-Qa'ida terrorist group which carried out attacks against US embassies, as well as the 9/11 attacks on the twin towers of the World Trade Center in New York in 2001 in which 3000 Americans were killed.

Some of the last remaining Buddhist monuments, four statues of Buddha, were destroyed by the Taliban in March 2001.

Despite large scale intervention in Afghanistan by the US and its allies, these intervening forces having now left the country, the Taliban has regained control of most of the areas it once controlled.

Bangladesh

In the 12th century Muslim invaders conquered the formerly Hindu area. British rule lasted from the 18th century to 1947, when East Bengal became part of Pakistan.

After a period of West Pakistani domination, the Awami League based in the East won control of the national assembly in 1971. Riots broke, assembly sessions were postponed, and Pakistani troops attacked on 25 March. Next day Bangladesh independence was proclaimed and in the ensuing civil war one million were killed and 10 million fled to India.

War between India and Pakistan broke out on 3 December 1971, Pakistan surrendering on 16 December. Mujibur Rahman became prime minister but was killed in a coup on 15 August 1975. During the 1970s Bangladesh sided with India and the USSR in response to US support of Pakistan, and much of the economy was nationalized.

On 30 May 1981, President Ziaur Rahman was killed in an unsuccessful coup attempt by army rivals. Vice President Abdus Sattar assumed the presidency but was ousted in a coup led by army chief of staff General Ershad in March 1988. In 1991 Bangladesh adopted a parliamentary system of government.

In April 1991 a devastating cyclone struck, killing more than 131,000. Chronic poverty has been made worse by the decline of jute as a world commodity.

In early 1996 political turmoil forced the election of a new prime minister. On December 12 Bangladesh signed a treaty with India over the long-disputed rights to water from the Ganges River. A cyclone in May 1997 left an estimated 800,000 people homeless.

China

A succession of dynasties and inter-dynastic kingdoms ruled China for 3,000 years until foreign rule came with the Mongols in the Yuan dynasty (1271-1368) and Manchus in the Ch'ing dynasty (1644-1911), but these did not alter the underlying and ancient culture.

During the 19th century Russia, Japan, Britain and other powers controlled parts of China.

In 1895 China ceded Korea, Taiwan and other areas.

From 1894 until 1945 there were conflicts with Japan.

China became a republic on 1 January 1912 after the Wuchang Uprising led by the Nationalist Party.

In 1928, the Kuomintang, led by Chiang Kai-shek, unified China nominally, but a bloody purge of Communists amongst its ranks fomented hostilities that would continue for decades. In 1949-50 communist armies took over mainland China and the Kuomintang government moved to Taiwan, 90 miles from the mainland, in December 1949.

The People's Republic of China, led by Mao Zedong, was proclaimed in September 1949.

In February 1950 the USSR signed a 30-year treaty of "friendship, alliance, and mutual assistance." In November China sent armies into Korea to fight US troops, forcing a stalemate in the Korean War.

Under Mao economic development was slow and in 1957 he admitted that 800,000 people had been executed in the period 1949-54 to curb violent factionalism, opponents claiming much higher figures.

Relations with the USSR deteriorated in the 1960s and the USSR reduced its aid to China.

In 1971 the Taiwan government was expelled from the UN and replaced by the People's Republic.

In 1979 China established formal diplomatic relations with the US and by the mid 1980s extensive economic reforms had been made, incorporating market-oriented incentives.

On 4 May 1989, 100,000 people marched in Beijing, demanding political reforms. As unrest spread martial law was imposed on May 20. Troops entered Beijing on June 3-4, tanks and armoured personnel carriers rolled though Tiananmen Square, and an estimated 5,000 were killed and 10,000 injured, hundreds more being arrested.

From 1990 – 2010 China enjoyed rapid economic growth. In recent years growth has slowed but still remains much stronger than in the US and most of Europe.

India

Muslim invasions of India began in 712 AD and statues were smashed, temples demolished, palaces plundered, vast numbers of men slaughtered, and their women and children enslaved. The invaders of the port city of Debal took only three days to slaughter all its inhabitants.

At one point the governor of Iraq, Hajjaj, rebuked the armies of Muhammad Quasim for showing mercy on the infidel:

O true believers, when you encounter the unbelievers strike off their heads ... henceforth, grant pardon to no-one of the enemy, and spare none of them, or else all will consider you a weak minded man.

Hajjaj demanded that all the able bodied Indian men were to be killed, and that all their sons and daughters were to be enslaved or retained as hostages. More than 10,000 men were slaughtered by Quasim at the town of Brahminabad (Hammond, 2010).

In the eleventh century Mahmud of Gazhni invaded India seventeen times, ordering the slaughter of 50,000 Hindus at Somnath, one Muslim writer summarizing the results as:

Mahmud utterly ruined the prosperity of the country and performed these wonderful exploits, by which Hindus became like atoms of dust scattered in all directions ..."

Will Durant in his *The Story of Civilization* describes the Muslim invasion of India as *"probably the bloodiest story in history."* The ancient cities of Barasani, Mathura, Uggain, Maheshwar, Jwalamukhi and Dwarka were sacked, the populations massacred, and every temple destroyed. (Hammond, 2010).

In 1351 AD Firuz Shah ordered that all Hindus be killed and all Hindu temples be destroyed, and mosques were built on the sites of many of the razed temples.

On February 24, 1568, after the Battle of Chitod, the Mogul emperor Akbar ordered that 30,000 captured Hindus be executed.

Shaj Jahan, who built the Taj Mahal, was the fifth Mogul emperor and a grandson of Akbar. He killed all but one of his male relatives, had 5,000 concubines, and had incestuous sex with his daughters Chamani and Jahanara. In only 30 years he launched 48 military campaigns against non-Muslims. In the town of Benares, he destroyed 76 Hindu temples. When he captured a Portuguese enclave near Calcutta he drowned or burnt alive 10,000 inhabitants, enslaving another 4,000, killing those who refused to convert to Islam.

The negative views of Sir Vidia Naipaul about four Islamic countries are noted in Chapter 28. His views on India were still more negative. He visited the country three times and wrote three books about it: *An Area of Darkness* (1967), *A Wounded Civilization* (1977), and *India: A Million Mutinies Now* (1990).

In the first of these he said: "The crisis of India is that of a decaying civilization, where the only hope lies in further swift decay."

In the second he wrote: "The crisis of India is not only political or economic. The larger crisis is of a wounded old civilization that has at last become aware of its inadequacies and is without the intellectual means to move ahead.

Hinduism . . . has exposed Indians to a thousand years of defeat and stagnation. It has given men no idea of contract with other men, no idea of the state . . . Its philosophy of withdrawal had diminished men intellectually and not equipped them to challenge; it has stifled growth."

Nirad Chaudhiri, an Indian writer born in the subcontinent, thought India "torpid" and "incapable of a vital civilization of its own unless it is subjected to foreign influence." He thought Indian spirituality "a fragment of the Western imagination . . . there is no creative power left in India. Indian colleges and universities have never been congenial places for research, outside of Indological studies" (Watson, 2001).

Indonesia

Proto-Malay peoples migrated to Indonesia from mainland Asia before 1000 BC. Commercial relations were established with China in about the 1st century AD, and Hindu and Buddhist cultural influences from India began to take hold. Indian traders brought Islam to the islands in the 13th century and it took hold throughout the islands, except for Bali, which retained its Hindu religion and culture.

European influence began in the 16th century, and the Dutch ruled Indonesia from the late 17th century until 1942, when the Japanese invaded. Sukarno declared Indonesia's independence in 1945, which the Dutch granted, with nominal union to the Netherlands, in 1949, and Indonesia dissolved this union in 1954.

The suppression of an alleged coup attempt in 1965 resulted in the deaths of more than 300,000 people the government claimed to be communists, and by 1968 General Suharto had taken power. His government forcibly incorporated East Timor into Indonesia in 1975-76, with much loss of life.

In the 1990s the Indonesia was beset by political and economic problems, and Suharto was deposed in 1998 and replaced by vice president B.J. Habibie.

Muslim leader Abdurrahman Wahid was elected president in 1999 but was sacked in 2001 after being implicated in scandals. He was replaced by vice president, Megawati Sukarnoputri, the eldest daughter of Sukarno.

In 1999 the people of East Timor voted for independence from Indonesia. The Indonesian Army invaded, killing 1,000 – 2,000 people. Australian forces landed and repelled the Indian forces and East Timor was granted independence.

Japan

Japan's history began with the accession of the legendary first emperor, Jimmu, in 660 BC. The Yamato court established the first unified Japanese state in the 4th-5th century AD. During this period, Buddhism arrived in Japan from Korea. For centuries Japan borrowed heavily from Chinese culture, but it began to sever its links with the mainland by the 9th century. The Fujiwara family held sway through the 11th century.

In 1192 Minamoto Yoritomo established Japan's first bakufu, or shogunate. The Ashikaga shogunate (1338-1573) was marked by warfare among powerful families and unification was not achieved until the late 1500s.

During the Tokugawa shogunate (1603 -1867), the government imposed a policy of isolation. Under the leadership of Emperor Meiji (1868-1912), it adopted a constitution (1889) and began a program of modernization and Westernization.

Japanese imperialism led to war with China (1894-95) and Russia (1904-5) as well as to the annexation of Korea (1910) and Manchuria (1931).

During World War II Japan attacked US forces in Hawaii and the Philippines (December 1941) and occupied European colonial possessions in South Asia.

In 1945 the US dropped atomic bombs on Hiroshima and Nagasaki, and Japan surrendered to the Allied powers.

US post war occupation of Japan led to a new democratic constitution in 1947. In rebuilding Japan's ruined industrial plant, new technology was used in every major industry and strong economic recovery followed, particularly in the 1960s, 1970s and 1980s.

Myanmar

The Burmese arrived from East Tibet before the 9th century, displacing earlier cultures, and a Buddhist majority was established by the 11th century.

In 1271 the Mongol dynasty of China conquered Burma and ruled it as a Chinese tributary until the 16th century.

Britain subjugated Burma in 3 wars in the period 1824-1884, ruling it as part of India until 1937, when it became self-governing. Independence from the Commonwealth was granted in 1948.

General Ne Win governed from 1962 to 1988, first as military ruler and then as constitutional president. His regime drove Indians from the civil service and Chinese from commerce. The economy was socialized and the country became isolated and economically weak, the UN granting it less-developed status in 1987.

Ne Win resigned in July 1988 after waves of antigovernment riots. The rioting continued and the military seized power again in September, changing the country's name to Myanmar.

On 27 May 1990, the first free multiparty elections in 30 years were held, and the main opposition party won decisively, but the military refused to hand over power.

High-profile opposition leader Aung San Suu Kyi, who had been awarded the Nobel Peace Prize in 1991, was held under house arrest from 20 July 1989 until 10 July 1995. After her release the military government continued to harass and imprison her supporters.

New UN sanctions took effect on 21 May 1997.

On 23 July 1997 Myanmar was admitted to ASEAN.

North Korea

Japan seized Korea in 1905, but after WW2 the north was occupied by the Soviet Union and the south by the US, and sporadic fighting accorded along the 38th parallel (latitude 38 degrees North).

On 25 June 1950 North Korea invaded South Korea, beginning a war in which 3 million people were killed and capturing about a third of South Korea. UN forces reclaimed this territory, and in July 1953 an armistice was signed, but to this day there is still no peace treaty.

South Korea is now thriving economically but the North is largely sealed off from the outside world and is one of the poorest countries in the world.

North Korea carried out its first nuclear test in October 2006. The following year it agreed to dismantle its nuclear facilities and provide full details of its nuclear program in exchange for food aid, at the same time signing a peace deal with South Korea. To this day, however, North Korea retains its nuclear weapons and occasionally conducts missile tests to demonstrate its military strength.

Pakistan

When the British left India in 1947, they were forced by Muslim leaders, who wanted their own Islamic homeland, to divide the subcontinent into India and Pakistan. The territory acceded to Pakistan was divided into eastern and western sections on either side of northern India.

In November 1971 East Pakistan began a civil war and broke away to create the independent nation of Bangladesh.

The top leadership group of the Taliban is the Quetta Shura based since circa 2001 in the city of Quetta in the Balochistan province of Pakistan.

Members of Pakistan's Inter-Services Intelligence (ISI) are believed to have attended meetings of the Quetta Shura and supported the Taliban.

In 2009 the Pakistani government acknowledged the existence of Quetta Shurah for the first time and since that time several of its members have been detained at various locations in Pakistan.

Having hidden out for many years in the mountains of southern Afghanistan, Osama Bin Laden moved to a town near Peshawar (in NW Pakistan) circa 2000, finally being captured and killed there by American troops.

OBL was traced by having an NGO children's aid agency visit the "compound" he and his 4 wives were living in (gutless Arab – hiding behind 4 women + countless young suicide bombers etc.). The visitor obtained DNA samples from the children living there, and these led back to OBL, so that a raid was duly organized and, when a fire fight broke out OBL was shot dead.

The Philippines

Discovered by Ferdinand Magellan in 1521, the islands were colonized by the Spanish, who retained control until the Philippines were ceded to the US in 1898 following the Spanish-American War.

The Commonwealth of the Philippines was established in 1935 to prepare the country for political and economic independence, which was delayed by World War II and the Japanese invasion.

The islands were liberated by US forces 1944-45, and the Republic of the Philippines was proclaimed in 1946 with democratic government.

In 1965 Ferdinand Marcos was elected president. He declared martial law in 1972, and it lasted until 1981. After 20 years of dictatorial rule, he was driven from power in 1986 and democracy re-established.

During the 1990s the government tried to come to terms with independence fighters in the southern islands.

Sri Lanka

Colonists from northern India subdued the indigenous Veddahs circa 543 BC, but their descendants, the Buddhist Sinhalese still make up most of the population. Hindu descendants of Tamil immigrants from southern India are about 20% of the population.

Parts of Sri Lanka were occupied by the Portuguese in 1501 and by the Dutch in 1658. The British seized the island in 1796 and it became part of the Commonwealth as Ceylon in 1948. In 1972 Ceylon became the republic of Sri Lanka.

Prime Minister Bandaranalke was assassinated in September 1959, being replaced by his widow after new elections. In 1970 she was elected again.

1971 saw economic problems and terrorist raids by ultra-leftists, thousands of whom were executed. In the mid-1970s foreign-owned plantations were nationalized.

Tensions between the native Sinhalese and militant Tamil separatists resulted in civil war in the early 1980s, the president was assassinated by a Tamil rebels in 1993, and 50,000 were killed by the late 1990s.

Conclusions

As in Africa, there are many countries with large Muslim populations in Asia, many of them having suffered a great deal of ethnic/religious conflict, particularly Afghanistan, Pakistan and India.

Indonesia has the world's largest Muslim population of more than 150 million and is seen as a potential future threat by other Asia-Pacific countries.

Chapter 19

EUROPE

The high contracting powers solemnly declare . . .
that they condemn recourse to war and renounce it . . .
as the instrument of their national policy towards each other . . .
The settlement or the solution of all disputes or conflicts of whatever
nature or of whatever origin they may be which may arise . . .
shall never be sought by either side except by pacific means
Aristide Briand, draft 20 June 1927, later incorporated into the Kellogg
Pact, 1928, in *Le Temps* 13 April 1928.

Great Britain

The early inhabitants of Britain were Celtic-speaking peoples. Julius Caesar invaded and took control of the area 55-54 BC. The Roman province of Britannia endured until the 5th century and included present-day England and Wales.

In the 5th century Nordic tribes of Angles, Saxons, and Jutes invaded Britain. The invasions had little effect on the Celtic peoples of Wales and Scotland.

Christianity began to flourish in the 6th century.

During the 8th-9th century, Vikings, particularly Danes, raided the coasts of Britain. In the late 9th century Alfred the Great repelled a Danish invasion, which helped bring about the unification of England.

William the Conqueror led the Norman conquest of England which began with the Battle of Hastings in 1066.

From the 11th century, Scotland came under the influence of the English throne.

Henry II conquered Ireland in the late 12th century.

During the reign of Edward I, statute law developed to supplement English common law, and the first Parliament was convened.

In 1314 Robert Bruce won independence for Scotland.

The Tudors became the ruling family of England following the Wars of the Roses (1455-85).

Henry VIII, who reigned from 1485 to1509, established the Church of England and incorporated Wales as part of England.

The reign of Elizabeth I (1558-1603) began with the defeat of the Spanish Armada in 1558.

The English Civil Wars erupted in 1642 between Royalists and Parliamentarians, ending in the execution of Charles I (1649). After 11 years of Puritan rule under Oliver Cromwell and his son (1649-60), the monarchy was restored by Charles II.

Great Britain's American colonies won independence in 1783. War with revolutionary France followed, and later with the empire of Napoleon (1789-1815).

Britain was the birthplace of the Industrial Revolution in the late 18th century, and it remained the world's foremost economic power until the late 19th century.

During the reign of Queen Victoria, Britain's colonial expansion reached its zenith, though the older dominions, including Canada and Australia, were granted independence in 1867 and 1901 respectively.

The United Kingdom entered World War I allied with France and Russia in 1914.

The United Kingdom entered World War II in 1939. Throughout the post war period and into the 1970s, the UK continued to grant independence to its overseas colonies and dependencies, beginning with India in 1948.

The UK participated with UN forces in the Korean War (1950-53). In 1956 it intervened militarily in Egypt during the Suez Crisis. In 1982 it defeated Argentina in the Falkland Islands War.

After continuing strife in Northern Ireland the UK agreed to establish an assembly in Northern Ireland. In 1997 referenda approved in Scotland and Wales devolved power to both countries, though both remained part of the United Kingdom.

Northern Ireland

The long-running conflict between Catholics and Protestants in Northern Ireland was summarized in Chapter 15. This continues to a limited extent to this day, but on a much smaller scale than at its peak in the 1960s.

The original IRA began around the time of WW1 in an attempt to drive the British out of Northern Ireland. Following the war, revolutionary disorder erupted in Ireland, and in 1921 the Irish Free State was granted dominion status. The six counties of Ulster, however, remained in the United Kingdom as Northern Ireland.

The Provisional IRA was formed in December 1969 and its political wing Sinn Fein, was created in the following month. They began raising money and guns, seeking help from Irish groups in the US to do so.

In October 1970 the Provisional IRA Council decided on a full military campaign. On February 6, 1971, the first British soldier was killed in the new campaign. On 30 January, 1972, which came to be known as Bloody Sunday, the British military killed 13 civilians during a response to Catholic demonstrations. In March 1973 the British government announced that it would rule Northern Ireland directly from London and "the paramilitary groups on both sides continued trying to score political points through violent means for nearly twenty years" (Suter, 2008).

Finally a truce began in August 1994. Some of the Provisionals disagreed with it and formed breakaway groups such as the Irish National Liberation Army and the Real IRA. These continue fighting, but now conflict is mainly between criminal gangs over drugs.

By 2005, the Provisional IRA had claimed to have decommissioned most of its weapons under a 1997 ceasefire agreement. Of the 3,500 people who died in the sectarian conflicts in Northern Ireland between 1969 and 2001, about 48% were killed by the Provisional IRA, 30% by Protestant paramilitary groups, and the rest by the British Army.

Despite centuries of conflict Northern Ireland still remains part of Britain and Suter (2008) concludes that now "the ballot is achieving more than the bullet could," and that the violence achieved little and simply "fed on itself and just kept going. The IRA's violence led to Protestant revenge attacks, many of which resulted in the deaths of innocent Catholics."

Greece

The earliest urban society in Greece was the Minoan civilization, which reached its peak on Crete circa 2000 BC.

The mainland Mycenaean civilization arose circa 1600 BC following a wave of Indo-European invasions.

Circa 1200 BC a second wave of invasions destroyed the Bronze Age cultures, and a dark age followed, after which classical Greece began to emerge circa 750 BC as a collection of independent city-states, including Sparta and Athens.

The civilization reached its zenith after repelling the Persians at the beginning of the 5th century BC and began to decline after the Peloponnesian War at the century's end.

In 338 BC the Greek city-states were taken over by Philip II of Macedon, and Greek culture was spread by Philip's son Alexander the Great throughout his empire.

The Romans, themselves heavily influenced by Greek culture, conquered the Greek states in the 2nd century BC.

After the fall of Rome, Greece remained part of the Byzantine Empire until the mid-15th century, when it became part of the expanding Ottoman Empire.

After the war of 1821-29 Greece won independence from Turkey.

Greece was occupied by Nazi Germany during World War II, after which civil war followed and lasted until 1949, when communist forces were defeated.

In 1952 Greece joined NATO.

A military junta ruled the country from 1967 to 1974, when democracy was restored and a referendum declared an end to the Greek monarchy.

In 1981 Greece joined the European Community, the first eastern European country to do so.

Upheavals in the Balkans in the 1990s strained Greece's relations with some neighbouring states, including the former Yugoslav entity that became the Republic of Macedonia.

Cyprus

Cyprus was inhabited by the early Neolithic Age, and by the late Bronze Age it had been settled by Mycenaeans and Achaeans, who introduced Greek culture and language.

Ruled over the centuries by the Assyrian, Persian, and Ptolemaic empires, it was annexed by Rome in 58 BC and was part of the Byzantine Empire in the 4th-11th century AD.

Cyprus was conquered by Richard I in 1191.

It became part of the Venetian empire from 1489.

It then fell to the Ottoman Turks in 1571-73 and, after incurring heavy losses, they inflicted unspeakable cruelties and mutilations on Christian prisoners.

In 1878 the British assumed control and Cyprus became a British crown colony in 1924. It gained independence in 1960.

Conflict between Greek and Turkish Cypriots led to the establishment of a UN peacekeeping mission in 1964. In 1974, fearing a movement to unite Cyprus with Greece, Turkish soldiers occupied the northern third of the country and Turkish Cypriots established a functioning government, which obtained recognition only from Turkey.

A UN peacekeeping mission was sent but conflict has continued to the present and reunification talks have remained deadlocked.

Italy

Italy has been inhabited since the Stone Age.

The Etruscan civilization arose in the 9th century BC and was overthrown by the Romans in the 4th-3rd century BC.

Barbarian invasions in the 4th-5th century AD destroyed the Western Roman Empire. Italy's political fragmentation lasted for centuries but did not diminish its impact on European culture, notably during the Renaissance.

From the 15th to the 18th century, Italian lands were ruled by France, the Holy Roman Empire, Spain, and Austria.

When Napoleonic rule ended in 1815, Italy was again a group of independent states but reunification was completed by 1870 with the inclusion of Sicily and Sardinia.

Italy joined the Allies during World War I, but social unrest in the 1920s brought to power the Fascist movement of Benito Mussolini, and Italy allied itself with Nazi Germany in World War II.

Defeated by the Allies in 1943, Italy proclaimed itself a republic in 1946. It was a charter member of NATO (1949) and of the European Community.

Since World War II Italy has experienced rapid changes of government but has remained socially stable and is a key member of the European Union.

Spain

Muslim armies conquered Spain and parts of Southern France but at the Battle of Tours in AD 732 the Franks drove the Muslim armies out of France and they withdrew behind the Pyrenees Mountains into Spain.

Spain under the Islamic Moors suffered. In 920 AD Caliph Abd-Er-Rahman III put the inhabitants of Muez to the sword and destroyed the cathedral at Pamplona. Cordova, Zarajoza and Merida were burned to the ground, all adult males executed, and all women and children enslaved.

All the Jews of Grenada were slaughtered in 1066 AD, and in 1126 AD the Christians of Grenada were deported to Morocco.

The 'Pact of Umar' forced Christians to pay a crippling poll tax or 'jizya', and a land tax or 'haraj', and give up their seats to Muslims should they want to sit down. Christians were not allowed to carry weapons, ride on saddles, display the cross in public, sell wines, raise their voices in church services or funeral processions, or build houses higher than those of Muslims (Hammond, 2010).

In 1492 the Spaniards conquered Grenada, finally freeing Spain from centuries of tyrannical Muslim rule.

Russia

The region between the Dniester and the Volga rivers was inhabited from ancient times by various peoples, including the Slavs. The area was overrun in the 8th century BC-6th century AD by successive nomadic peoples, including the Sythians, Sarmatians, Goths, Huns, and Avars.

The Vikings briefly dominated Novgorod, Kiev, and other centres, but were quickly absorbed by the Slav population.

The Vikings ruled Novgorod from c. 879 and seized Smolensk and Kiev in 882, the latter becoming the capital of Kievan Rus, a confederation of principalities. It lost supremacy in the 11th-12th century to independent principalities, including Novgorod and Vladimir. Novgorod ascended in the north and was the only Russian principality to escape the domination of the Mongol Golden Horde in the 13th century.

In the 14th-15th century the princes of Moscow gradually overthrew the Mongols, and Russia began to expand.

Russia was invaded by Napoleon in 1812, and after his defeat in 1815 Russia received most of the grand duchy of Warsaw.

Russia annexed Georgia, Armenia, and Caucasus territories in the 19th century, also advancing southward against the Ottoman Empire.

Russia was defeated in the Crimean War.

Chinese cession of the Amur River's left bank in 1858 marked Russia's expansion in the Far East.

Russia sold Alaska to the US in 1867.

Its defeat in the Russo-Japanese War led to an unsuccessful uprising in 1905.

In World War I it fought against the Central Powers.

The Russian Revolution of 1917 brought most of the former empire under Communist control and organized it as the Russian Soviet Federated Socialist Republic (RSFSR).

The RSFSR joined other soviet republics in 1922 to form the USSR (Union of Soviet Socialist Republics).

The Cold War between the USSR and the West lasted from 1945 until circa 1990, though vestiges of the suspicions of that period remain today.

The USSR had global ambitions, for example, according to Zubok (2007):

The Politburo "discovered" Africa at the same time that it began its support for the Arab nationalists. From the beginning the Soviets acted on the ideological premise that decolonization of the continent would be a major blow to world capitalism and a great victory for Communism. Ivan Maisky wrote to Khrushchev and Bulganin in December 1955 that "the next act of the struggle for global domination of socialism will unfold through the liberation of colonial and semi-colonial people from imperialist exploitation". He added: "At the same time, the loss of colonies and semi-colonies by the imperialist powers must accelerate the victory of socialism in Europe, and eventually in the USA."

The USSR was dismantled in 1991 and the Russian SFSR was renamed and became the leading member of the Commonwealth of Independent States. It adopted a new constitution in 1993.

During the 1990s Russia was beset with economic difficulties, political corruption, and conflicts with independence movements, particularly in the largely Muslim republic of Chechnya, the latter conflict continuing to the present day.

Chechnya

Chechnya is part of the Checheno-Ingush autonomous republic of the former USSR in south-western Russia in the northern Caucasus Mountains bordering on Georgia. It declared independence from the USSR in 1991 but Russian troops invaded and it became a republic within Russia in 1992, as did Ingushetia.

It is populated mainly by Chechens, a Muslim ethno-linguistic group. Chechnya's demand for independence from Russia in 1992 led to an invasion by Russian troops in 1993-94. Fighting led to severe devastation of the area. A cease-fire agreement was reached in 1996, but fighting resumed in 1999. The capital, Grozny (pop. est.: 400,000), is a major oil centre with pipelines to the Caspian and Black seas, and it suffered heavy damage in both periods of fighting.

The Ukraine

Different parts of the area were invaded and occupied in the first millennium BC by the Cimmerians, Scythians, and Sarmatians, and in the first millennium AD by the Goths, Huns, Bulgars, Avars, Khazars, and Magyars.

Slavic tribes settled there after the 4th century and Kiev was its chief town. The Mongol conquest in the mid-13th century decisively ended Kievan power.

Ruled by Lithuania in the 14th century and Poland in the 16th century, it fell to Russian rule in the 18th century. The Ukrainian National Republic, established in 1917, declared its independence from Soviet Russia in 1918 but was reconquered in 1919 and made the Ukrainian Soviet Socialist Republic of the USSR in 1923.

The north-western region was held by Poland 1919-39.

The Ukraine suffered a severe famine in 1932-33 and more than 5 million Ukrainians died of starvation in an unprecedented peacetime catastrophe. Overrun by Axis armies in 1941 in World War II, it was further devastated before being retaken by the Soviets in 1944.

In 1986 it was the site of the Chernobyl accident, at a Soviet-built nuclear power plant.

With the break-up of the USSR the Ukraine declared independence in 1991.

In recent years there has been conflict between Russian-supported rebel forces and government forces in the region containing important port cities such as Odessa and Berdyansk. Currently there is, supposedly, a ceasefire, but conflict continues with considerable intensity.

Yugoslavia

The Kingdom of the Serbs, Croats, and Slovens was created after the collapse of Austria-Hungary at the end of World War I. The country signed treaties with Czechoslovakia and Romania in 1920-21, marking the beginning of the Little Entente.

In 1929 an absolute monarchy was established, the country's name was changed to Yugoslavia, and it was divided without regard to ethnic boundaries.

Axis powers invaded Yugoslavia in 1941, and German, Italian, Hungarian, and Bulgarian troops occupied it for the rest of World War II.

In 1945 the Socialist Federal Republic of Yugoslavia was established to include the republics of Bosnia and Herzegovina, Croatia, Macedonia, Montenegro, Serbia, and Slovenia.

Internal ethnic tensions flared up in the 1980s, causing the country to collapse. In 1991-92 independence was declared by Croatia, Slovenia, Macedonia, and Bosnia and Herzegovina, and the new Federal Republic of Yugoslavia (containing roughly 45% of the population and 40% of the area of its predecessor) was proclaimed by Serbia and Montenegro.

Still fuelled by long-standing ethnic tensions, hostilities continued into the 1990s, particularly in Bosnia. Despite the Dayton peace accord (1995), sporadic fighting continued and was followed in 1998-99 by Serbian repression and expulsion of ethnic populations in Kosovo.

Conclusions

There has, of course, been a great deal of conflict in Europe for over two thousand years, affecting almost every part of it except for the most remote and inhospitable regions that are largely uninhabited.

From 1350, for 300 years Turkish Muslims invaded Christian villages in the Balkans to exact an annual 'blood levy' in which one in five Christian boys were forced into the Sultan's armies, an additional burden to the crippling Jizya tribute tax. This has, according to Hammond (2010): "left such a deep scar on the collective memory of Balkan Christians, especially the Serbs and Bulgarians, that it continues to contribute to the hostilities of Bosnia and Kosovo."

Fortunately, with the creation of the Euro zone and it's common currency (the Euro), future conflict in most of Europe seems less likely, though the current conflict in the Ukraine is, of course, an example of the fact that there will always be some conflict over territory, religion etc. – all we can hope to do is minimize it.

Chapter 20

NORTH AMERICA

> *Unless drastic reforms are made, we must accept the fact that*
> *every four years the United States will be up for sale,*
> *and the richest man or family will buy it.*
> Gore Vidal, *Reflections upon a Sinking Ship,* June 6, 1968.

American settlement

Since Christopher Columbus sighted the Bahamas on 12 October 1492, North America has seen a great deal of conflict, initially between native tribes and colonizing forces, then between competing colonial forces, parts of what are now the USA and Canada having been colonized by the British, Dutch and Spanish.

On 8 September 1644 British troops seized New Netherland from the Dutch, renaming it New York. The Dutch recaptured the colony in 1673, but ceded it to Britain in 1674.

In 1676 many Indians were killed in New England.

In 1682 William Penn arrived in Pennsylvania, and in 1683 he signed a treaty with the Delaware Indians, making payment for Pennsylvania lands.

In 1682 France claimed lower Mississippi River country, calling it Louisiana, also building outposts in Illinois and Texas. In 1699 French settlements were established in Mississippi and Louisiana.

In Queen Anne's War of 1701-1713 British-Colonial troops captured the French fort of Port Royal, Nova Scotia, and France surrendered Nova Scotia by treaty in 1713.

In 1754 the French and Indian War began with the French occupying Fort Duquesne (Pittsburgh). In 1755 the British moved Acadian French from Nova Scotia to Louisiana. In 1759 the British took Quebec from the French, and in 1763 France signed a peace treaty giving Canada and the Midwest to Britain.

The American Revolution

In May 1773 East India Company tea ships were turned back at Boston, New York and Philadelphia. In October a cargo ship was burned at Annapolis, and on December 16 cargo was thrown overboard at the 'Boston Tea Party'.

On 5 September 1774 the First Continental Congress held in Philadelphia called for civil disobedience against the British. The American Revolution of 1775 – 83 followed, George Washington being named commander in chief in June 1775 by the Continental Congress, who adopted the Declaration of Independence on July 4.

In 1776 France and Spain agreed to provide the revolutionary forces with arms. In June a British sea attack at Charleston, South Carolina, was repulsed. In August Washington, with 10,000 men lost the Battle of Long Island and evacuated New York.

In June 1777 British troops moved from Canada but were forced to surrender at the Battle of Saratoga in upstate New York.

In 1778 France provided increased financial and material support, including a fleet, helping force the British to evacuate Philadelphia in June.

In May 1780 Charleston fell to the British, but in October a British force was defeated near Kings Mountain NC.

In 1781 Washington, aided by French forces, forced British forces to surrender on Yorktown Peninsula in Virginia.

In March 1782 Britain's cabinet agreed to recognize US independence and on 3 September 1783 Britain and the US signed the Paris peace treaty recognizing American independence, Congress ratifying it on 14 January 1784.

Conflict with British forces resumed, however, in the War of 1812, during which several American ships were sunk and British forces landed in Maryland. The British suffered a number of major defeats, however, until a peace treaty was signed at Ghent on 24 December 1814.

US territory expands

In 1803 Napoleon sold all of Louisiana, stretching to the Canadian border to the US, doubling the US in area.

In 1811 local Indians were defeated in the battle of Tippecanoe in Indiana.

In 1819 Spain ceded Florida to the US.

In 1832 the Black Hawk War saw Sauk and Fox Indians pushed west across the Mississippi River.

In 1835 Seminole Indians began attacks in protest against plans to relocate them. The 8-year war ended in August 1841 and they were sent to Oklahoma.

In 1838 Cherokee Indians were removed from Georgia to Oklahoma.

On 1 May 1841 the first emigrant wagon trail with 47 people left Missouri for California, arriving on 4 November.

In 1843 more than 1,000 settlers migrated from Missouri to Oregon.

In 1835 Texas seceded from Mexico, beginning a decade of conflict. US troops assaulted Mexico City in 1847 and subsequently Mexico was forced to cede most of the present-day south-west USA.

In 1850 California was admitted as the 31st state, whilst Utah and New Mexico were made territories.

In 1867 Russia sold Alaska to the US for $7.2 million.

In 1890 the Battle of Wounded Knee, the last major conflict between US troops and Indians, took place in South Dakota. About 200 Indian men, women, and children, and 29 soldiers were killed.

The American Civil War

On 8 February 1861 seven southern states declared themselves the Confederate States of America with Jefferson Davis as president. Federal arsenals and forts were overtaken and Civil War began when Fort Sumter in Charleston SC was captured on April 18. By May, eleven states had seceded.

On 1 January 1863 President Lincoln issued the Emancipation Proclamation freeing "all slaves in areas of rebellion."

Union forces won a major victory at Gettysburg PA July 1-3, 1863, and the entire Mississippi River was in Union hands by 4 July 1863.

On 9 April 1865, 27,000 Confederate troops surrendered to Union forces, 31,000 more surrendering 9 days later.

The last rebel troops surrendered on May 26.

Conflicts over slavery

In 1713 slaves revolted in New York, six committing suicide and 21 being hanged. In a second rising in 1741, 13 slaves were hanged, 13 burned, and 71 deported.

In 1808 importation of slaves was made illegal, but about 250,000 slaves were imported illegally from 1808 to 1860, mostly to the South.

On 6 December 1865 the 13th amendment, abolishing slavery, was ratified by congress.

In 1866 the Ku Klux Clan was secretly formed in the South to terrorize blacks who voted. It was disbanded in 1869-71 but reorganized in 1915.

War with Spain

On 15 February 1898 the US battleship 'Maine' was blown up at harbour in Havana, killing 200.

The US responded by blockading Cuba to aid independence forces on 22 April, declaring war on Spain on 24 April.

On 1 May US forces destroyed a Spanish fleet in the Philippines. Guam was taken 20 June and from July 25 to August 12 Puerto Rico was taken.

Annexation of Hawaii was signed by President William McKinley on 7 July.

On 10 December 1898 Spain ceded the Philippines, Puerto Rico, and Guam, also approving independence for Cuba.

WW1

On 7 May 1915 the British ship Lusitania was sunk by German submarines with the loss of 128 Americans, German passengers having been warned of the attack.

On July 28 1915 US troops landed in Haiti and under a 16 September treaty it became a virtual US protectorate. US troops were withdrawn in 1934.

In August 1916 the US purchased the Virgin Islands from Denmark. On 29 November the US established a military government in the Dominican Republic.

On 31 January 1917 Germany declared unrestricted submarine warfare. On 3 February the US cut diplomatic ties with Germany.

On April 6 the US formally declared war on Germany, a conscription law being passed on May 18. The first US troops arrived in Europe on June 26, and by July 1918 more than a million US troops were in Europe.

The allied counter-offensive was launched on 18 July 1918, an armistice ending the war being signed on 11 November.

WW2

On 17 May 1938 the Naval Expansion Act was passed.

In January 1939 the President sought an increase in the US defence budget.

On 5 September 1939 the US declared its neutrality in the European war.

On 3 June 1940 the US began selling surplus war material to Britain. On 3 September it agreed to give Britain 50 of its oldest destroyers.

On 11 March 1941 the Lend-Lease Act provided $7 billion in military credit for Britain. In November Lend-Lease for the USSR was approved.

On 7 July the US occupied Iceland.

On 7 December Japan attacked Pearl Harbour, Hawaii, sinking or damaging 19 ships and killing 2,300. The US declared war on Japan on 8 December, and on Germany and Italy on 11 December.

In 1942 the US government moved 110,000 Japanese-Americans from the West Coast to detention camps, their detention lasting three years.

On 9 July 1943 Britain and the US invaded Sicily, then invading the mainland on 3 September.

On 6 June 1944 allied forces landed at Normandy, the greatest amphibian landing in history.

On 20 October 1944 US forces landed in the Philippines.

On 19 February 1945 US forces landed on Iwo Jima and it was taken on 16 March after heavy casualties.

On 7 May Germany surrendered and May 8 was declared V-E Day.

On 6 August 1945 a nuclear bomb was dropped on Hiroshima, killing about 90,000 people, another being dropped on Nagasaki on 9 August, killing about 40,000 people. On 14 August Japan agreed to surrender, formally doing so on 2 September. By the end of 1945 the death tolls in Hiroshima and Nagasaki were estimated to be 140 and 70 million respectively, whilst by 1950 they were estimated to be 200 and 140 million.

The Cold War

At the Yalta conference of 4-11 February 1945 in the USSR's Crimea, Roosevelt, Churchill and Stalin agreed that their three countries and France would occupy Germany, and that the Soviet Union would enter the war against Japan.

At the Potsdam conference of 17 July to 2 August, the US, USSR and Britain agreed on occupation zones in Europe. Many felt that the USSR was allowed control of too much of Europe at this conference.

The USSR having moved in many troops to take control of much of Eastern Europe after WW2, the Cold War between the USSR and the West began and lasted until the USSR was dismantled in December 1991.

It involved economic sanctions imposed on the USSR by the West, the building of the Berlin Wall, and occasional political skirmishes such as the Cuban Missile Crisis of 1962.

Further wars and political conflict

After WW2 the US was involved in several wars, including those in Malaya in the 1950s, Korea (1950-53), Vietnam (1954-75), Iraq (1991, 2003) and Afghanistan (2006-2011)

The US was also involved in the overthrow of left-wing governments in South America, Europe and Africa, particularly during the 1960s to the 1980s.

Racial conflict

In July 1863 in riots in New York blacks were hanged by mobs and 1,000 people were killed or wounded.

In the Southern states of the US, public facilities were segregated according to the Jim Crow laws from the late 19th century into the 1950s.

On 21 June 1943, 34 were killed and 700 injured during a race riot in Detroit, and 6 were killed in a riot in the Harlem section of New York City.

On 17 May 1954 the Supreme Court ruled racial segregation in public schools unconstitutional, on 31 May 1955 ordering "all deliberate speed" in integration of public schools. In March 1955, 101 Southern congressmen called for massive resistance to the Supreme Court desegregation rulings.

In 1957 federal troops were used to enforce a court order to remove guards preventing black students from access to an all-white high school in Little Rock.

On 1 February 1960 four black college students staged a sit-in when refused service at a supermarket. By September 1961 more than 70,000 black and white students had participated in sit-ins.

In 1961 "Freedom Rides" were begun to protest segregation in interstate transport.

On 1 October 1962 the first black student was allowed entry to the University of Mississippi after 3,000 troops stopped riots.

On 11 June 1963 the University of Alabama was desegregated after Governor George Wallace stepped aside when confronted by National Guard troops.

On 28 August 1963, 200,000 people marched on Washington in support of equal rights and to hear Martin Luther King's celebrated "I have a dream" speech. King was assassinated on 4 April 1968.

The civil-rights movement and the Civil Rights Act of 1964 helped end segregation in education and the use of public facilities, but socially sanctioned racial discrimination continues.

Canada

French explorer, James Cartier, who reached the Gulf of St. Lawrence in 1534, is generally regarded as Canada's founder, but English seaman John Cabot sighted Newfoundland in 1497, whilst Vikings are believed to have reached the Atlantic coast centuries earlier.

The French began settlement by establishing Quebec City in 1608, and Montreal in 1642, declaring New France a colony in 1663.

Britain acquired Acadia (later Novia Scotia) in 1717 and, after military victories over French forces, captured Quebec in 1759, and took control of the rest of New France in 1763.

The War of 1812 between Great Britain and the US was fought mainly in Upper Canada and ended in stalemate in 1814.

In 1837 there were rebellions in Upper and Lower Canada (later called Ontario and Quebec) demanding more democratic government. Britain responded by uniting the two parts into one colony, Canada. Thus union lasted until 1 July 1867, when the British North America (BNA) Act created the Dominion of Canada, consisting of Ontario, Quebec, and the former colonies of Nova Scotia and New Brunswick.

Canada was proclaimed a self-governing Dominion under the British Empire Act in 1931. The Constitution Act of 1962 allowed Canada to change its constitution, severing the last formal legislative connection with Britain.

In the late 1980s concerns about preserving French culture sparked a separatist revival, culminating in the Charlottetown agreement which recognized Quebec as a "distinct society", but this was defeated in a national referendum in 1992. Another referendum in 1995 was lost by a slim margin.

In May 1992 voters in the Northwest Territories approved the creation of a self-governing homeland for the 17,000 Inuit of the territories.

Conclusions

Having been colonized by European powers only relatively recently in recorded history, North America has not experienced as much conflict and war as Europe and the Middle East. The War of Independence, of course, was a notable exception, as was the American Civil War.

Chapter 21

CENTRAL & SOUTH AMERICA

Poor Mexico, so far from God, and so near to the United States.
Porfirio Diaz,
referring to the beginning of the Mexican War (1846-48), *attrib.*

Argentina

Nomadic Indians roamed the Pampas when the Spaniards arrived, 1515-16, led by Juan Diaz de Solia. Nearly all the Indians were killed by the late 19th century and, after a long period of disorder, the colonists won independence in 1816.

Large-scale Italian, German, and Spanish immigration in the decades after 1880 brought about modernization. In the 1920s social reforms were enacted, but military coups prevailed from 1930 to 46 until the election of General Juan Peron as president.

Peron and his wife, who died in 1952, effected labour reforms but also suppressed freedom of speech and the press, closed religious schools, and ran the country into debt.

A 1955 coup exiled Peron, who was followed by a series of military and civilian regimes. Peron returned in 1973, again being elected president, and his wife, Isabel, was elected vice president. He died 10 months later to be succeeded by his wife, who became the first woman head of state in the western hemisphere.

Ms Peron was ousted by a military junta in 1976 amidst charges of corruption. Under siege from leftist guerrillas, the army killed 5,000 people and jailed and tortured many others.

On 9 December 1985, 5 former junta members were found guilty of human-rights abuses and murder.

On 2 April 1982 Argentine troops seized control of the British-held Falkland Islands for which both countries claimed sovereignty. Britain sent a task force and blockaded the islands by both sea and air. Fighting began on May 1, during which several hundred were killed when a British destroyer was destroyed, and an Argentinean cruiser being used for military purposes was sunk.

On 21 May British troops landed on East Falkland Island, eventually surrounding the capital Stanley. The Argentinean troops surrendered on 14 June and the Argentinean president resigned on 17 June.

Democratic rule was restored in Argentina in 1983 when the Radical Civic Union won national elections.

The nation was plagued by severe political and financial problems by 1989 and a newly elected government introduced harsh economic measures to curb inflation, reduce government spending, and reduce foreign debt.

On 18 July, 1994, about 100 people were killed in the terrorist bombing of a Jewish cultural centre in Buenos Aires.

Bolivia

The Incas overtook the region from Indian inhabitants during the 13th century. Spanish rule began in the 1530s, and ended in 1825 after the Venezuelan statesman Simon Bolivar led a revolt of South American colonies against Spanish rule.

After a series of wars from 1879 to 1935, Bolivia lost its Pacific coast to Chile, the oil-rich Chaco to Paraguay, and rubber-growing areas to Brazil.

From 1951 to 1964 a reformist government nationalized tin mines and tried to improve the lot of the Indian majority, but was overthrown by a military junta. A series of coups and countercoups continued until 1981, when the military junta elected a president.

In July 1982 the junta retook power amid growing economic crises and foreign debt problems, and elections for a new president, who had formerly been dictator of a military junta from 1971-1978, was elected.

US pressure on the government to reduce Bolivia's output of cocoa, the raw material for cocaine, led to clashes between police and cocoa growers, also increasing anti-US feeling amongst Bolivians.

Brazil

Portuguese navigator Pedro Alvares Cabrai is believed to have been the first European to reach Brazil in 1500, when the area was sparsely settled by various Indian tribes, only a few of which have survived, mostly in the Amazon basin.

In following centuries Portuguese colonies extended inland, bringing with them large numbers of African slaves.

Under pressure from Napoleon's army, in 1808 the King of Portugal moved the seat of government to Brazil. After the king's return to Portugal, the king's son proclaimed the independence of Brazil on 7 September 1822, and crowned himself emperor. He was deposed in 1889, and a republic called the United States of Brazil proclaimed. In 1967 the country was renamed the Federative Republic of Brazil.

In 1930 a military junta took power and Gétulio Vargas became dictator until he was forced out by the military in 1945. A democratic regime followed from 1945 until 64, during which period the capital was moved from Rio de Janeiro to Brasilia.

In 1964, after economic policies had aggravated inflation, the army took control and the next five presidents were all military leaders who imposed censorship and suppressed opposition amid claims of torture. When the official opposition party made gains in the 1974 elections there was some relaxation of censorship.

Thanks to its fertile soils, vast mineral resources, and huge workforce, Brazil became the leading industrial power of Latin America in the 1970s, during which agricultural output soared.

Brazil returned to civilian rule in 1985 via democratic presidential elections. Recession followed, however, in the early 1990s. In 1992, President Fernando Collor de Mello, who had been elected in 1989, was impeached for corruption and resigned, a new president being elected in December 1992.

Chile

Northern Chile was under Inca rule before the Spanish conquest of 1536-1540, the southern Araucanian Indians resisting until the late 19th century. It gained independence by 1818, and defeated Peru in 1836-39, and Bolivia in 1879-84, gaining mineral-rich northern land.

In 1970 Salvador Allende Gossens, a Marxist, became president with a third of the national vote. His government improved conditions for the poor, but financial and political chaos followed and a military junta led by General Augusto Pinochet seized power on 11 September, 1973, saying that the president had killed himself. Pinochet held power for 17 years, during which time no elections were held, the media were tightly controlled, and about 3,000 people were executed, died under torture, or disappeared.

Before allowing democratic elections which it lost, the military government took steps to shield its members and Pinochet granted himself a lifetime seat in the Senate, giving him immunity from prosecution. In October 1998, however, he was arrested in London when he went there for medical treatment. He was held on an international warrant issued in Spain that charged him with human rights violations during his dictatorship, including the torture of 94 Spanish captives.

The case went to the House of Lords and ran for 16 months, but in the end he was deemed to be to sick to stand trial in Spain and allowed to return to Chile. There, however, he lost his status as senator for life and was arrested several times. Finally, based on charges relating to abductions that took place in 1973, he was placed under house arrest and died thus in December 2006 (Suter, 2008).

In 1994 a Chilean human rights group announced a revised estimate of more than 3,100 deaths from human rights violations during Pinochet's rule.

Columbia

Spain subdued the local Indian kingdoms in the 1530s and ruled Columbia and neighbouring areas as New Granada for 300 years. Independence was granted in 1819, Venezuela and Ecuador broke away in 1829-30, and Panama withdrew in 1903.

In 1948-58 'La Violencia', a plague of rural and urban violence, claimed 200,000 lives. Much of this was caused by right-wing paramilitary groups who killed peasant farmers and stole their land to protect and advance the interests of multinational companies who financed their terrorism.

Attempts at land and social reform have failed to reduce massive social problems, and after 50 years of violence hundreds of thousands of people have been killed.

In Columbia the Revolutionary Armed Forces of Columbia (FARC), a powerful and wealthy terrorist organization, formed in 1957 as the guerrilla arm of the Colombian communist party, continues to cause trouble.

FARC is heavily involved in the drug trade, exporting large amounts to the US, to which it is politically opposed.

In the 1980s government activity against local drug traffickers led to a series of retaliatory killings. On 18 August 1989, the ruling party's candidate for the presidential elections was assassinated. In 1990 two more presidential candidates were assassinated.

On 1 July 1992, the head of the Medellin drug cartel escaped from prison, allegedly with the aid of military and prison officials, but was killed by government troops on 1 December 1993.

Charges that it had received money from the Cali drug cartel for its 1994 campaign engulfed the administration of Ernesto Samper Pizano in scandal, but in June 1992 the legislature voted not to impeach him.

Government actions have reduced Columbian drug trade, but it still remains a major problem.

Cuba

When Fidel Castro came to power in 1959 the US immediately imposed sanctions, most of which remain today.

Despite the Cuban missile crisis of 1962, Cuba itself never posed any direct threat to the US. Cuba under the leadership of Raul Castro is beginning to embrace free enterprise and many believe continuing sanctions are counterproductive and simply prevent the rise of a politically active middle class (Suter, 2008).

Guantanamo Bay

Since 11 September 2001, more than 3,000 people associated with al-Qa'ida have been arrested or killed in 90 countries. Up to 600 members of al-Qa'ida and the Taliban have been held at the US Naval Station at Guantanamo Bay in Cuba.

There they have no right of appeal against their arrest and can only be tried by military tribunal, if at all. Britain objected to this, and its nationals were sent to Britain where most were released without trial.

In February 2006, an independent UN panel of experts called for Guantanamo Bay prison to be shut down. In June 2006 the US Supreme Court ruled that the trials at Guantanamo Bay were illegal under American and international law. Since then the American government has passed further legislation about military tribunals, but this has also been challenged in the Supreme Court (Suter, 2008).

Ecuador

Ecuador was conquered by the Incas in AD 1450, and came under Spanish control in 1534. Under the Spaniards it was a part of the viceroyalty of Peru until 1740, when it became a part of the viceroyalty of New Granada.

Ecuador gained its independence from Spain in 1822 as part of the republic of Gran Colombia, and in 1830 it became a sovereign state.

A succession of authoritarian governments ruled into the mid-20th century, and economic hardship and social unrest prompted the military to take a strong role.

Border disputes led to war between Peru and Ecuador in 1941 and the two fought periodically until agreeing to a final demarcation in 1998.

The economy was depressed in the 1980s by reduced oil prices and earthquake damage.

In the 1990s social unrest caused political instability and several changes of heads of state. In a controversial move to help stabilize the economy, the US dollar replaced the sucre as the national currency in 2000.

El Salvador

El Salvador has a developing economy based on trade, manufacturing, and agriculture, with coffee, sugarcane, and cotton the major export crops.

The Spanish arrived in the area in 1524 and subjugated the Pipil Indian kingdom of Cuzcatlán by 1539. The country was divided into two districts, San Salvador and Sonsonate, both attached to Guatemala. When independence came in 1821, San Salvador was incorporated into the Mexican empire, and upon its collapse in 1823, Sonsonate and San Salvador combined to form the new state of El Salvador within the United Provinces of Central America.

From its founding, El Salvador experienced a high degree of political turmoil, and was under military rule from 1931 to 79, when the government was ousted in a coup. Elections held in 1982 set up a new government and in 1983 a new constitution was adopted, but civil war continued through the 1980s. An accord in 1992 brought an uneasy truce.

As in other countries in central and South America, Marxist rebels have often been active, the government receiving US support to maintain power.

Mexico

Mexico was in habited by advanced Indian civilizations including the Mayans who build large stone pyramids and invented a calendar. The Aztecs overcame the Toltecs and founded what is now Mexico City.

In the period 1519 to 21 Spanish conquest destroyed the Aztec empire. After revolts in 1810, 1812 and 1821 a republic was declared in 1823.

Mexican territory extended into the present American southwest and California until Texas revolted and established a republic in 1836, but this was not recognized by Mexico.

In the US-Mexican War of 1846-48 Mexico lost its lands north of the Rio Grande.

In 1864-67 an Austrian archduke was king thanks to French military support until US pressure forced France to withdraw. In 1877-80 and 1884-1911 the dictator Porfirio Diaz ruled until fighting by rival forces led to a new constitution in 1917.

The Institutional Revolutionary Party (PRI) dominated politics from 1929 until the late 1990s and it contained radical opposition by strong measures.

Mexico established a free trade agreement with the US and Canada which took effect on 1 January 1994.

That same day guerrillas of the Zapatista National Liberation Army (EZLN) began an uprising in southern Mexico until a peace accord was signed on 2 March 1994.

On 23 March the presidential candidate of the governing PRI was assassinated at a political rally. The new PRI candidate won the election on 21 August.

In early 1995 an austerity plan and promises of US aid saved Mexico's currency from collapse.

In August 1996 Popular Revolutionary Army guerrillas attacked government targets.

In the July 1997 elections the PRI failed to win a congressional majority for the first time since 1929.

Panama

The land was inhabited by American Indians when the Spanish arrived in 1501. The first successful Spanish settlement was founded by Vasco Nunez de Balboa in 1510

Panama was part of the viceroyalty of New Granada until it declared its independence from Spain in 1821 to join Colombia. In 1903 it revolted against Colombia and was recognized by the US, to whom it ceded the Canal Zone.

The completed canal was opened in 1914 and its jurisdiction reverted from the US to Panama in 1999.

An invasion by US troops in1989 overthrew the de facto ruler, General Manuel Noriega.

Panama joined the World Trade Organization in 1997.

Peru

Spain conquered Peru in 1533, enslaving the native Incas.

In 1821, Argentine liberator José de San Martin captured Lima, the seat of the Spanish viceroys, but the Spanish were finally routed by Simon Bolivar in 1824.

On 3 October 1968 a military coup occurred, followed by socialist programs. Escalating food shortages and foreign debt led to another coup in 1976.

Democracy was restored in 1980 but Peru was plagued with economic problems and terrorist attacks by the leftist 'Shining Path' group.

The leader of Shining Path was captured in 1992, guerrilla activity was curtailed, and the economy began to boom.

Peru's repressive antiterrorism tactics drew international condemnation, however, and on 17 December 1996 Tupac Amara guerrillas infiltrated a reception at the embassy in Lima. Hundreds of hostages were taken, but most were soon released. Peruvian soldiers stormed the embassy on 22 December, freeing 71 of the remaining hostages: 1 hostage, 2 soldiers, and all 14 guerrillas were killed.

Venezuela

Venezuela has been inhabited by indigenous peoples for millennia. In 1498 Christopher Columbus sighted it, and in 1499 the navigators Alonso de Ojeda, Amerigo Vespucci, and Juan de la Cosa traced the coast.

A Spanish missionary established the first European settlement at Cumana circa 1520. In 1718 it was included in the viceroyalty of New Granada and was made a captaincy general in 1731.

Venezuelan Creoles led by Francisco de Miranda and Simón Bolívar led the South American independence movement, and though Venezuela declared independence from Spain in 1811, it was not assured until 1821.

Military dictators generally ruled the country from 1830 until the overthrow of Marcos Pérez Jiménez in 1958. A new constitution adopted in 1961 marked the beginning of democracy.

As a founding member of OPEC Venezuela enjoyed relative economic prosperity from oil production during the 1970s, and its economy has remained dependent on the world petroleum market.

In 1999 the government of Hugo Chavez introduced socialist reforms which were resented by the US.

That same year a devastating rainstorm killed thousands in and around Caracas.

Despite it having the largest oil reserves in the world, Venezuela has severe economic problems, in part because of a massive fuel subsidy that reduced the price of petrol to a small fraction of normal levels, resulting in a thriving petrol-smuggling trade to Columbia. Such measures have reduced government spending on education and health drastically and resulted in social problems, there being 20,000 murders per year in Venezuela, and Caracas has the second-highest murder rate in the world.

Conclusions

Like Northern America, South America was colonized by European powers only relatively recently in recorded history.

Prior to that time there is evidence of conflict between competing groups, particularly the Incas and native Indian tribes.

In the last several decades there has been much political instability in much of South America, and several revolutions.

Behind the scenes the US has played a part in these, seeking to install governments to its liking, that is, those of a more conservative nature rather than more socialist governments.

Chapter 22

AUSTRALASIA

Australia

The native Australian Aborigines arrived 40,000-60,000 years ago, and estimates of the population at the time of European settlement in 1788 range from 300,000 to more than 1 million.

The Dutch landed in 1616 and the British in 1688, but the first large-scale expedition was that of James Cook in 1770, which established Britain's claim to Australia's east.

The first English settlement, at Port Jackson (1788), consisted mainly of convicts and seamen.

By 1859 the colonial nuclei of all Australia's states had been formed, but the Aboriginal population declined sharply with the introduction of European diseases and weaponry, the Tasmanian Aborigines being completely exterminated.

Britain granted its colonies limited self-government in the mid-19th century, and an act federating the colonies into a commonwealth was passed in 1900.

Australia fought alongside the British in World War 1, notably at Gallipoli, and again in World War 2.

US troops were stationed in Australia during World War 2, helping prevent Japanese invasion.

Australia joined the US in the Korean and Vietnam wars, introducing conscription for the latter in the late 1960s.

In 1999 the East Timorese crisis began with attacks by anti-independence militants on civilians, and expanded to general violence throughout the country, centred in the capital Dili. The violence erupted after a majority of eligible voters in the population of East Timor chose independence from Indonesia. Some 1,400 civilians are believed to have died. A UN force (INTERFET) consisting mainly of Australian Defence Force personnel was deployed to East Timor to establish and maintain peace.

Since the 1960s the government has sought to deal more fairly with the Aborigines, and a loosening of immigration restrictions has led to a more heterogeneous population.

In the last two decades the number of refugees seeking political asylum in Australia has increased considerably and recently measures have been taken to discourage illegal shipping of asylum seekers to Australia.

Passport confiscation in Australia

In April 2015 the US military targeted an Australian fighting in Syria for assassination because of his association with Jabhat al Nusra, al-Qa'ida's official affiliate in the ongoing conflict in Syria.

Around the same time another Australian in Syria fighting for al Nusra posted on the Internet a statement ridiculing the Islamic State terrorist group for it having lost the city of Idlib to al Nusra. Idlib was the second major city in Syria captured by al Nusra in a year.

In Australia there is growing concern about more than a hundred young men having gone to the Middle East to fight for Islamic State and other terrorist groups.

Several Australian women have also gone to fight for ISIS or support them by marrying the men of ISIS.

On 18 April 2015 the Melbourne Herald Sun newspaper reported that 30 Australians had been confirmed to have died fighting for Islamic State.

As a result of such reports the Australian government has placed travel bans on several young Muslims suspected of radical tendencies, preventing them from leaving the country.

The Australian government is also planning to cancel the passports of dual-citizens who have left the country to join terrorist groups.

In May 2015 it was reported that up to a dozen Australian jihadists fighting with IS in the Middle East had said that they wanted to return to Australia. Australia's Prime Minister, Tony Abbott, responded by saying that he would ensure that they were incarcerated.

New Zealand

Polynesian occupation dates to circa AD 1000.

New Zealand was first sighted by Dutch explorer Abel Tasman in 1642 and the main islands were charted by Capt. James Cook in 1769.

It was made a British crown colony in 1840.

The Wellington area was the scene of warfare between colonists and native Maori through the 1860s.

The capital was moved from Auckland to Wellington in 1865, and in 1907 the colony became the Dominion of New Zealand.

New Zealand administered Western Samoa from 1919 to 62, and participated in both world wars. Whilst the culture is predominantly European, much traditional Maori culture and art has been preserved.

When Britain joined the European Economic Community in the early 1970s, New Zealand was forced to expand its export markets and diversify its economy. It has also become more independent in its foreign relations.

Today there are circa 350,000 Maoris in New Zealand, and six of 120 members of the House of Representatives are elected directly by the Maori people.

Papua New Guinea

The area has been inhabited since prehistoric times.

The Portuguese sighted the coast in 1512, and in 1545 the Spanish claimed the island.

The first colony was founded in 1793 by the British.

In 1828 the Dutch claimed the western half as part of the Dutch East Indies.

In 1884 Britain annexed the south-eastern part and Germany took over the north-eastern sector. The British part became the Territory of Papua in 1906 and passed to Australia, which also governed the German sector after World War I.

After World War II, Australia governed both sectors as the Territory of Papua and New Guinea. Dutch New Guinea was annexed to Indonesia in 1969 as the province of Irian Jaya. Papua New Guinea achieved independence in 1975 and joined the British Commonwealth.

Long-running disputes and conflicts with Bougainville independence fighters were largely resolved in 1997.

Fiji

Archaeological evidence shows that the islands were occupied in the late 2nd millennium BC and had developed pottery by 1300 BC.

The first European sighting was by the Dutch in the 16th century. In 1774 the islands were visited by Captain James Cook, who found a mixed Melanesian-Polynesian population with a complex society.

Traders and the first missionaries arrived in 1835.

In 1857 a British consul was appointed, and in 1874 Fiji was proclaimed a crown colony.

Fiji became independent as a member of the Commonwealth in 1970, and was declared a republic in 1987 following a military coup.

Elections in 1992 restored civilian rule and a new constitution was approved in 1997.

Conclusions

Australasia has been relatively free of conflict, though both Australia and New Zealand have, for example, been pulled into such wars as WW1 and WW2 by 'big sister' England.

Australia too was heavily involved in the Vietnam War, and also the relatively small conflict in East Timor in the late 1990s.

Politically Australia is now run to a considerable extent by Australian media baron and now US citizen (to reduce taxes in the US) Rupert Murdoch – for example, he got Bob Hawke elected (via his newspapers and their BS) in 1983, even though he normally pushes, as one might expect from an oligarch in an oligarchical society, for the conservative Liberal/National Party coalition.

Thus, when Michael Moore was trying to publish his book *Stupid White Men ... and Other Sorry Excuses for the State of the Nation,* he had some difficulty at first:

The response I got was the publishing world's equivalent of "fuck off." They wanted a significant rewrite, they were not going to budge on their insistence that I censor large portions of the book, and, yes, they wanted that $100,000 check made out from me to Mr. Murdoch's enterprise.

He was, of course, talking to Harper Collins who did actually publish the book anyway. Later in the book, however, he complains, for example, about overuse of the death penalty in the US, a complaint which we suppose many would agree with.

PART 3
WORLD WAR 3

Chapter 23

THE SEEDS OF CONFLICT

In 1956 Professor W.A. Lewis calculated that if the world population were to double every 25 years (a rate of increase currently observable in some parts of Africa and Asia), it would reach 173,500 thousand million by the year 2330, at which time there would be standing room only, since this is the number of square yards on the land surface of the earth.
John Carey, *The Faber Book of Science* (1995),
'The Menace of Population.'

The seeds of conflict

Human population has grown exponentially since the industrial revolution began in Europe in the middle of the 18th century. The quotation above reminds us that, not only will we begin to suffer overcrowding before very long, but we are also damaging the planet as well (Mohr, 2012b).

With this massive growth in population, and thus increasing scarcity of fast vanishing resources, comes increasing risk of conflict (Heywood, 2012). Now, with about a third of the human population undernourished, and with the disparity between the rich and poor growing ever wider, the seeds of conflict continue to be sown.

In the second half of the last century there were more than 100 wars fought in more than 60 countries (Bell & Hall, 1991) and it seems likely that this carnage will continue.

Now we have economic warfare in progress which may eventually spark armed conflict between such economically competitive countries as China and the USA (Clark 1967).

In addition, extremist Islamic terrorists still talk of building a global Islamic empire or caliphate and continue to orchestrate terrorist attacks around the world.

The main concern, of course, is that sooner or later future wars will involve nuclear and biological weapons.

Too many people

The world's human population is, in our opinion, now at least twice that which can be sustainable for the long term.

Table 23.1. Human population since 10,000BC, N = population in millions, Year = thousands AD.

N	1	5	27	50	200	300	400	500	600	750	1000
Year	-10	-5	-2	-1	0	0.5	1	1.5	1.65	1.75	1.8

Table 23.1 shows human population (millions) since 10,000BC, when we reached our first million. It then took 10,000 years to reach 200 million, but only another 1000 years to add a further 200 million, 10 times the rate of increase.

Table 23.2 shows the date at which the human population reached 1 billion, 2 billion etc., including UN projections for when it will reach 8, 9, and 10 billion.

Table 23.2. Dates for population in billions, * = United Nations Population Fund estimates, 31/10/2011.

N	1	2	3	4	5	6	7	8*	9*	10*
Year	1800	1927	1960	1974	1987	1999	2011	2025	2043	2083
+ yrs		127	33	14	13	12	12	14	18	40

As shown in Table 23.1, it was 11,800 years after 10,000BC before we reached 1 billion, that is, about 50,000 years since Homo sapiens sapiens first left behind evidence of religion, recorded events, and art.

Then, as shown in Table 23.2, it was only another 127 years until a further billion people were added, reducing to a minimum of 12 years to have added another billion people in both 1999 and 2011. Needless to say, a further billion people in 12 years is like the speed of light compared to a tortoise when we compare it to 50,000 years to reach the first billion.

This reflection does, indeed, remind us that some authors have compared our population to that of a deadly viral or bacterial infection spreading over the planet, one that gobbles up resources and spoils and pollutes the planet at an increasingly rapid rate.

Ironically, our population began to exponentiate more rapidly with the coming of the industrial revolution in Europe (Cipolla, 1974), since then many improvements in living conditions such as sewerage, and medical advances such as antibiotics, having reduced mortality rates and increased longevity considerably.

In Table 23.2 it is assumed that the rate of population increase is slowing, and this indeed is the case. Thus some "experts" predict our population will peak at between about 9 and 10 billion somewhere between 2050 and 2100.

There are those that doubt that the planet can support 8 billion people, the present authors feeling that half that number is all that we could hope to sustain with a truly modern standard of living rather than a subsistence one.

Alarmingly, population growth is more rapid in the poorest, most backward countries, and thus from 1990 to 2008 Africa's population increased by 55%.

In the period 1990 to 2010 India's population increased by 40.2%, Bangladesh's by 41.3%, Nigeria's by 62.4%, and Pakistan's by 55.3% (in March 2013 their respective populations were 1.27B, 154M, 170M, 182 M).

In March 2013 India's population density was 386.5 people per square kilometre, compared with 1068 /sq. km in Bangladesh, 226.7/sq. km in Pakistan, 183.7/sq. km in Nigeria, 141.5 /sq. km in China, 32.3/sq. km in the USA, or about 3/sq. km in Australia.

It is estimated that in 2050 Africa's share of the human population will be 20.8%, up from 13.8% in 2005, whereas in the same period Europe's share of population will have declined from 11.3% to about 5%.

Africa is a dry but populous continent, and in recent decades there have been mass migrations of conflict ridden and starving people from some of its poorest countries such as the Central African Republic, Chad, Nigeria, and the Sudan (particularly the Darfur region), such countries having a life expectancy of only about 50.

For decades there have also been mass migrations from other countries that have suffered conflict and regime change, Vietnam being an example in recent decades.

The result is thousands of 'boat people' trying to arrive in freer and more prosperous places such as Australia and Europe. Ultimately, the stresses of exponentiating population and diminishing resources can only lead to an escalation of conflict around the world.

The global arms industry

The arms industry is one of the world's two largest, along with the illegal drugs trade.

During World War 2 the US made a fortune out of the lend-lease program which sold weapons to 35 countries including the UK, China, the USSR, the Netherlands, Belgium and the Free French. By the end of the war lend-lease appropriations had totalled $48B.

In departing from office President Dwight Eisenhower coined the term 'military-industrial state', warning against the "military-industrial complex" having too much influence, a situation that has come to pass (Wheen, 2004).

The US remains the world's largest manufacturer of military equipment and weapons. In the period 1970 – 76 the US made arms sales to almost 100 countries. In 1976 some of their best customers were Australia ($0.41B), Germany ($0.21B), Iran ($1.3B), Israel ($0.92B), Jordan ($0.43B), Korea ($0.63B), Saudi Arabia ($2.5B), Switzerland ($0.45B), and Taiwan ($0.22B), (Sampson, 1977).

The UK is the second biggest arms dealer in the world, Israel being one of its main customers. Indonesia used UK-supplied weapons, including rockets from Hawk aircraft, to attack East Timor in the 1990s, killing a third of the population. An Indonesian source confessed to using torture on citizens (Thomas, 2006).

Then, of course, there is the second-hand arms business, an example being Israel selling 100,000 AK-47s, 300,000 artillery shells, thousands of tank engines, and ten aging Hercules aircraft to Iran, the total for the deal being a billion dollars (Ben-Menashe, 1992).

Farcically, it was converted Bell helicopters that were sold to Iraq by Cardoen, a well-known Chilean arms dealer, and then used for biochemical warfare against the Kurds (Clarkson, 1998). Cardoen also began building a chemical weapons plant outside Baghdad, one reason why the USA began the first Iraq war.

The Muslim threat

When English scholar of Arabic E.W. Lane first visited Egypt almost 200 years ago he predicted that contact with European civilization "will, probably, in the course of time, materially diminish the [Muslim] feeling of fanatical intolerance." In the final edition of his book *Modern Egyptians,* however, he said that his original "prediction has not yet been fulfilled; on the contrary, European innovations in the dress and domestic manners and customs of grandees, and of persons in the employ of government, have enormously increased the fanaticism of those who belong to the religious and learned profession, and generally speaking, the bulk of the population."

According to Harris (2007):

"Muslim contact with the West had not led to an abandonment of fanaticism, but, on the contrary, to an intensification and revitalization of it.

. . it has given Islam the capacity to expand, not merely through conquest of territory but through conquest of hearts and minds."

Harris concludes that whilst the "tradition of reason" has "ennobled the West and that alone gives it a claim to superiority over other cultures, and not our wealth or our military power," our 'live for the moment' ethos leaves us vulnerable to cultures like Islam in which individuals, instead of following their own bliss, are willing to die – and alas, kill – in order to impose their cultural traditions on those who have lost all sense of the precious value of their own."

World War 3

We believe that Word War 3 was sparked in 1948 when the state of Israel was established in the British Protectorate of Palestine – giving birth to the PLO which Heywood (2012) feels pioneered international terrorism. Since then wars between Israel and the many surrounding Arab countries have occurred in every decade, whilst conflict with Palestinian militants occurs almost every week.

Since then conflict between Arab nations and the West has occurred in every decade, ranging from Nasser's occupation of the Suez Canal in 1956 to US-led invasions of Iraq in 1991 and 2003, and Afghanistan circa 2006, with Western forces still involved in conflicts in the region.

Some see 9/11 as the starting point of WW3 (Harris, 2007), but that attack was planned by al-Qa'ida whose leader, Osama Bin Laden, had publicly declared war against America in 1998, al-Qa'ida having bombed the World Trade Center in 1993. Al-Qai'ida then bombed US embassies in Kenya and Tanzania in 1998.

In that 1998 public declaration one of Bin Laden's three main demands was the return of Israeli-occupied lands to the Palestinians.

Chapter 24

ECONOMIC, INFRASTRUCTURE & CYBER WARFARE

> *Despite doubts about Amiri's reliability, the U.S. intelligence community stuck by the information he provided.*
> *Based in part on the information provided by Amiri, as well as information provided by Mossad, on September 27, 2009, President Obama and the leaders of Great Britain and France publicly accused Iran of building a secret underground uranium enrichment facility one hundred miles south of Tehran on the grounds of an Islamic Revolutionary Guard Corps base at Fordow, located outside the holy city of Qom. At the time of the announcement, the Qom site was far from complete, but the analysts believed that at the rate construction was going it would be ready by 2010.*
> Matthhew M. Aid, *Intel Wars, The Secret History of the Fight Against Terror*, Bloomsbury, New York (2012).

Economic warfare

During WW2 Churchill created a Ministry of Economic Warfare to help weaken Hitler's regime. Since that time economic sanctions have been targeted at dozens of countries, including South Africa and the USSR.

In September 1973 OPEC increased its oil price by 70%, increasing it a further 130% in December, thus quadrupling oil prices in just a few months (Batra, 1998).

There were further increases in 1975, 1977, 1979, and 1980, by which point the oil price had risen from about 3 dollars a barrel to about 35 dollars a barrel.

At the time the authors thought that this amounted to an economic war against the West and, indeed, it contributed to the present economic woes in Europe and the USA.

A concern now is that major oil-producing countries could destabilize the US by switching from US dollars to Euros as the currency in which oil is priced.

An article in the August 20-21, 2011 edition of *The Weekend Australia* reported on an economic war game conducted at the Warfare Analysis Laboratory in Maryland USA in 2009. There were 5 teams, America, Russia, China, Pacific Rim, and a 'grey' team representing criminal and terrorist organizations.

They were surrounded by an enormous array of screens normally used to simulate nuclear world war. The China team won and the article points out why China is a "huge threat." China is the biggest holder of US debt so that: "If China were to dump this debt it would totally screw with the [US] economy."

Infrastructure warfare

A recent article in the *Far Eastern Economic Review* pointed out that US ports have only "superficial" security and that a terrorist attack on them using a weapon of mass destruction would bring the entire container system to a halt.

Information warfare (IW) is another threat to which the US is particularly vulnerable and it seems likely that some of the most sophisticated 'viruses' that have been let loose on the Internet may be deliberate IW.

Another example of IW, perhaps, recently the US has become concerned about Chinese hackers gaining access to banking and other information.

If hostile organizations can disrupt the banking systems or the stock exchanges of their major opponents such as the US and UK then serious damage could be done (Adams, 1998; Alexander, 1999).

IW is, of course, only a particular form of *infrastructure warfare* and poisoning water supplies, disrupting power and oil supplies, destroying bridges and hijacking aircraft are just a few of the many alternatives open to terrorists.

September 11, of course, was a spectacular example of such warfare. That numerous anthrax letters were posted around the country, resulting in the closure of public buildings for long periods, was perhaps another. Here there was, perhaps, no great aim to cause loss of life but, more important perhaps, to cause panic and disruption.

Another example of 'media spin', akin to brainwashing over time, the anthrax attacks were written off as having originated locally and being of little consequence. That is unlikely, and further such attacks of this kind are likely.

Cyber warfare

In the last two decades cyber warfare has increased
Wikileaks, headed by Julian Assange, brought the issue to worldwide attention when it leaked masses of information about US military activities, including footage of an American helicopter gunning down innocent civilians during the second US invasion of Iraq (Dreyfus & Assange, 2011).

Melbourne's *Herald-Sun* newspaper reported on 17/6/2015 that "SWEDISH prosecutors want to interview Wikileaks founder Julian Assange in London over sex assault allegations by the end of July". In September 2015 it was reported that all but one of the Swedish charges had 'legally expired' and had been dropped.

As a result, however, Assange has been holed up in the Chilean embassy in London to escape arrest for charges of sexual misconduct in Sweden for several years

Another noted 'whistleblower' is Edward Snowden, a former National Security Agency (NSA) employee who left his home in Hawaii in May 2013, travelling to Hong Kong to leak lots of sensitive US documents. Charged with espionage by the US he found refuge at an undisclosed location in Moscow.

In June 2015 it was reported that the records of four million US government employees had been stolen by hackers, cyber search 'vectors' suggesting the hacking had been done in East Asia.

China and Russia had committed such acts before this with similar MO (modus operandi), of particular concern being the hijacking of sensitive business data that might disadvantage global US business operations, and also hijacking of 100,000 US Department of Internal Revenue records.

To carry out such mischief, of course, the computer nerds doing it must be able to deal with codes (Abelson et al., 2008; Dreyfus & Assange, 2011), and computers have a lot to do with coding and, of course, a very primitive computer was used to help break the Enigma Code, Alan Turing being given much of the credit for that breakthrough (Hodges, 1985).

Conclusion

All those records governments keep of us, the million CCTV cameras on the streets of London, and America's Echelon spy program, for which there is a base somewhere somewhat remote in Australia, which monitors all phone calls and Internet communications in the world, its massive computers searching for key words such as 'bomb' that might pick up an email or phone chat to or from a terrorist – all those scrutinies and thus lack of privacy are a reminder that:

In Orwell's imagined London, only O'Brien and other members of the Inner Party could escape the gaze of the telescreen. For the rest, the constant gaze was a source of angst and anxiety. Today, we willingly accept the gaze. We either don't think about it, don't know about it, or feel helpless to avoid it except by becoming hermits. We may even judge its benefits to outweigh its risks. In Orwell's imagined London, like Stalin's actual Moscow, citizens spied on their fellow citizen.

Today, we can all be Little Brothers, using our search engines to check up on our children, our spouses, our neighbours, our colleagues, our enemies, and our friends. More than half of adult Internet users have done exactly that (Abelson et al., 2008).

Chapter 25

THE NUCLEAR THREAT

> *Today every inhabitant of this planet must contemplate*
> *the day when this planet may no longer be habitable.*
> *Every man, woman and child lives under a nuclear sword of*
> *Damocles, hanging by the slenderest of threads, capable of*
> *being cut at any moment by accident or miscalculation or madness.*
> JF Kennedy, Address to the UN Assembly, NY Sept. 1961.

Nuclear warfare

The atom was first split at the Cavendish Laboratories in Cambridge in 1931, one of the team responsible being the first author's father (Mohr, 2012a). This led to the Manhattan project in which the first atomic bomb, a 20-kiloton implosion-type device, was tested in New Mexico on July 16th 1945.

On August 6th 1945 a 13-kiloton gun-type bomb was dropped on Hiroshima, killing from 70 to 100 thousand people and injuring as many again. Three days later a 22-kiloton implosion-type bomb was dropped on Nagasaki, killing about 40,000 people, the smaller number of fatalities being because of the hilly terrain.

In Hiroshima there was complete destruction for a radius of about a mile, severe damage for a radius of about 1.5 miles, and minor damage occurring up to a radius of four or five miles. There was massive fallout, thousands of tons of radioactive soil and dust flying up to 100,000 feet into air and spreading over a radius of more than 100 miles.

Table 25.1. US & Soviet Nuclear Armaments (Bethe, 1991).

	US	USSR
Delivery vehicles		
Intercontinental Ballistic Missiles (ICBMs)	1,050	1,400
Submarine Launched Ballistic Missiles (SLBMs)	630	950
Bombers	350	140
Total	2,030	2,490
Warheads		
ICBMs	2,150-2,250	5,500-6,400
SLBMs	4,750	1,750-1,900
Bombers	2,500-3,500	280-550
Total	9,400-10,500	7,530-8,850
Equivalent megatons		
ICBMs	1,300	5,900
SLBMs	800	1,200
Bombers	3,500	900
Total	5,600	8,000

Table 25.1 shows strength of the USSR and USA nuclear arsenals circa 1990. Note that in table 25.1, 2 megatons = 1.59 equivalent megatons. The latter is the best measure of the area that can be destroyed, whereas megatons are the best measure of fallout.

Circa 1990, China had circa 350 nuclear warheads, the UK circa 150, and France circa 200 (Bell & Hall, 1991).

Hydrogen or fusion-type bombs are far more destructive than fission bombs. In 1952 the US tested a 10.4 megaton hydrogen bomb and in 1961 the USSR tested a 58 megaton hydrogen bomb.

Relatively new, neutron bombs are designed to kill people, not destroy infrastructure. They release ten times as much radiation as atomic bombs and can be fired by artillery, as well as carried in missiles or dropped from aircraft.

Since 1945 there have been at least 15 occasions when the use of nuclear weapons has been seriously considered (Bell & Hall, 1991):

> In 1946 the US threatened to use fission bombs if the USSR did not withdraw troops from Azerbaijan.
> At least 5 misreadings of radar led to consideration of the nuclear option.
> The US has considered limited nuclear war 7 times.
> The 1962 Cuban missile crisis and the 1973 Yom Kippur war.

In the Cuban missile crisis of 1962 the US and USSR came very close to all-out nuclear warfare. Indeed, according to the documentary movie *The Fog of War* by Errol Morris, Castro had recommended that the USSR launch its nuclear arsenal on the USA, knowing full well that Cuba would be wiped off the map.

Circa 1990 only 5 countries had nuclear weapons, now that number is about a dozen, making eventual nuclear warfare increasingly likely.

Dirty bombs

Disturbingly, recent reports (June, 2015) that ISIS has begun collecting radioactive material from hospitals to make 'dirty bombs' have caused concern.

Such reports occurred a few years ago, then the concern being al-Qa'ida, but ISIS, of course, is hardly unconnected in thinking and operations from 'AQ.'

Conclusion

So is there a real threat of nuclear war sometime in the future? All through the Cold War they sure thought so.

So why not now foresee an even greater degree of threat than back then since, as we've said already in this book, WW3 really began when the state of Israel was created in the then British mandate of Palestine in 1948.

Chapter 26

THE BIOCHEMICAL THREAT

At the main Russian BW research facility Vektor
a scientist named Ustinov accidentally infected himself
with Marburg virus. In the 15 days it took him to die
a new more virulent strain developed in his bloodstream.
The Russians called it Marburg Variant U
and weaponized it for delivery by SS16 and SS17 rockets.
GA, PE & RS Mohr, *Brainwashed Zombies* (2018).

Biological warfare

Biological warfare (BW) dates back to Roman times when dead soldiers were thrown into the water supplies of cities under attack.

During air raids in the 1930s the Japanese dropped porcelain canisters of fleas infected with plague on the Chinese. These and other primitive biological weapons killed thousands in rural areas of Manchuria (Alibek, 2000).

During WW2 the Russians dropped tularemia on the stalled German Panzer divisions freezing on the outskirts of Stalingrad (Alibek, 2000).

It is well known that Sadam Hussein used chemical weapons on the Kurds in Northern Iraq in the late 1980s, and other countries in the Middle East, including Israel, have engaged in biological weapons (BW) research.

Table 26.1. Soviet & US peak BW agent production levels in metric tons per year (Miller et al., 2001).

Agent	USA	Soviet U
staphylococcal enterotoxin B	1.9	0
tularemia	1.6	1,500
Q fever	1.1	0
anthrax	0.9	4,500
Venezuelan equine encephalitis	0.8	150
botulinum	0.2	0
bubonic plague	0	1,500
smallpox	0	100
glanders	0	2,000
Marburg	0	250

As shown in Tables 26.1 and 26.2, the USSR had an enormous BW research program with some 50 research centres and storage facilities (Alibek, 2000).

Table 26.2. Other Russian BW agents (Alibek, 2000).

Argentinian haemorrhagic fever (Jinin)
Bolivian haemorrhagic fever (Machupo)
brucellosis
dengue fever
Ebola virus
epidemic typhus
Lassa fever
Russian spring-summer encephalitis

After WW2 the US also implemented a large BW research program, though not nearly as extensive as that of the USSR (see Tables 26.1 and 26.2). The US program was based mainly at one facility, Fort Detrick in Maryland.

In this massive arsenal the haemorrhagic filoviruses Ebola and Marburg are the most frightening because they are highly contagious and liquefy the body's organs.

At the main Russian BW research facility Vektor a scientist, Ustinov, was accidentally infected with Marburg virus. It took 15 days to kill him, developing into a new, more virulent strain that was called Marburg Variant U and weaponized for delivery by Soviet rockets.

To date there have been no large scale BW attacks but in December 1943 news arrived in London that Germany intended to use a pilotless plane or rocket called the V-1 to deliver biological weapons. US intelligence learnt that they intended to use botulinum and the US had already developed an antidote to botulinum. By the summer of 1944 they had manufactured 4,000 gallons of this antidote, enough to immunize 700,000 troops (Regis, 1999).

In the spring of 1944 a worried Winston Churchill asked the US to provide him with 500,000 anthrax bombs. Churchill wrote in a memorandum, *"We should regard it as a first instalment."*

The Americans set up for production, aiming to produce a further 500,000 anthrax bombs for their own use. The task was never completed owing to the first atomic bomb test in July 1945, and then its use on Hiroshima and Nagasaki in August, ending the war a month later.

That Germany, the US and UK were preparing for massive BW warfare towards the end of WW2 suggests that there is a serious risk of BW warfare on a large scale at some time in the future.

In March 2013 the Syrian government, which has not joined a convention banning the use of chemical weapons, claimed that rebel forces had used chemical weapons in a rocket attack, a claim refuted by the rebels.

Conclusions

Enormous nuclear and biological arsenals having been established, all history suggests that they are likely to be used eventually.

The 1972 the Biological and Toxic Weapons Convention bans the development, production and deployment of biological weapons.

In contravention of this the Soviet Union is believed to have continued anthrax research which resulted in an anthrax outbreak at Sverdlovsk (now Yekaterinburg) in 1979 which killed 64 people.

Shortly after the 9/11 attacks on New York there were a series of anthrax mailings, the first victim of which was Robert Stevens, a photo editor at a Florida newspaper, who was admitted to hospital on 2 October 2001, and died three days later. The perpetrator was never found and since then much more money has been spent on precautions against bio-terrorism (Suter, 2008).

After Iraq's use of chemical weapons in 1990 an international treaty banning chemical warfare was established, but this bind governments and not 'non-state' organizations such as terrorist groups (Suter, 2008).

In March 2013 the Syrian government claimed that rebel forces had carried out a rocket attack using chemical weapons, a claim which the rebels denied, saying that they did not have rockets. As usual, who did what is hard to know. The rebels have had support from the US, which might have included short range rockets, whilst until now the Syrian government has not joined a UN convention banning the use of chemical weapons.

In late May 2015, there were reports that ISIS was recruiting top scientists to work on producing advanced biochemical weapons. As Table 26.1 suggests, this is a frightening prospect.

Chapter 27

SOCIALISM VS. OLIGARCHY

Democracy

The city states of classical Greece and Rome were direct democracies in which the people directly spoke and voted at meetings, though in both cases this was limited to men and then only property holders in Rome.

Aristotle's remark about oligarchy which opens this chapter is an important reminder that, as then, we do not have *real* democracy today. The populations of the Greek city-states of his time rarely exceeded 10,000 people, all the 'citizens' of which voted with black and white stones on the questions of the day in open forum.

Aristotle's complaint was that it was only the men, and not women or slaves, who were allowed this privilege and slavery, of course, can hardly be equated with democracy.

As noted in Chapter 2, Rome's Senate eventually allowed both patrician and plebeian members, but then only when the plebs had become property holders.

In the modern era we invariably have representative democracies, though some degree of direct democracy is usually available through referendums. The latter are usually rare, and usually unsuccessful, but in Switzerland they may be initiated by a petition of 50,000 voters.

The Westminster System

In most of the world today we do not have anything like real democracy. We have, in fact, Westminster type *parliamentary democracy,* a very brief history of which is (Mackenzie, 1950):

Pre 1066 (Saxon times). The barons and King met each year at Easter, Whitsun and Christmas.

1258 (in the reign of Henry III). A meeting of the barons of England at Oxford was the origin of the *House of Lords.*

1264. Simon de Montfort, on the King's behalf, organized a meeting of two knights from each county.

1265. Two citizens from each county were included in the latter meeting, constituting the origin of the *House of Commons.*

In the reign of Elizabeth I the puritans became the first party and were the opposition to the crown.

In the reign of Charles I the cavaliers and roundheads emerged as two opposing political forces.

1681. The origin of the names *Whig* and *Tory.*

This system has evolved in England, Australia and New Zealand into the two main parties being a conservative party, which supports the capitalist ruling class, and a labour party which traditionally supported the workers.

The conservative party is said to be *right wing* and the labour party *left wing*, a fine example of the power of emotive language.

Now, however, big business has considerable influence over both parties and the policies of the labour party are sometimes more conservative than those of its opposition conservative party.

The result is a revolving door parody of democracy in which stooges become our leaders for relatively brief periods, but their policies are greatly influenced by the business sector and the economic imperialism of traditional allies in war, in Australia these being the US and UK.

In this parody the 'fat cats' of the public service wield more influence in policy-making than do average members of parliament (Self, 1977).

Socialism

There have been a variety of socialist ideas, for example:

(1) Saint-Simon (1760 – 1825) who envisaged a just society directed by a technocratic elite.

(2) Utopian Robert Owen (1771 – 1858) built a model factory town in New Lanark, Scotland.

(3) Utopian communal experiments such as Brook Farm, Massachusetts (1841 – 1847) were tried in the USA.

(4) Bakunin (1814 – 1876) was a prominent anarchist who spread his views throughout Europe. Anarchists oppose any form of government, believing that individuals should be free to express themselves without any external control.

(5) Marx (1818 – 1883) posited the inevitable triumph of socialism in the industrial countries through a historical process of class conflict. His statement in the opening quotation for this chapter was "an exaggeration when he made it in the middle of the nineteenth century. By the middle of the twentieth century it had become almost an understatement" (Brown, 2009).

Socialism refers to the 'means of production' being owned by the state, whereas *communism* refers to the means of production being owned by the people. The two terms are often confused but in a modern society it is doubtful that communism is practical. It is doubtful, for example, that the very large companies required in some industries, many of these now transnational ones, can be effectively run by just the people in a particular community.

What is clear, however, is that the 1848 Marx-Engels manifesto was anti-capitalist and this was the real spirit of the 1917 Russian revolution, a spirit which many believed would eventually spread globally. This revolution created a socialist state with a long term view towards forming a communist society.

Marxists argue that the capitalist *class* accumulates increasingly more capital or a 'surplus value' in fact created by the workers. The working class, therefore, are left to accumulate misery or, as Marx put it:

> *In proportion as capital accumulates, the lot of the labourer be his payment high or low, must grow worse.*

Critics of this view will point out that in practice state ownership leads to totalitarian government which makes the people worse off, rather than better.

Marxists argue that in capitalism monopolies or oligopolies eventually develop, in turn influencing the political system so that totalitarianism can result.

In defence against this view critics of Marxism will argue that it is better to reform the capitalist system, not replace it, for example by introducing antimonopoly laws.

Theoretical arguments aside, revolutions have always occurred when there are high levels of unemployment and poverty. Capitalism, however, relies upon a substantial pool of unemployed to keep the price of labour down (Sweezy, 1946). As a result, some studies found little reduction in poverty in the USA in the years 1947 - 1960 (Townsend, 1970) whereas socialism has reduced poverty and famine in China dramatically (Maxwell et al., 1977).

Capitalism

While so-called democracy prevails in most of the world, the reality is that, with the world's markets becoming increasingly global, transnational companies and thence unrestrained capitalism provides the power and influence that runs the politics of most countries.

In the 1930s John Maynard Keynes proposed that a multiplier effect existed such that small increases in government spending in the community have a much greater effect upon the productivity of the nation.

This *fiscal* approach was widely adopted by many countries in the West to stimulate flagging economies.

Milton Friedman and other economists favour the free market or *monetarist* economic philosophy. This stems from the 17th century and is based on the equation (Wonnacott & Wonnacott, 1979):

$$MV \text{ (aggregate demand)} = PQ \text{ (aggregate supply)}$$

where
M = the amount of money in circulation (per year)
V is its velocity of circulation (in transactions per year)
P = the price of goods in circulation
Q = the quantity of goods in circulation (per year)

Here V is the only relatively stable quantity and is based on the fact that, when you buy a product, the money you pay for it will be passed on quite soon as wages for somebody in the company you bought the product from. Then that person spends their wages on food and other necessities, and so on. Typically V takes a value of around 4 in modern economies.

This little or no government monetarist approach has led to more rampant capitalism than ever before. As a result an 'establishment' that effectively rules capitalist countries is formed (Blondel, 1963).

This establishment deplores the mildest hint of socialism and thence government ownership of industry, or even influence over industry. *They* tell government to reduce company taxes further and to cut back on government spending to do it and governments continue to heed them.

Effectively running military-industrial countries, the barons of capitalism ensure that their governments fight the evil threat of socialism.

In the 1970s David Rockefeller funded the Trilateral Commission which in 1975 funded a meeting of multinational corporate executives to consider the "excess of democracy" afflicting advanced capitalist countries and to "rationalize the US economy through capitalist dominated planning and in conjunction with other leading capitalist nations to reassert US authority on a world scale" (Crough et al., 1980).

Proposals for change

Some authors suggest that inequality in capitalist societies should be reduced by reducing the inheritability of wealth by increasing death duties (Broom et al., 1980).

This is an unpopular proposal to both the rich and the middle class. As a result the Australian state of Queensland abolished death duties many years ago and other states only apply them to large fortunes.

Marxists aim to equalize incomes, penalizing effort as well as inheritance (Jencks et al., 1975).

A more original and interesting proposal was made by Peter Jay (1981), a former economics editor of *The Times*:

- - that the enterprises which create the wealth, the firms, the corporations, should belong to, be owned by, should have their directors exclusively appointed by, and their net assets and their residual earnings should belong to, and exclusively to, the people who work at them.

Jay suggested that it is an accident of history, not a law of economics, that the entrepreneur has tended to be the person who supplied the risk capital.

He proposed that in modern economies worker-owned companies should be able to raise debt finance from banks and equity finance from shareholders in the usual way.

Capitalists are happy to have their workers become shareholders, of course, because shareholders do not have to be paid dividends in bad times whereas banks always require interest to be paid on loans.

Jay's proposal goes a lot further and might eliminate the absurd salaries, share and rights bonuses, and retirement packages we see today. Indeed, it would only seem fair that *all* workers for a corporation should receive share issues as a non-taxable part of their income.

A criterion that the modern welfare economist employs in deciding whether a given change is 'efficient' was developed by Vilfredo Pareto (Buchanan & Tullock, 1962). This relies on the ethical postulate that the 'welfare' of a group of individuals is said to be increased if

[1] Every individual in the group is better off, or if
[2] At least one member of the group is better off, without any member of the group being made worse off.

Here it should be noted that a person is deemed better off when they move from one position to another freely of their own choice, that is, 'better off' is subjectively evaluated. A common example might be people who reduce their working hours and salary in order to improve their overall quality of life.

There are clearly many changes that can be made to either of the capitalist and socialist extremes that might result in a compromise that might improve the overall position of people. That monarchies no longer play an active role in government in the world is an example that significant change is indeed possible.

Russia and China

The Soviet Union, like any large hierarchical organization, was not without corruption, members of the Party elite having access to special cars, airplanes, department stores and vacation sites (Yeltsin, 1990).

The imminent collapse of the Soviet Union was not without tensions, for example an attempt on Boris Yeltsin's life in 1989 which was probably carried out by the KGB, making one think, of course, of Vladimir Putin, ultimately president after Yeltsin's 1991-1999 term.

Not surprisingly, therefore, Yeltsin's autobiography says: "I can foresee that a fierce, hard struggle lies ahead over the future of the army and the KGB" (Yeltsin, 1990).

Yeltsin also decried the "state's monopoly of property ownership," saying: "Only when the land is worked by the people who own it will the country be fed."

On politics he said: "My view is that we still need to grow and mature toward a real, civilized, multiparty system."   It is now safe to say that Russia's system has changed and some aspects of socialism, such as centralization of power, have been much reduced.   Before the USSR was dismantled, however, there had long been changes such as a greater tendency to pay highly skilled workers more, less interventionist government, and slow opening up to outside (and hence not state) capital.

Nevertheless, with people from the 'old guard' like Putin still in control Russia is still only perhaps halfway democratic, the government still being somewhat authoritarian. An example of this, perhaps, there is only 13% personal tax, the mining industry paying a large share of the government's tax take.

China does not appear likely to suffer the same fate as the Soviet Union which was ethnically diverse and only about half Russian, ultimately leading to ethnic divisions and dissolution. In contrast, China is about 93% Han Chinese with much greater ethnic cohesion (Calder, 1997).

In addition, because of China's "mass-based agrarian revolution and Mao's emphasis on egalitarianism" its government has been more responsive to the feelings of the populace, whereas the Soviet leadership was more dictatorial (Calder, 1997).

China, of course, is not immune from corruption. Some claim, for example, that corruption by government officials is rife, some having siphoned off large amounts of money to remote banks, eventually investing the laundered money in the US and elsewhere.

One of the Chinese companies involved in this activity, Longtop Financial had Deloitte as their auditor for six years but, after recent forensic investigations, Deloitte felt forced to quit.

China, having experienced massive economic growth in recent decades, is now the biggest holder of US debt, so that the aforementioned corruption (according to Deloitte) may, in fact, be part of how that came about, perhaps with some degree of official encouragement from the Chinese government at large.

Convergence of the systems

Not long ago some economics texts asked the question about socialism and capitalism: "Are the systems converging?"

In the USA and like countries there is some disenchantment with the two-party system that may begin to crystallize somewhere. In Australia in 2013, for example, three independents and the Greens party held the balance of power in both the legislative lower house of representatives, and the upper house or senate which is required to approve legislation from the lower house.

In Westminster the Tories vs. Whigs farce has changed to Tories versus New Labour, with the Liberal-Democrats on the fringe as usual.

A former Australian finance minister wrote in his 2011 book *Dumbing Down Democracy* that politicians now consider appearances far more important than outcomes, lamenting that the resulting "sideshow syndrome" was eroding informed democracy as the basis of decision-making.

Thus we conclude that the politico-economic systems of both the 'east' and the 'west' will doubtless continue to change slowly. Whilst current trends are towards freer capitalist markets it is certain that this trend may be slightly reversed at some point.

Socialist parties remain strong in many countries in Europe, for example Belgium where the Belgian Worker's Party was founded in 1885, gaining 27 seats in the 1983 election.

After WW1 the party abandoned its revolutionary Marxist stance and became a regular coalition partner in Belgian governments, often leading them in the 1950s and 1960s. The socialists had 37% of the vote in the mid-1950s but their popularity has since declined, though they still remain a significant force in Belgian politics.

The communist party in Russia might currently have less than 50% of the vote but that might not last. Thus Russia could be counted as roughly 7 or 8 on the 'commie scale' at present, as could China, with India perhaps about 6. Then, of course, Vietnam and North Korea are strictly socialist.

Some countries in South America and much of Africa, on the other hand, are in a state of economic collapse, as usual, and God only knows what 'colour' their politics is. In some cases not simply 'red' to whatever extent, but often the politics of chaos one supposes.

Operation Condor

Operation Condor was a secret project involving six Latin-American countries established at a military intelligence meeting in Chile on 25 November 1975. The six countries – Chile, Argentina, Brazil, Bolivia, Paraguay and Uruguay – agreed to form teams to track down, monitor and assassinate political opponents of the ruling regimes.

A joint information centre was established by the Chilean secret police and many left-wing opponents of the military regimes in the region who had fled into neighbouring countries were found and killed.

Operation Condor also carried out operations internationally, for example in Italy and the US. In September 1976 the former Chilean foreign minister Orlando Letllier was killed in a car bomb explosion in Washington DC, but it was not until 1993 that the former head of Chile's military intelligence, Manual Contreras, was given a seven-year sentence by a Chilean court for the murder.

Conclusions

The 1905 Russian revolution was in part owing to Leon Trotsky who was "a revolutionary who did not fit neatly into one camp or the other." (Brown, 2009).

According to Brown (2009):

The first of three revolutions which culminated in Bolshevik takeover in late 1917 occurred against a background of appalling social conditions in the Russian cities, poverty in the countryside, and a lack of basic political rights and freedoms.

The French and the 1917 Russian revolutions, of course, involved a good deal of conflict. As noted earlier in Chapter 15, the latter provoked espionage on the part of the UK government aimed at supporting the White Russian army's resistance to the revolution.

Since World War 2, after Stalin had annexed much of Europe, the Cold War between the USSR and the US and UK led to a very wasteful and costly arms race. Indeed, the US and USSR may have come close to nuclear war during the Cuban Missile Crisis.

In the second half of the last century there were numerous wars against socialism, including:

(1) That fought against communist revolutionaries in Malaya circa 1950.

(2) The bitter war in Korea in the early 1950s.

(3) The costly Vietnam war which the US ultimately lost comprehensively.

In addition, the US and its allies have surreptitiously overthrown "dictators," many of them of socialist inclination, in several countries around the world, particularly in Africa and central and South America.

Capitalists largely control government in the USA and like-minded countries, of course, and the entrenched elites in such countries will always resist efforts to create free market societies. Thus "a ruling class that has been accustomed to dominating a servile population" is a "hard habit to break once acquired" (Harris, 2007).

Finally, as always, conflict continues around the world, most noticeably at present continuing terrorism by Muslim extremists and jihadis wanting to rape the world.

Indeed, there is no end to this in sight, in part because no end to the conflict between Israel and the displaced Palestinian peoples is in sight.

In addition, it is not hard seeing "the world's only super power", the USA, one day becoming involved in conflict with China. Indeed, the CIA has conducted simulated economic war games against China in which the US lost, China's growing economic power being, of course, in part at the expense of the USA and thus a source of grievance to it.

At present, indeed, there is considerable tension amongst China's neighbours about its territorial ambitions in Nepal, South Vietnam, and the China Sea, and its building of several artificial islands in order to claim fishing rights in the areas surrounding them.

In addition, conflict continues in several parts of the world where ethnic groups such as the Kurds and Tamils continue to seek to form independent nations.

Finally, we should note that for about a century Western pollies have called socialists "communists" – an ignorant and incorrect use of the term.

A true commie lives in a commune such as ancient tribal man did, and one or two small religious sects in the USA still do, but socialism refers to the ownership of industry on any scale belonging to the government, as it largely did in the USSR (Brown, 2009).

In the stupid oligarchical West we bemoan the fact that to pay of government debt stupid pollies have always sold off airlines, power companies, telcos, etcetera to the point that, in the end, there is nothing left to sell.

Then, to satisfy big biz (and thence the billionaire-salaried CEOs/owners thereof), they have removed all tariffs long ago so cheap labour can be used in Asia, Africa etcetera for the products of transnational companies, thus putting millions in the US etc. out of a job and onto the dole, drugs etc. (which some biz bods sell too, of course) – and so forth.

Then, because economists who spout 'econobabble' are stupid, they increase interest rates to supposedly reduce inflation, but as the first author has proved (and observed from the figures since the 50s), that in fact does the opposite – that is, as any dummy would expect intuitively: *Increasing interest rates increases inflation* (Mohr, 2014b).

Other reasons why economists, academics etcetera are stupid (relatively) are outlined in the chapter 'Econobabble' of a recent book (Mohr, 2014c).

So when you hear BS to the effect that you've never had it so good, don't believe it.

It is always coming from the mouths of pollies who are paid well enough, get 'free lunches' (+ bribes) from big biz, and have very good pensions after an easy 'hot air raving' job. If you can understand that situation somewhat, then you might want to think about 'real democracy' and go straight to Appendix B without passing GO.

Finally, with our 'stock market-like' Western economies we become accustomed to various kinds of "bubbles", for example in the housing market in Sydney, Australia in mid-2015, and we are inclined to believe that worse is yet to come for the US economy than the GFC of 2008, and such writers as George Soros are somewhat inclined to agree with us on that score, he citing the "supremist ideology" of the US, and it's sometimes unwise use of bombs etc. on terrorists that just radicalizes more Muslims, thence increasing their response, thus escalating things in the way that so often happens in wars – until you get "the war to end all wars", that is, and quotations on that issue appear at the end of the final chapter of this book (Soros, 2004).

As to our opinion on this, Michael Moore would agree with us, as his book *Stupid White Men ... and Other Sorry Excuses for the State of the Nation!* indicates (Moore, 2002).

As for peace negotiations, the 12 June 2015 edition of Melbourne's Herald-Sun newspaper reported that, during talks between Vladimir Putin and the Pope at the Vatican, the Pope had urged Putin to try to restore peace in the disputed region of the Ukraine. Putin's response was to point out that the economic sanctions that had been imposed on Russia to try and pressure them to end the conflict, in particular by preventing soldiers from Russia fighting with the rebels (perhaps as mercenaries) – those sanctions he said were going to cost Italian companies a billion dollars.

We can't guess what time frame Putin was thinking of in coming up with that number, but perhaps he meant that much each year as we can't be too sure about how long that conflict will go on. We guess a few more years, but it could be much more.

Chapter 28

ISLAMIC JIHAD

> *...there were no more than twenty-six days ... in which there was no war somewhere in the world ... on any given day ... there is an average of twelve wars going on somewhere in the world.*
> Anthony Sampson, *The Arms Bazaar* (1978),
> referring to the results of a study of the years 1945 - 1978.

Introduction

Islamic conflict has gone through three phases:

The first began when the prophet Muhammad and his followers fled from Mecca to Medina to escape persecution in 622. It then took only two years for them to convert the desert tribes to Islam, and the next six decades saw the faith expand from Saudi Arabia into the other Arab lands of the Middle East.

The second lasted a thousand years, during which Persia (now Iran), North Africa, southern Spain, Eastern Europe, the Indian subcontinent, and east to Indonesia were conquered. The Holy Land was also successfully defended against the European crusaders of the Middle Ages.

Those conquered were offered three choices, convert to Islam and be saved, pay a tax to the caliph, or be slaughtered. This period ended with defeat in Vienna in 1683.

From 1683 to 1945, the West counter-attacked and colonized Islamic areas and avenged the defeat of the crusades to the point at which Britain's Queen Victoria had more Muslim subjects than any other ruler in history in the Indian subcontinent, and in northern and eastern Africa.

Expansion of the West began with Diaz rounding the Cape of Hope to reach the Indian Ocean in 1488, and Columbus' discovery of the Americas. Thenceforth European colonisation and development left the Arab world a backwater. The subsequent rise of the European nation-state system was also a blow to the Islamic world which sees itself as a global community.

The third phase of Islamic conflict began with the creation of Israel in 1948, conflict continuing between Israel and its neighbours, particularly Palestine, to this day.

The threat of Islam is now greater than ever because today Muslims are almost 20 per cent of the world's population, in part because of greater breeding rates.

Islam defines Jihad as (Massoulié, 2003):

Literally "Holy War for the benefit of God." The individual must first purify himself, and then those close to him, and then if, under threat, he must take a stand against the enemies of Islam. In the sixties, as a result of Nasser's persecutions, the Muslim brother, Sayyid Qotb, radicalized this idea to "unholy" governments.

"The Greatest Conflict"

In the Forward to the book *Slavery, Terrorism and Islam* (Hammond, 2010), Dr George Grant writes:

"The greatest conflict of the past century has not been between Communism and Democracy. . . . It has not been between Socialism and Capitalism."

"The most convulsive conflict of the past century, and indeed the most convulsive conflict of the past millennium has undoubtedly been between Islam and Civilization; it has been between Islam and Freedom; it has between Islam and Order; it has been between Islam and Progress; it has been between Islam and Hope."

Indeed, Islamic conquest and slaughter goes back to Muhammad's early conquests so that: *"By the 10th Century, Muslims had annihilated 50% of all the Christians in the world of that time. Today, repression of Christian lands continues"* (Hammond, 2010).

A primitive religion

Muhammad's first marriage lasted 25 years, but after the death of his first wife he married at least another 15 wives, many of whom were widows or divorcees. One of his wives, Ayesha, was only six years old when she was given in marriage to him, and nine years old when he consummated the marriage, according to the Hadith.

In AD628 Mary The Copt, a Christian slave, was given to Muhammad by the governor of Egypt. When he married his daughter-in-law, Zainab, he claimed that Allah had instructed him to do so.

Muhammad died in 632 and the four Caliphas who followed the 'apostolic' tradition of Muhammad were Abu Bakr (d. 634), Umar (d. 633), Uthman (d. 656), and Ali who was Muhammad's cousin and son-in-law.

After the Battle of the Camel, in which 10,000 Muslims were killed, the governor of Syria, Mu'awiya, accused Ali of complicity in the murder of Uthman and engaged in battle but without a decisive result.

Soon after this Ali was assassinated and his eldest son Hassan was seen as rightful heir, but Mu'awiya opposed his succession and he fled, leaving Mu'awiya to rule the whole Islamic empire.

Then Ali's other son, Al-Hussein, was murdered on the orders of Calipha Yazid in October AD 680, his head being sent to Yazid in Damascus. This began the split between Sunnis and Shi'ites, the latter regarding Ali's sons as the only legitimate line of succession (Hammond, 2010).

For many years, if not decades, the Middle East has been in turmoil, and at present terrorism is rife in almost every country. Terrorism was discussed at modest length in Chapter 15 where it is seen that today most terrorism is Islamic in origin.

The present authors would contend that this is in part because much of the Koran is vengeful in nature and from its outset Islam was spread by violence, beginning with Muhammad's attack on Medina in 627AD, and then conquest of Mecca in 630AD (Mohr & Fear, 2014).

Islam is also in many ways a somewhat primitive religion, coming as it does some 600 years after Christianity. It disparages those who are not 'true believers' as infidels, often savagely attacking them, at the same feuding incessantly about its own sectarian differences in ideology, particularly those of the Sunni and Shiite sects.

One person who agreed with this view was Sir Vidia Naipaul who visited the four Islamic societies of Iran, Pakistan, Malaysia, and Indonesia (Watson, 2001).

He found Iran confused and angry: "the confusion of the people of high mediaeval culture awakening to oil and money, a sense of power and violation, and a knowledge of a great new encircling civilization. . . That civilization couldn't be mastered. It was to be rejected; at the same time it was to be depended upon."

Pakistan he found a found a fragmented country, economically stagnant, "its gifted people close to hysteria." He said the failure of Pakistan as a society "led back again and again to the assertion of the faith." As with Iran there was an emotional rejection of the West, especially its attitudes towards women. He found no industry, no science, the universities stifled by fundamentalism which "provides an intellectual thermostat set low."

The Malays he found had an "inability to compete" with the Chinese, who made up half its population and dominated the country economically.

Naipaul described the Islam of Indonesia as "stupefaction"; community life was breaking down, and the faith was the inevitable response.

He said that in all four places Islam drew its strength from a focus on the past that prevented development and kept its lagging behind the West. The "rage and anarchy" induced by this kept them locked in the faith.

Islamic slavery

The practice of slavery has existed for much of human history, and particularly in Rome and the Roman Empire where it lasted for several hundred years.

European involvement in the Trans-Atlantic slave trade to the Americas lasted three centuries, whereas Arab involvement in the slave trade has lasted fourteen centuries and continues in the Muslim world (Hammond, 2010).

In the American slave trade two out of every three slaves shipped across the Atlantic were men and the mortality rate was 10%. In the Islamic Trans Sahara and East African slave trade to the Arab world, two out of three slaves were women and the mortality rate was between 80 and 90%.

According to Hammond (2010): "While most of the slaves shipped across the Atlantic were for agricultural work, most of the slaves destined for the Muslim Middle East were for sexual exploitation as concubines, in harems, and for military service.

"While many children were born to slaves in the Americas, and millions of their descendants are citizens in Brazil and the USA to this day, very few descendants of the slaves that ended up in the Middle East survived."

While most of the slaves who went to the Americas married and had families, most of the male slaves destined for the Middle East were castrated, and most of the children born to the women were killed at birth.

About 11 million Africans were transported across the Atlantic, 95% going to South and Central America, mainly to Portuguese, Spanish and French possessions, and only 5% went to the United States.

At least 28 million Africans were enslaved in the Muslim Middle East. According to Hammond (2010):

. . . . it is believed that the death toll from 14 centuries of Muslim slave raids into Africa could have been over 112 million. When added to the number of those sold in the slave markets, the total number of African victims of the Trans Saharan and East African slave trade could be significantly higher than 140 million people.

That slavery still exists in the Muslim world is yet another indication of its backwardness, treatment of women in Islam as second rate citizens, if not sexual and domestic slaves, another (Hanna, 2015).

Islamic brutality and polygamy

As for sheer brutality, when a fire was reported at a girls school in Mecca, Muslim police forced the girls back into the burning building because in their haste to escape many had not put on their obligatory head coverings (Newsweek, 22/7/2002).

In Pakistan, Zahida Perveen, a 29 year-old mother of three, was disfigured when her husband attacked her after accusing her of being unfaithful and bringing shame to the family. He cut off her ears, tongue and nose, and then gouged out her eyes.

Iben Saud of Saudi Arabia reported having had over two hundred wives, but claimed that he had never had more than four at one time, and had thus not sinned in this respect.

Kamarudin Mohammad, a 72 year-old Malaysian policeman who had just had his 52nd wedding said: "I am not a playboy. He too claimed to have not had more than four wives at a time, his marriages having lasted on average of 193 days.

Islamic intentions

At a conference in Mecca in 1974 the World Islamic Organization adopted the following programme:
1. Muslim organizations should set up centres to resist Christian missionary activities.
2. Islamic radio and TV stations should be established.
3. All Christian activities, no matter the secular expression, should be stopped.
4. Christian hospitals, orphanages, schools and universities should be taken over.
5. Muslim organizations should set up Intelligence Centres about Christian activities.
6. All Christian literature should be banned in Muslim countries.

Muhammad declared Jihad (religious fighting) to be the second most important activity in Islam:

Allah's apostle was asked, 'What is the best deed?'
He replied, 'To believe in Allah and his Apostle.'
The questioner then asked, 'What is the next (in goodness)?'
He replied, 'To participate in Jihad in Allah's cause.'
The Hadith, Al Bukhari, Vol. 1, no. 25.

According to Hammond (2010):
Muslims in fact divide the world into two sectors: Dar-al-Islam (the House of Islam) and Dar-al-Harb (the House of War). The only countries considered to be at peace are those were Islamic law (the sharia) is enforced. Islam does not recognize the right of any other religion or worldview to exist.

Writing in *The Weekend Australian* of October 10-11, 2015, Anthony Klan reported that:
For the highly vocal Hizb ut-Tahrir Australia, the local arm of the global movement with as many as one million members, abolishing Australia's democracy, ideology and way of life is its purpose.

He suggested that this group should be banned in Australia, as it is "in several Middle Eastern countries."

Regarding the general issue of Islamic jihad, he wrote:

Recruiters portray such jihad as part of a distorted sense of religious obligation and social media is awash with religious references to the fighting [in Syria and Iraq].

The Six Pillars of Islam

These are:

1. *Shahada*, the open **confession** of faith.

2. *Salah*, the five daily **prayers**.

3. *Sawn*, fasting during the month of **Ramadan** during which Muslims can only eat from sunset to sunrise.

4. *Zakat*, the giving of **alms**.

5. *Hajj*, the **Pilgrimage** to Mecca at least once in a lifetime, given one has the means for it.

6. *Jihad*, Holy **War**.

Islamic Jihad

According to Hammond (2010), Islamic scholars identify many forms that Jihad can take:

1. The Jihad of Words, ravings aimed at inspiring Muslims with a sense of their own superiority whilst mocking and cursing the opposition.

2. The Jihad of Deception. When Muslims are small in number they follow the example of Muhammad's 83 followers who fled from persecution in Mecca to Abysinnia where they sought protection when the Meccans demanded their return as slaves by pointing out the Koran's references to the life of Jesus that corresponded to those in the Bible.

3. The Jihad of the Sword. Rejecting Islam equates to attacking it and therefore inviting Jihad so that any war against non-Muslims can be condoned as 'defensive'.

4. The Jihad of Taxation, an extortionist tax for non-Muslims.

5. The Jihad of Slavery. According to the sharia, Muslims are allowed to own and sell slaves and in Sudan the Islamic government uses slavery to encourage Arab northerners to attack Christians in the South.

6. The Jihad of sharia Law. The testimony of non-Muslims is not valid against a Muslim, and the death penalty is applied to those who renounce Islam and convert to another religion.

7. The Jihad of Polygamy. When many of his men were killed by Meccans in AD625 at the battle of Uhud, Muhammad allowed them to take up to 4 wives. This same policy now allows Muslims to increase in number twice as fast as other religions.

8. The Jihad of the Spirits. According to the Quran Muslims are not only humans, but spirits who fight for the spread of Islam both in life and after death.

Hammond concludes:

We need to have the courage and integrity to describe an intolerant religion of violence and oppression as it is. No Muslim has the freedom to change or leave his religion.

The huge block of over one billion Muslims presents the greatest political and military threat to the free world and the greatest missionary challenge to the Christian Church. Muslim states are the most severe persecutors of Christians, and Muslim terrorist groups are the most vicious hijackers, kidnappers, bombers and assassins. Islam is a challenge we cannot ignore.

How we choose to respond, in prayer, publication, projects and persistent vigilance will determine much of the course of history in the 21st Century.

Islam on the offensive

Harris (2007) points out that in the West we are largely accustomed to relative continuity of government:

So long as the various nations of the world went about their ordinary business, selecting their leadership in the same old corrupt or not so corrupt ways, it was quite easy to predict what figures would play a role on the world stage. Like the revolving door of leadership during the various parliamentary crises of the French Third Republic, new governments might be formed, but those that formed them were always the same old familiar faces. Similarly, in the United States, no one expects either the republicans or the democrats to pick a candidate for the next election whose name is not already a household word. The deck may be reshuffled, but it still contains the same old cards.

He then points out that this sort of 'relative continuity' does not exist in the Muslim world, so that it is difficult to predict who will be ruling Iraq, Iran, or Pakistan in a few years time, and that the leadership of Muslims nations is sometimes given to "wild cards" who were hitherto unknown to all but a few supporters.

This often makes it difficult for the West to know which side it should back in Middle East conflicts. In addition, it poses the problem of dealing with men who have risen the hard way, men of the people who are 'rabble rousers' or 'demagogues'.

Such leaders are unpredictable, leaving the West constantly guessing what their next move might be:

Herein lies the danger of the Western crisis of leadership: As our current crisis drifts aimlessly toward a world historical catastrophe in which policy is no longer an option and our leadership is forced simply to react to the events initiated by others, the people will become increasingly cynical and angry - - - as the system seems more and more inept, the search for radical alternatives will intensify (Harris, 2007).

In this way the pressures of widespread Islamic conflict, much of it directed against the West and thus involving Western military responses, may ultimately have a negative effect on both sides leading back towards the 'law of the jungle' and thence increasing conflict so that, what might already be termed World War 3, escalates with the widespread use of nuclear and biochemical weapons.

Chapter 29

WORLD WAR 3

> *We cannot let terrorist and rogue nations*
> *hold this nation hostile or hold our allies hostile.*
> George W. Bush, speaking in Des Moines, Iowa, 21 Aug. 2001.
>
> *Britain must, and I am sure will, stand shoulder to shoulder with the*
> *United States of America and peaceful nations across the world in*
> *deploying every possible resource to bring to justice the people*
> *responsible and make sure terrorism never prevails.*
> Tony Blair, statement, 11 Sep. 2001.

Introduction

Perhaps the first seed of WW3, that is, the current global scourge of Islamic terrorism, was the creation of the state of Israel in 1948 in the UN-mandated British protectorate of Palestine. Another such seed, of course, was the division of India to create the Muslim country of Pakistan to house much of the Muslim population of India, the motivation being to try and reduce Muslim-Hindu conflict. This 'state creation' was also a disaster, however, and conflict between migrating Muslims and Hindus is said to have killed some 1 million people, though perhaps the real death toll was much higher.

Since then dozens of Islamic terrorist organizations have been founded, the most notable of late being al-Qa'ida and Islamic State (IS) which rely on brainwashing young Muslim men via the Internet, sometimes with the help of local Muslim leaders and preachers.

The Munich massacre

On the eighth day of the 1972 Munich Olympics the Palestinian 'Black September' terrorist group killed two Israeli athletes and took nine others hostage. They demanded the release of 232 Palestinians held in Israeli prisons, two local terrorists held in Germany, as well as their own safe passage out of Europe.

When brief negotiations stalled the terrorists took their hostages to the military airport in Munich by helicopter for a flight back to the Middle East. German sharpshooters opened fire and the terrorists fired back, blowing up the helicopter and killing all nine hostages, along with one German police officer and five terrorists. Three terrorists were captured.

On 29 October a Lufthansa jet was hijacked by Arab terrorists demanding release of the three captured terrorists and the Germans agreed.

Israel responded with an air strike, using 75 aircraft to attack guerrilla targets in Lebanon and killing 66 with hundreds wounded. Then Mossad, Israel's foreign intelligence agency, created independent assassination teams to kill every Palestinian involved in the Munich massacre.

About 35 targets were selected, including the three terrorists released by West Germany. The first person killed was a cousin of Yasser Arafat who was an organizer of PLO terrorism in Europe. The next was the coordinator of the Munich operation.

In one incident the target was killed, but also a KGB agent who blocked the exit of the assassination team. In 1974 a freelance assassin seduced one of the Israeli assassins and killed him, but the Israeli's found and disposed of her.

When a person in Norway was killed because he looked like the target six Israeli's were captured and imprisoned for two years.

Of the three surviving terrorists directly involved in the Munich massacre, two were assassinated and the other died of natural causes.

The last person on the hit list was killed in a booby-trapped car in Beirut in 1979.

Mediterranean hijack

On 7 October 1985 hundreds of passengers on the cruise ship *Achille Lauro* were taken hostage by four members of the Palestine Liberation Front (PLF). They demanded the release of 50 Palestinians held by Israel.

The hostage crisis lasted for two days, during which the terrorists shot a wheelchair bound 69 year-old American because he was Jewish, throwing his body into the sea.

Egypt intervened and offered the terrorists safe harbour if they freed their hostages. The terrorists agreed and boarded an Egyptian jet but American Navy fighter planes surrounded it and forced it to land on the island of Sicily where the terrorists were arrested.

When Italy released one of the hijackers on parole in 1991 the family of the murdered American protested.

Other PLF members involved in the hijack are still at large, but in 2003 US troops captured the leader of the hijacking, Abu Abbas, in Baghdad.

Plane bombings

On 21 September 1988 a Pan Am Boeing 747 blew up over the Scottish village of Lockerbie killing 270 people, including 11 on the ground. An April 1990 British investigators announced finding an electronic component linking two Libyan agents to the explosion. The UN imposed sanctions on Libya to force it to hand over the two agents for international trial.

In March 1989 Libyan agents blew up a French UTA plane over Niger, killing 170 people, including the wife of the US ambassador to Chad.

Bombing of Jewish cultural centre

In 1994 a suicide bombing of the Jewish cultural centre in Buenos Aires killed 85 people and wounded 300. Investigators concluded that the attack had been carried out by Hezbollah on orders from Tehran. Only two years earlier the Israeli embassy in Buenos Aires was bombed, killing 29 people and wounding 200.

The Oklahoma City bombing

The 1995 Oklahoma City bombing, in which 168 people were killed, was the most spectacular act of terrorism on US soil before the September 11 attacks. It was in revenge for the mass deaths in 1993 of members of the Branch Davidian movement at Waco after a 51-day siege by federal agents.

The FBI charged Timothy McVeigh and Terry Nichols with the bombing but only McVeigh was convicted and executed on 11 June 2001. McVeigh's chief defence counsellor, however, found that McVeigh and Nichols had had contacts with Aryan Nation, other people with neo-Nazi sympathies and, most interesting of all, Nicholls had been to the Philippines several times where he had been in contact with Ramzi Yousef, who in turn had had contact with al-Qa'ida and Osama Bin Laden.

Ramzi Yousef was responsible for the 1993 bombing of the World Trade Centre, and for the plot to destroy Philippines Airlines Flight 434 in 1994 (Jones & Israel, 1998).

Such groups as Aryan Nation, if their rhetoric is to be believed, may pose a serious threat to the US in future:

> *I suspect Americans will begin engaging in terrorism*
> *on a scale the world has never known.*
> William Pearce, author of *The Turner Diaries* (1978)
> and leader of the National Alliance, a US neo-Nazi group.

The 9/11 World Trade Centre attacks

On 11 September 2001 the most spectacular terrorist attack in history took place. It had been planned by al-Qa'ida, which opposes non-Islamic governments, then led by the notorious Osama Bin Laden. Al-Qa'ida had also bombed the World Trade Center in 1993, killing six and injuring more than a 1,000.

Terrorists hijacked four passenger planes and crashed two of them into the upper levels of the Twin Towers of the World Trade Center in New York City. As Bin Laden would have expected, having a knowledge of structural engineering, the floors impacted fell, the resulting dynamic load on the floors below bringing those crashing down also, both buildings collapsing into a pile of smoking rubble within a few minutes.

The third jet crashed into the Pentagon building, and the fourth into a field near Pittsburgh after the passengers prevented it reaching another target building. All those on board the four planes were killed.

About 50,000 people worked in the World Trade Center, and almost 3,000 people were killed at the site on that fateful day, a hundred of them fire fighters and police.

About 23,000 people work at the Pentagon, and 120 people in it were killed.

After the twin towers were destroyed all New York City's airports were closed, and then all US flights were cancelled, those in the air over the US having to land at the nearest airport, those from other countries being redirected to Canada.

From that fateful day the USA's 'War on Terror' began in earnest.

Soon after the September 11 attacks numerous anthrax letters were posted around the country, resulting in the closure of public buildings for long periods. To this day it is now known who perpetrated these acts.

The Moscow theatre siege

On 23 October 2002, 40 to 50 armed Chechens, who claimed allegiance to the Islamist militant separatist movement in Chechnya, raided a Moscow theatre and took 850 hostages, demanding withdrawal of Russian forces from Chechnya and an end to the Second Chechen War.

The terrorists had bombs that could have brought down the ceiling and caused in excess of 80 percent casualties. After a two-and-a-half day siege and the execution of two female hostages, Russian security units pumped a chemical agent into the building's ventilation system and raided it.

All 40 of the attackers were killed, along with 130 hostages, but there were no casualties among the security units.

The use of the gas was widely condemned as heavy-handed, but the American and British governments deemed Russia's actions justifiable.

Some reports said the drug naloxone was successfully used to save some hostages.

The Madrid Subway bombings

Since the 9/11 attacks in the US, many European cities had been on high alert for terrorist attacks.

Three days before a Spanish election, on 11 March 2004 suicide bombers detonated ten bombs on four commuter trains in Madrid. Seven of the explosions were in or close to Madrid's main station, the Atocha station, the other three exploding near Atocha.

The first three bombs exploded just after 7:30 AM inside Atocha station, severely damaging several carriages and killing at least 34 people, wounding dozens of others.

At the same time four more bombs exploded on a second train, killing 59 people and wounding many others.

Three more bombs exploded on two trains en route to Madrid, killing at least 85 and wounding many others.

Later police found three more unexploded bombs at Atocha station, two of them in backpacks.

A cell phone was found in one of these backpacks, leading to the arrest of several men, one of whom had ties to al-Qa'ida. Then, when police were closing on a suspect apartment a bomb exploded in it, killing the occupants.

Spanish authorities searched worldwide for other suspects and in October 2007 Spain's National Court convicted 21 men of the Madrid bombings, finding another seven not guilty (Weil, 2013).

The Madrid subway attacks were the worst terrorist attack in Spain's history.

The London Underground bombings

On 7 July 2005 at about 8:50 AM bombs planted by terrorists exploded in three trains shortly after they had left King's Cross under-ground station.

A train which had been waiting in the tunnel 100 yards away from Aldgate Street was severely damaged and eight people killed.

A second bomb exploded in a train between King's Cross and Russel Square stations, killing 27 people.

The third bomb exploded in a train arriving at Edgeware Road, blowing holes in several nearby trains and killing 7 people.

Almost an hour after the last Underground explosion a bomb exploded on the upper deck of a Number 30 double-decker bus as it stopped at the junction of Upper Woburn Place and Tavistock Square. The roof of the bus was ripped off and fourteen people killed.

The fourth bomb had also been intended for an Underground train but the bomber, 18 year-old Hasid Hussain, was turned back from the Underground because the Northern Line station was closed.

The four bombings killed 56 people, including the four bombers, and injured 700 others, some very seriously. Al-Qa'ida claimed responsibility (Weil, 2013).

Australian plot

In 2005, police Operation Pendennis raided two terrorist cells in Melbourne and Sydney inspired by Melbourne man Abdul Nacer Benbrika. It was believed that the Sydney cell was close to launching a major attack.

Eighteen men were prosecuted and sentenced, one for 28 years. Most, however, have been released, some of them then going overseas to fight with IS, others radicalizing young men in Australia who left to fight with IS.

The 2011 Oslo bombing

In 2011, 32 year-old Anders Behring Breivik, a body-builder and committed Christian, posted messages on the Internet saying he wanted to keep Muslims out of Norway.

At around 3:30 PM on 22 July 2011 a huge blast shook the centre of Oslo, severely damaging the offices of Norway's Prime Minister and other government buildings. Eight people were killed and dozens injured.

Breivik had planted the bomb, then driving to catch a ferry to the island of Utoya disguised as a policeman and carrying a fake police ID card, a pistol, and an automatic rifle.

On Utoya, Norway's Labor Party was holding a summer camp for hundreds of young people, most of them less than 20 years old.

On arriving, Breivik told people to go to the main building on the island to watch news of the Oslo bombing. Then he put on earplugs and rushed in and began shooting people. Many ran out of the building but Breivik pursued them to the water's edge and into caves and shot them, one person drowning while trying to escape, other being shot while trying to swim to safety.

When police arrived an hour after the shooting had begun Breivik was still shooting. When the police found him he surrendered and was later convicted and jailed.

Eight people died in the Oslo bombing, and more than 200 were injured. The death toll at Utoya was 69, with more than 100 injured. The attacks were the worst massacre in Norway's modern history (Weil, 2013).

Kenyan shopping centre attack

In 2013 the Al Shabab terrorist group attacked the crowded Westgate shopping centre in Kenya, inflicting many casualties.

Nigeria

According to Amnesty International, Boko Haram kidnapped 2000 women in Nigeria in the period January 2014 to March 2015.

In April 2014 Boko Haram abducted 219 Nigerian schoolgirls from Chibok, in the north-eastern state of Borno. It was believed that they had been split into three or four groups and held at different Boko Haram camps.

In May 2014 Boko Haram released a video message showing 100 of the girls in Muslim dress and reciting verses of the Koran. The message said that the women had been converted to Islam and been "married off".

Women who have escaped from Boko Haram have told of being kept in overcrowded prisons, being forced to cook and clean, and being forced to marry Islamist fighters.

According to the Melbourne Herald-Sun newspaper (15/4/2015): *"One human rights advocate who interviewed more than 80 abducted women and girls after their escape said that in 23 cases they had been raped either before arrival at camps or after forced marriage."*

In May 2015 Boko Haram were reported to have fired rockets into a Nigerian city, the Nigerian army returning fire.

MH370

On 8 March 2014 Malaysian Airlines flight MH370 disappeared en route from Kuala Lumpur to China with 227 passengers on board. Despite extensive searches, it was not until 16 months later that parts of the plane were found on Reunion Island near Madagascar. Such a location suggests that the plane might have been high-jacked by Islamic terrorists (as in the 9/11 attacks) and then flown to a remote location and ditched. No other sensible explanation is plausible as pilot error could not take a plane so far off course.

Sydney attack

In December 2014 a self-styled Muslim preacher held about 20 people hostages in a Sydney café for several hours. When police heard shots they stormed the café and killed him, hitting him with several bullets to do so, but two hostages were also killed during the siege and several others injured.

The Charlie Hebdoe siege

In 2006 riots broke out in various parts of the Muslim world about cartoons published in an obscure periodical in Denmark. According to Harris (2007): *"What to liberal Westerners appeared to be a harmless cartoon led to outbreaks of lethal violence in Afghanistan and Nigeria, where Muslims seized and murdered Christians in the streets."*

On the morning of 7 January 2015 two masked brothers, Said and Cherif Kouachie, armed with Kalashnikovs and a rocket-launcher, invaded the offices of the French satirical magazine *Charlie Hebdoe* because it had published cartoons mocking the prophet Muhammad.

Eleven people were killed and eleven injured in the offices by the Muslim fanatics, and after leaving they killed a police officer.

The gunmen identified themselves as belonging to the Yemen branch of al-Qa'ida. Several related attacks followed in the Île-de-France region in which five more people were killed and another eleven wounded.

France raised its alert to its highest level and deployed soldiers in Île-de-France and Picardy. When the brothers took hostages at a signage company in Dammartin-en-Goële on 9 January they were shot dead when they emerged from the building firing.

On 11 January, about 2 million people, including more than 40 world leaders, met in Paris for a rally of national unity, and 3.7 million people joined demonstrations across France. The phrase *Je suis Charlie* was a common slogan of support at the rallies and in social media. The remaining staff of *Charlie Hebdo* continued publication, the following issue's print run being 7.95 million copies in six languages, in contrast to the typical print run of 60,000 in only French.

Harris (2007) argues that, in contrast to Islamic fundamentalists, Christian fundamentalists are not fanatics, an example being peaceful protests when copies of the Ten Commandments were removed from a court house in Alabama in which: "None lifted a finger to stop the process - - no one was killed; no one received a scratch."

Myanmar refugee crisis

In the first half of 2015 yet another refugee crisis began when members of the Muslim minority in Myanmar fled, claiming persecution by the Buddhist majority, many of them on boats run by people smugglers. Many of the boats, as usual, were old and leaky, and many people died on them as they floated aimlessly in the sea after being refused entry by various countries, before a few countries agreed to intervene and save them.

On one boat survivors reported that Muslims threw many Christians overboard, so that other passengers had to form a human shield to protect a few remaining Christians still on board from the same fate.

Saudi Arabia attacked

In early April 2015 Somalia-based terrorist group Al Shabaab captured and killed 140 Kenyan University students, first separating out Christian students to be killed.

Christians drowned by Muslims

On 18 April 2015, Melbourne's *Herald-Sun* newspaper reported that Muslims on a boat full of Libyan asylum seekers off the coast of Africa threw 12 Christians overboard. It was reported that survivors told a "dreadful" story of "forcefully resisting attempts to drown them, forming a veritable human chain in some cases".

Melbourne plots

On 18 April 2015 police arrested five young men over an alleged plot to kill police officers with knives and swords during Melbourne's centenary Anzac Day celebrations.

Melbourne police had been alerted by police in England who had discovered suspicious communications between a 14 year-old from the north-western city of Blackburn and the Melbourne men. In one of these he had urged the Melbourne teenagers to carry out a knife, car or gun attack, suggesting they run over a policeman and then decapitate him.

More than 200 officers conducted seven raids at 3:30 AM, finding knives, swords and IS material. Two men were kept in custody, one being charged with preparations for, or planning, terrorist raids. Two others were charged later.

One of those arrested told police that a school friend of his had recently been killed fighting in Iraq or Syria.

It is believed that one motive of the would-be terrorists was to avenge the death of Numan Haider, a Muslim man who had been shot and killed by police after he attacked and stabbed two of them on 23/9/2014. Two of the group had been to Haider's funeral, whilst the two leaders of the group had frequented a controversial Islamic group run by a "firebrand" Islamic cleric.

Haider had attended lectures by this cleric at the Al-Furqan Information Centre in Melbourne where the cleric, Harun Mehicevic, had in 2012 told his followers not to take the oath of citizenship pledging allegiance to an 'unbeliever' government. He is reported to have ended each lecture by saying that Allah would help the mujahideen (holy warriors) build an Islamic State for Muslims.

A senior IS recruiter from Melbourne who went overseas to fight with IS had ties to the Al-Furqan centre and was alleged to have communicated with the men accused of the 2015 Anzac Day terror plot in Melbourne.

The Ukraine

In recent years there has been conflict between Russian-supported rebel forces and government forces in the region containing important port cities such as Odessa and Berdyansk. Currently there is, supposedly, a ceasefire, but conflict continues with considerable intensity.

Trade sanctions against Russia for supporting the rebel forces in Ukraine were put in place but had little effect, and it is still quite likely that a separate Russian-speaking province in the north of the Ukraine might eventually achieve independence.

Islamic State terror

In June 2014, the group then known as Islamic State in Iraq and Levant (ISIS) attacked the city of Mosul, population 1.8 million, in northern Iraq. Confronted by as few as 800 militants, about 30,000 Iraqi soldiers fled, leaving behind US armoured vehicles and weapons.

At the end of June 2014, ISIS renamed itself Islamic State and formally declared the establishment of a "caliphate", demanding allegiance from Muslims worldwide.

In August 2014, IS attacked the semi-autonomous Kurdistan region, forcing the inferior Kurdish forces to flee, leaving IS free to kill many men and boys, and rape and enslave many women and girls.

Early in 2015, IS captured the key city of Tikrit, a major embarrassment to the Iraqi government and the US.

In May 2015, Islamic State terrorists herded an audience into an ancient Roman amphitheatre in Syria and publicly shot 20 captives in front of them.

April 2015

In April 2015, Iraqi government forces retook Tikrit after a month-long offensive.

The following short article comes from Melbourne's Herald-Sun newspaper on 15 April, 2015:

IRAQ has exhumed the remains of 164 military cadets massacred by Islamic State terrorists and dumped in mass graves in Tikrit, the Human Rights Ministry has said.

The remains were discovered at ex-president Saddam Hussein's palace compound.

They are among an estimated 1700 victims from a military academy tricked by IS gunmen into boarding buses last year then all shot.

May 2015

In late May 2015, there were reports that ISIS was recruiting top scientists to work on producing advanced biochemical weapons. As Table 26.1 suggests, this is a frightening prospect.

Most disturbing of all, reports that ISIS has also begun collecting radioactive material from hospitals to make 'dirty bombs' have caused concern. Such reports occurred a few years ago, then the concern being al-Qa'ida, but ISIS, of course, is hardly unconnected in thinking and operations from 'AQ'.

June 2015

On 8 June 2015 a BBC interviewer on the 'Hard Talk' program was bemoaning the fact that relative peace was still not forthcoming in Nigeria after many years, and the hostilities of Boko Haram which had resulted in the death of 50,000 people and displaced half a million.

On Wednesday 10 June, 2015, Melbourne's *Herald-Sun* newspaper carried a report from Syria headed "Virgins sold cheap" which began:

Teenage girls abducted by Islamic State fighters are being sold in slave markets "for as little as a packet of cigarettes", says the UN envoy on sexual violence.
The article ended with:

A recent UN report said close to 25,000 foreign fighters from over 100 countries were involved in conflicts, with the largest influx into Syria and Iraq. Ms Bangura [the envoy] said the abuse of women and girls was "medieval", because IS wanted to "build a society that reflects the 13th century.

That same paper on (14/6/15) had an article beginning:
Turkey terrorist link probe.
THE Turkish government will investigate a terrorist recruitment network with an Australian extremist at its head.

On Saturday 20 June, 2015 an article in Melbourne's *Herald-Sun* newspaper began: ***JIHADI TEACHER***

A NOTORIOUS jihadi in Syria has boasted of helping a young Melbourne extremist make a bomb.

The Herald Sun has obtained transcripts of encrypted messages in which hacker and bomb-maker Junaid Hussain – acknowledged as one of Islamic State's most dangerous operatives – claims that he "mentored" a young Australian to develop a deadly weapon from easily accessible materials.

The young Australian was caught before he could blow up people at Australia's annual Anzac Day commemoration ceremony in Melbourne – a typical "we're tougher than you" etcetera act of Muslim terrorism.

On Saturday June 27, 2015 an article in the *Herald-Sun* was headed: **WORLD TERROR STRIKES**
19 die in Tunisia: 13 killed in Kuwait: French beheading

In the same edition, another article told of a border city in Syria being brutally attacked by ISIS, and of the Turkish President being accused of "allowing" ISIS forces to cross the border.

On June 29, 2015, page 7 of *The Australian* newspaper carried an article which began:
"UK's worst terror toll in a decade
SOUSSE: [in Tunisia] Britain has endured its blackest day at the hands of Islamist-inspired terrorism in a decade, with at least 15 Britons – including three members of the same family – among the dozens killed in the Tunisian carnage."

July 2015

The *Herald-Sun,* Thursday July 2, 2015 carried four articles involving ISIS in some way:

(1) The ISIS-linked terrorist who killed 38 people on a Tunisian beach a few days earlier was said by a hotel worker to be "laughing and smiling as he massacred his 38 victims with an AK-47 assault rifle."

(2) *A FRENCH prosecutor has confirmed that the man who beheaded his boss and tried to blow up a gas factory had a "terrorist motive" and links to Islamic State in Syria.*

(3) *ABOUT 1200 prisoners, including al-Qaeda suspects and convicted murderers, escaped from a prison in south-western Yemen after Shi'ite rebels let them out.*

(4) **'IS BEHEADING PEOPLE, KILLING CHILDREN, RAPING AND BEATING WOMEN, IT REALLY GOT TO HIM IN THE END'**
and reported that an Australian man had gone to fight with the Kurdish YPG, known as the People's Defence Unit, because he was disillusioned with the brutality of ISIS, but was killed by a land mine laid by Islamic jihadist forces.

In early July 2015 it was reported that Syrian rebels led by the al-Nusra front had successfully begun an offensive against the northern city of Aleppo.

On July 2, 2015, it was reported that Islamic State had released a video showing them executing 25 captured Syrian soldiers.

On July 8, 2015, it was reported that attacks by Boko Haram militants seeking to overtake Nigeria had killed 300 people in a week.

On July 21, 2015, it was reported that rebel bombing in of a major city in Yemen had killed 57. The next day it was reported that shelling near the same city had killed almost 100.

August 2015

In early August 2015 jihadists associated with Islamic State carried out a suicide bombing of a mosque inside a police compound in Saudi Arabia, killing at least 15 people.

In early August reports surfaced that British jihadis planned to blow up the Queen during 70th anniversary of VJ Day celebrations.

In mid-August it was reported that Australia was considering joining the US in bombing strikes on IS targets in Syria, an activity it was already undertaking in Iraq. By mid-September 2015 Australian planes had begun this campaign.

On August 15 it was reported that a truck bomb had killed 67 and wounded 150 at a market in a Shi'ite neighbourhood in Baghdad. Such bombings continue in Iraq on an almost daily basis.

On August 20 the Australian government reported that, over a period of about 10 months, 336 potential jihadists had been prevented from leaving the country for hotspots such as Iraq and Syria. In two linked groups of 2 and 5 men each was carrying $10,000 in cash.

On 21/8/2015 the *Herald-Sun* reported that the archaeologist in charge of the ancient ruins of Palmyra in Syria had been beheaded by Islamic State militants and his body hung in the main square. Subsequently, IS then set about destroying ancient temples and monuments in the city.

In the *Weekend Australian* of August 22-23 it was reported that Israel blamed Iran for firing four rockets into the Upper Galilee and Golan Heights territories, the latter having been partly seized from Syria during the 1967 war, also blaming Iran for periodic fire into the Golan. In response Israel launched artillery and air strikes against 14 Syrian military posts.

On August 23 it was reported that a heavily armed Moroccan had opened fire on a train travelling from Amsterdam to Paris, wounding two and injuring three before being overcome by passengers, two of whom were members of US military forces.

September 2015

Early in September 2015 a UNICEF report said that more than 13 million children were being denied education because of Middle East conflicts, UNICEF having documented 214 attacks on schools in Syria, Iraq, Libya, Sudan, Yemen, and the Palestinian territories during 2014.

On the 1st of September Melbourne's *Herald-Sun* newspaper reported that the Islamic group Boko Haram had killed 68 villagers in northeast Nigeria, bringing the death toll of their six-year uprising to nearly 20,000.

On the 2nd a IS suicide bomber killed 28 people at a Shi'ite mosque in the Yemeni capital of Sana'a. IS, which considers Shi'ites to be heretics, had claimed similar mosque bombings.

On the 9th the *Herald-Sun* reported that Germany's foreign intelligence agency had "information that IS used mustard gas in northern Iraq." There have also been reports of IS using mustard gas in Syria.

In mid-September fears of civil war in Turkey were reported as Government forces continued major operations against militants of the Kurdistan Workers' Party (PKK) and thousands of demonstrators took to the streets to protest against many bloody PKK attacks.

On the 20th a series of bomb blasts at a mosque in north-eastern Nigeria attributed to Boko Haram killed at least 117 people.

Many such attacks had occurred since a new President had come to power late in May, vowing to crush the insurgency.

Throughout the month the refugee crisis in Europe deepened with more than a million refugees expected to have arrived by the end of 2015. By the middle of the month Hungary and neighbouring countries had begun closing off their borders to prevent migrant access, prompting urgent talks to set migrant quotas for all EU countries.

Towards the end of the month it was reported that after over four years of conflict in Syria 250,000 people had been killed and that 12 million Syrians were in need of assistance, nearly half of them children.

It was also reported that US intelligence estimated that nearly 30,000 foreign fighters, perhaps 250 of them American, had gone to Iraq and Syria, many to join Islamic State.

On the 29th of September the Taliban captured the city of Kunduz in northern Afghanistan, the first time the insurgents had captured a major urban area since the 2001 US-led invasion of the country. More than 600 prisoners, including 140 Taliban, were released from the city's jail.

October 2015

In early October 2015 Russia began air strikes against IS and rebel forces opposing the Assad government. The US, which had supported the anti-Assad rebels, protested but Australia's foreign minister, Julie Bishop, was supportive of Russia's efforts, saying that "all transition options" should be considered, and that, in the short term at least, Assad and Iran should play a role in any peace process in Syria.

The *Weekend Australian* of October 3-4 reported that Iran believed that the US-led air campaign against IS had failed, and that:

The original Obama idea of training rebel forces who would simultaneously fight both Assad and Islamic State turns out to have been a strategic fantasy.

Foreign editor Greg Sheridan wrote:

The Russian moves transform strategic calculations in Syria and have left Washington completely flat-footed and almost irrelevant. The Russians now control the narrative.

Obama has become that most grotesque of strategic players – an impotent enemy and a dangerous friend.

Reports of civilian casualties from the first Russian air strikes soon emerged, but these were followed by reports of an American air strike on a hospital in the embattled city of Kunduz in Afghanistan. The hospital, run by Medicine sans Frontiers, reported many casualties and patients were burnt alive in their beds, also disputing US claims that insurgents were hiding in the hospital.

The final death toll was 22, including several medical staff, and the US military later apologized for this "tragic event."

On Friday October 3rd a 14-year old Muslim boy fatally shot a police worker in the back of the head at point-blank range outside a Sydney police station, before being killed by police. Only the day before the shooting his sister had left Australia for the Middle East.

In response to the shooting police raided four homes, two of them linked to convicted criminals, and arrested two young men, one a 16-year old who had been to school with the shooter and who had previously been charged with waving an IS flag at a nun and threatening to kill Christians.

On October 16 it was reported that police had charged a 22-year old man with supplying the gun used in the killing, and also an 18-year old man with giving it to the killer at a nearby mosque shortly before the killing.

In early October 2015, it was reported that ISIS groups were forming in Australian jails, and that there were at least 30 members of an ISIS gang in Goulbourne jail in NSW, forcing management to reserve a section of the prison for Muslims after threats were made to behead prison staff.

By early October 2015, Islamic State group forces had advanced to the outskirts of Aleppo, Syria's second city, killing one of the senior commanders of Iran's Revolutionary Guards.

In early October it was reported that IS was recruiting heavily in Indonesia where the government reported circa 1000 Indonesians to be fighting for IS and its allies in Iraq and Syria. It was also reported that Islamic State's 20 mosques in Indonesia were regularly collecting money to support IS, whilst many schools encouraged extremism, some giving classes in bomb-making. In mid-October it was reported that two churches in Indonesia had been attacked and destroyed.

By mid-October several Israelis and Palestinians had been killed by renewed urban conflict in the region, and talk of a third intifada having begun, a Hamas spokesman said: "The intifada is intensifying."

On Friday 16th of October, Palestinians torched a sacred Jewish site in the West Bank, Palestinians having called for a "Friday of revolution" against Israel after it was announced that men less than 40 years of age would be barred from the main weekly prayers at the "flashpoint" Al-Aqsa mosque.

On the same day President Obama announced that a planned withdrawal of nearly all of US forces [about 10,000] serving in Afghanistan was to be deferred until 2017.

That same day, it was also reported that 300 Cuban troops were to being sent to Syria to man Russian tanks fighting Islamic State.

The Weekend Australian of October 17-18 (2015) reported that the organization funding a mosque planned for the Victorian city of Bendigo, the Australian Islamic Mission, "has received financial support from an organization accused of channelling support funds to terrorists." That organization, Human Appeal International Australia, was reported to be one of 36 organizations banned by the Israeli government since 2008 because it "channelled funds to Hamas," in particular to hospitals in the Gaza strip run by Hamas, one such hospital being reported by *The Washington Post* as housing Hamas' headquarters.

November 2015

Conflict between Israelis and Palestinians having continued throughout October, in early November there seemed no end in sight to what had been termed by some Palestinians a third intifada, despite rallies by thousands of Israelis calling for Israeli-Palestinian peace talks.

Throughout October Russia stepped up its air strikes against ISIS and other rebels in Syria, on October 30 being reported to have flown 71 sorties and struck 118 terrorist targets in 24 hours.

On November 1, the US announced that it was going to deploy up to 50 special operations soldiers to assist Kurdish and Arab forces in northern Syria.

Conflict continued in Nigeria, mosques in two north-eastern towns having been bombed in late October.

Throughout October the flood of mostly Muslim refugees from Syria, Iraq and Northern Africa continued, despite attempts in some European countries to close their borders By November the situation had reached crisis point, encouraging greater international efforts to combat Islamic terrorism that had caused the flood of refugees.

On Friday 13th terrorist attacks occurred at 6 sites in Paris, killing 129 people, and wounding 350 more, about 100 critically. Six attackers killed themselves with suicide bomb vests, a seventh being shot by police. At one site, a popular concert venue, the attackers opened fire on the crowd at random with automatic rifles, killing nearly 100 people.

A US terrorism expert now working at Royal Melbourne Institute of Technology said that the attacks were a "game changer", saying that ISIS now had "franchises" in several countries. On Melbourne radio a caller blamed the Muslim religion, and the acronym ISIS bears witness to that view.

2016

Table 29.1 summarizes Islamic terror attacks in 2016 reported in the media and on the Internet by Wikipedia and other sites.

Table 29.1. Summary of Islamic terror attacks in 2016.

Location	Date	Description	Deaths	Injuries
Afghanistan	January 1	A Taliban suicide bomber. French restaurant in Kabul.	2	15
India	January 2	Jaish-e-Mohammed militants. Indian air base.	7	
Iraq	January 3	Five Islamist suicide bombers. Iraqi military base.	15	22
Afghanistan	January 4	Militant + truck with explosives. Compound near Kabul's airport.	0	30
Libya	January 7	Islamist militants + truck bomb. Police training camp in Zliten.	50+	100+
France	January 7	Moroccan Islamist attacked police with meat cleaver.	1	0
Libya	January 7	A car bombing at a checkpoint in the Libyan oil port of Ras Lanuf.	7	11
Egypt	January 8	2 armed militants stormed the Bella Vista Hotel in Hurghada.	0	3
France	January 11	15-yo Turkish ISIL 'fan' attacked teacher at Jewish school in Marseille.	0	1
Iraq	January 11	ISIL gunmen detonate suicide vests in a shopping mall.	20	40+
Turkey	January 12	ISIL suicide bomber targets tourists in the historical centre of Istanbul.	11	15
Indonesia	January 14	Attack by 4 in Jakarta orchestrated & funded by ISIL in Syria.	2	24
Somalia	January 15	Al-Shabaab terrorists attack African Union Kenyan army base in El-Adde.	63+	?
Burkina Faso	January 15	Islamist gunmen attacked restaurant in capital Ouagadougou.	20+	15+
Pakistan	January 21	Attack on Bacha Khan University. The Taliban claim responsibility.	22	

Location	Date	Description	Deaths	Injuries
Somalia	January 22	Al-Shabab attack on restaurant.	20	
Cameroon	January 25	Boko Haram insurgents. Suicide bombing in market in Cameroon.	25	62
Nigeria	January 30	Boko Haram gunmen raided a Nigerian village.	65	136
Ivory Coast	March 13	al Qa'ida gunmen storm 3 hotels in beach resort Grand-Bassam.	18	
Iraq	March 20	ISIL suicide bombers attack municipal building In Anbar.	24	
Belgium	March 22	Suicide bombings at Brussels Airport and in Brussels Metro.	35	300+
Yemen	March 25	Three ISIL suicide bombers strike checkpoints in city of Aden.	29	
Iraq	March 25	Suicide bomber at a football stadium in Iskandariya. ISIL claim responsibility.	30	95
Pakistan	March 27	Taliban suicide bombing targeted Christians in a park.	70	300
Afghanistan	April 19	Taliban attack security team protecting VIPs in Kabul.	64	347
Bangladesh	April 23	University professor hacked to death in Rajshahi. ISIL claim responsibility.	1	
Bangladesh	April 25	2 gay rights activists killed in Dhaka. Al-Qaeda affiliated group responsible.	2	
Iraq	May 11	Car bomb attack on a market in Baghdad. ISIL claims responsibility.	40	60
United States	June 12	Shooting at nightclub in Orlando, FL. Shooter pledged allegiance to ISIL.	49	53
France	June 14	Magnanville: Policeman & wife killed by man swearing allegiance to ISIL.	2	
Jordan	June 21	ISIS soldier infiltrates refugee camp at army post near Rukban.	6	14
Pakistan	June 22	An assassination claimed by splinter group of Taliban.	1	

Location	Date	Description	Deaths	Injuries
Turkey	June 28	Shootings + suicide bombings at airport in Istanbul.	45	230
Bangladesh	July 1	Gunmen killed 20 hostages in Dhaka. ISIL claimed responsibility.	20	
Iraq	July 3	2 bomb attacks in Baghdad.	300+	221+
Indonesia	July 4	Suicide bomb at Java police station.	1	1
Iraq	July 7	Suicide bombers and gunmen attack holy site in Baghdad.	56	75
France	July 14	Bastille day attack in Nice.	87	434
Germany	July 18	17-yo Afghan refugee attack with knife & hatchet on a train.	1	5
Germany	July 24	Suicide bombing by IS follower at wine bar in Ansbach.	1	15
France	July 26	2 ISIS followers kill priest killed in church in Rouen.	3	
Pakistan	August 8	Suicide bombing at a government hospital in Quetta.	77	100+
New York	Sept. 17–19	3 three bombs exploded in NY by Islamic jihadist.		31
India	Sept. 18	Militants attacked on army HQ	18	19
United States	November 28	2016 Ohio State University attack by Muslim Somali refugee.	0	11
Pakistan	November 12	Bomb at the Shah Noorani shrine in Balochistan. ISIL responsible.	56	102
Egypt	December 11	A suicide bomber at church in Cairo. ISIL claimed responsibility.	29	47
Germany	December 19	Truck driven into Christmas market at Berlin church.	12	56

2017

Table 29.2 summarizes Islamic terror attacks in 2017 reported in the media and on the Internet by Wikipedia and other sites.

Table 29.2. Summary of Islamic terror attacks in 2017.

Location	Date	Description	Deaths	Injuries
Iraq	January 2	Suicide bomber + truck attacked Shia market in Baghdad. IS claimed attack.	36	52
Afghanistan	February 8	IS militants attack convoy of aid workers of the Red Cross in Northern Afghanistan.	6	0
Afghanistan	Feb. 11	Taliban car bomber at Lashkargah bank.	7	21
Pakistan	Feb. 16	Suicide bomber at shrine in Sehwan.	88	100+
Iraq	February 19	2 suicide bombings hit districts recently retaken from Islamic State in E. Mosul.	5	0
Pakistan	February 21	3 suicide bombers with guns & grenades in Tangi near Afghanistan border.	7	22
Egypt	February 22	Two Coptic citizens killed in Al-Arish by IS-affiliated group.	2	0
Afghanistan	February 28	Infiltrator from Taliban allowed militants into Lashkar Gah outpost.	12	0
Afghanistan	March 8	IS gunmen dressed as medics attacked a military hospital in Kabul.	40+	50+
Iraq	March 8	2 Islamic State suicide bombers at wedding party in Hajaj near Tikrit.	26	67
England	March 22	Car driven into pedestrians on Westminster Bridge.	6	49
Russia	April 3	Islamist bomber on St. Petersburg metro.	5	15
Egypt	April 9	Bombings at Christian churches in Tanta & Alexandria.	47	100+
France	April 20	Man with AK-47 on Champs-Élysées had a note re. Islamic State and had previous contacts with IS.	2	3

Location	Date	Description	Deaths	Injuries
England	May 22	Suicide bomber attacks Manchester pop concert.	22	129
Egypt	May 26	Gunman attacks convoy of Christians.	28	22
United Kingdom	June 3	Van hits pedestrians on London Bridge and nearby shoppers then stabbed.	11	48
France	June 6	Man attacks guard at Notre Dame. Video pledging allegiance to ISIS was found.	0	2
Iran	June 7	Parliament and shrine in Tehran hit by ISIS suicide bombers and gunmen.	22	43
Iraq	June 9	Suicide bombing in Karbala. Attack claimed by ISIL.	30	36
Pakistan	August 7	Taliban militants in truck with explosive material clash with CT squad in Lahore.	2	35
Spain	August 18	3 attacks in Barcelona by 12 IS members.	15	120
Somalia	October 14	Truck bombing in Mogadishu. Al-Shabaab is suspected to have carried out the attack.	587	316
United States	October 31	IS followers drive truck into cyclists and runners on a bike path in Manhattan.	8	12
Egypt	Nov. 24	40 men attack Sufi mosque in al-Rawda.	311	122

2018

Tables 29.3 and 29.4 summarize the main Islamic terror attacks killing or wounding large numbers of people in 2018 reported in the media and on the Internet by Wikipedia and other sites. Numbers of dead attackers are shown in ( ).

Table 29.3. Islamic terror attacks in January to May 2018.

Location	Date	Description	Deaths	Injuries
Iraq	Jan. 15	Bombings in Baghdad.	38	105
Afghanistan	January 20	Attack at Inter-Continental Hotel in Kabul.	40	22
Afghanistan	January 24	Attack on Save the Children office in Jalalabad.	6	27
Afghanistan	Jan. 27	Ambulance bombing in Kabul.	103	235
India	Feb. 10-11	Attack in Sunjuwan.	7(+3)	11
Russia	Feb. 18	Shooting at church in Kizlyar.	6	5
Somalia	Feb. 18	Attack in Mogadishu attack.	45	36
Burkina Faso	March 2	Attacks in Ouagadougou.	30	85
Afghanistan	March 21	Suicide bombing in Kabul.	33	65
France	March 23	Attack & hostage taking at Carcassonne and Trèbes.	5	15
Somalia	April 1	Attack on African Union base in Bulo Marer.	59 (+30)	?
Afghanistan	April 22	Suicide bombing in Kabul.	69	120
Afghanistan	April 30	Suicide bombings in Kabul.	29	50
Nigeria	May 1	Suicide bombings in Mubi.	86	58
Libya	May 2	Attack on High National Elections Commission in Tripoli.	16	20
France	May 12	Knife attack in Paris.	1	4
Indonesia	May 13	Suicide bombings in Surabaya.	25	55
Belgium	May 29	Attack in Liège.	4	4

Table 29.4. Islamic terror attacks in June to November 2018.

Date		Dead	Injured	Location	Perpetrators
June 1	Gun+mortar attack	72	Unknown	Moqokori, Somalia	Al-Shabaab
6	Bombings	20	110	Baghdad, Iraq	Islamic State (suspected)
8-9	Shootings	65	17	3 districts in Afghanistan	Taliban
11	Suicide bombing	17 (+1)	40	Kabul, Afghanistan	Islamic State
16	Suicide bombing	36 (+1)	65	Rodat District, Afghanistan	Islamic State
16	Suicide bombings	43 (+6)	84	Damboa, Nigeria	Boko Haram
17	Suicide bombing	25 (+1)	50	Jalalabad, Afghanistan	Islamic State
23	Grenade attack	2	156	Addis Ababa, Ethiopia	Unknown
23	Grenade attack	2	47	Bulawayo, Zimbabwe	Unknown
July 9	Shootings, shelling	27 (+6)	40	Latakia District, Syria	Ansar al-Islam and Fursan al-Iman
10	Suicide bombing	22 (+1)	75	Peshawar, Pakistan	Tehrik-i-Taliban Pakistan
11	Shootings, shelling	40	10	2 districts in Afghanistan	Taliban
13	Bombing	5	37	Bannu, Pakistan	Ittehad-ul-Mujahideen
13	Suicide bombing	149(+1)	186	Mastung, Pakistan	Islamic State
14	Shooting	62	50	Geidam, Nigeria	Boko Haram
22	Suicide bombing	23 (+1)	107	Kabul, Afghanistan	Islamic State
25	Suicide bombing	31 (+1)	40	Quetta, Pakistan	Islamic State
25	Suicide bombings, shootings, + hostages	255(+63)	180	As-Suwayda Governorate, Syria	Islamic State

Date		Dead	Injured	Location	Perpetrators
Aug. 3	Shooting, suicide bombings	48 (+2)	70	Gardez, Afghanistan	Islamic State
15	Suicide bombing	48 (+1)	67	Kabul, Afghanistan	Islamic State
28	Bombing	2	36	Isulan, Philippines	Bangsamoro Islamic Freedom Fighters
30	Shooting, Ambush	31	19	Borno State, Nigeria	Boko Haram
Sept 4-5	Shootings, Stabbings	42	?	Bria, Central African Republic	Séléka(suspected)
5	Suicide bombings	26 (+2)	91	Kabul, Afghanistan	Islamic State
10	Ambush, Shooting	52(+42)	27(+many)	Khamyab District, Afghanistan	Taliban
11	Suicide Bombing	68 (+1)	165	Momand Dara District, Afghanistan	Islamic State(suspected)
12	Suicide Car Bombing	6 (+1)	42	Saladin Governorate, Iraq	Islamic State
22	Mass shooting	25 (+5)	70	Ahvaz, Iran	IS & Ahvaz Nat. Resistance (suspected)
Oct. 2	Suicide bombing	14 (+1)	40	Kama District, Afghanistan	Islamic State
8	Shooting, kidnapping	18	157	Borno State, Nigeria	Boko Haram
10-13	Shooting, Kidnappings, Bombings	37(+58)	100+	Deir ez-Zor Governorate, Syria	Islamic State
20	Bombings, suicide bombing	18 (+1)	62	Kabul, Afghanistan	Taliban and Islamic State(suspected)
23	Car bombing	7	40	Qayyarah, Iraq	Islamic State

Date		Dead	Injured	Location	Perpetrators
Oct. 23	Kidnapping	0	125 kidnapped	Giro District, Afghanistan	Taliban
26-27	Shooting, ambushes, suicide bombings	70	106	Al-Baghuz Fawqani, Syria	Islamic State
27	Suicide car bombing	7 (+1)	37	Maidan Wardak Province, Afghanistan	Taliban
Nov. 9	Suicide + car bombings & shootings	58 (+6)	106	Mogadishu, Somalia	Al-Shabaab
11-12	Shootings	50 (+1)	19 (+3)	Farah Province, Afghanistan	Taliban
18	Shooting	96 - 100+	Several	Borno State, Nigeria	Boko Haram
18	Kidnapping	0	50 (kidnapped)	Gamboru, Nigeria	Boko Haram
20	Suicide bombing	55 (+1)	94	Kabul, Afghanistan	Islamic State(suspected)
23	Suicide Bombing	33 (+1)	56	Kalaya, Pakistan	Tehrik-i-Taliban Pakistan(suspected)
23	Suicide Bombing	27 (+1)	57	Khost Province, Afghanistan	Taliban(suspected)

Conclusion

The foregoing tables of terror attacks emphasize the enormous global problem that Islamic terrorism poses, with major attacks occurring every few days, and attacks killing at least a few people occurring daily.

A consequence of the widespread Islamic terrorism in recent years has been enormous numbers of refugees fleeing their strife-ridden homelands to seek asylum in Europe.

The front page article in the *International Express* of August 10, 2016, was:

EU'S MIGRANT CRISIS IS COLLOSAL

British borders face threat from terrorists and smuggling gangs.
A FLOOD of migrants into the EU is leaving Britain open to terrorist attacks and people smugglers, MPs have warned.

The article said that 227,316 migrants had arrived in Europe in the first 6 months of 2016, more than 1.2 million asylum applications having been made in EU nations in 2015. It concluded: *The EU external border must improve security, including deploying specialist equipment to fingerprint and check everyone against security databases. This is not happening. Terrorists do not see borders as barriers to their barbarism.*

Another article in the same newspaper said that:

According to a former head of the UK Border agency: *Britain is home to at least a million illegal migrants who may never be found. - - There are thought to be as many as 20,000 migrants camped along the northern French coast waiting for a chance to reach Britain.*

World War 3, as we call it, and now the Pope agrees, has been going on too long – and it is far more serious and nasty than most realize. Just two of many possible examples are:

[1] From day 1 almost, the first author felt sure that Malaysian Airlines flight MH370 was deliberately downed as an act of Islamist terrorism and jihad in March 2014. In July 2016 it was reported that the pilot had used a home flight simulator a couple of days before the actual flight to plot and simulate the very wayward flight path needed to ditch the plane thousands of miles off course in the Southern Pacific Ocean.

[2] The first author has for several years felt sure that the summer rash of deliberately lit bush fires in Australia and the USA are acts of Islamist jihad, that is, a form of *infrastructure warfare*, and, indeed, in some cases in Australia, at least, this has been proved to be the case.

Perhaps a letter by 'Jason' printed in Melbourne's Herald-Sun newspaper on 5/7/2016 sums up the jihad problem well, saying that action is needed to deal with it, just as action is also needed cut back Australia's growing deficit:

During 2015 alone there were 2865 Islamic attacks in 53 countries – 27,626 were killed and 26,149 injured. By all means just ignore it and it will go away. Like the spending problems.

Another reader's letter to the same newspaper on 28/7/16 said: *SO UNESCO declares Islam as the "most peaceful religion of the world".*

Who made that decision? Is UNESCO a Muslim-dominated organization? Where were the (unreported) terrorist attacks, massacres, etc, committed by Bahais, Buddhists, Christians, Hindus, Jews, Sikhs, Rastafarians, Zoroastrians, or others in this century? Thousands have been listed involving "the religion of peace".
I'm really scared now. Probably won't go to church next Sunday.

A reader's letter in *The Age* on 29/7/2016 says:
Major French media outlets are to no longer print the names and photos of terrorists and terror suspects, thereby denying them posthumous glorification in the case of death or notoriety in the case of living. This will deny them a platform to promote their ideals of hate. All Western media should follow suit.

In Australia, *The Weekend Australian* reported on 30/7/2016 that: *Australia's foreign espionage agency* [ASIS] *has stripped officers from across its Southeast Asian and central Asian station, sending spies to the Middle East in an urgent bid to meet the growing threat posed by Islamic State.*

On 4 August 2016 it was reported that a "high level assessment" ranked Australia as third most likely to be victim of a "crowd sourced" terrorism attack, after the US and France.

On August 20 a column in the *Weekend Australian* said:
We now know political correctness doesn't just place worrying limits on how freely we discuss Islamist extremist terrorism – it also dangerously inhibits our ability to fight it.

As shown in Tables 29.3 and 29.4 Islamic terror attacks are continuing throughout the Middle East and much of Africa to this day.

They also continue elsewhere around the world, particularly in Europe, the UK, the US, and Australia.

In Australia for example:

(a) In mid-November 2018 a Muslim man carried out a knife attack in Melbourne, killing a police officer and wounding a couple of other people, before being shot and killed by police.

(b) On November 20, 2018, three Muslim men were arrested in Melbourne for planning terrorist attacks. The men had been refused passports to travel to Syria just a couple of years earlier, and were believed to have been inspired by and/or followers of ISIS>

The bottom line is really that, the madness of Islamist terrorism and jihad having gone on for some 1500 years in the name of the satanic Muslim religion, non-Muslims are losing patience, so how much longer should we as a community tolerate it?

Chapter 30

CONCLUSIONS

> *... the sword of Muhammad and the Quran are the most fatal enemies of civilisation, liberty, and truth which the world has yet known ... an unmitigated disaster parading as God's will . . .*
> William Muir (1819-1905), Orientalist.

Islam is on the rise

According to Burke (2011):

[In Egypt] *In 1986, there had been one mosque for every 6,031 Egyptians, according to government statistics. By 2005, there was one mosque for every 745 people – and the population has nearly doubled. As elsewhere too, anti-Americanism in Egypt remained at a historically high level.*

Support for suicide bombing in Egypt had dropped from around 33 to 8 per cent after a wave of attacks in the middle of the decade before stabilizing at around 15 per cent.

Islamic jihad

Before the crusades began, prominent Islamic scholar Abu Ala Al-Mawardi produced a formal blueprint for Islamic government reiterating division of the world into the House of Islam, where sharia law is enforced, and the House of War – the rest of the world with which Islam is in a permanent state of war.

He made it clear that Jihad was an obligation for all Muslims who could use tactical cease fires, but could never abandon Jihad until all unbelievers had been subjugated (Hammond, 2010).

When the Muslim Brotherhood was founded in 1928 five tenets were laid down, the fifth being (Massoulié, 2003):

I believe that the Muslim has the right to bring Islam to life by the renaissance of its various peoples, and that the banner of Islam should cover mankind, and that each Muslim should educate the world in Muslim principles. And I promise to fight to achieve this aim as long as I live, and to sacrifice everything I have to this end.

Serge Tritkovic in *The Sword of the Prophet* observes that:

... the massacres perpetrated by Muslims in India are unparalleled in history, bigger in sheer numbers than the holocaust, or the massacre of the Armenians by the Turks; more extensive even than the slaughter of the South American native populations by invading Spanish and Portuguese. They are insufficiently known in the outside world, however ... Ghandi and Nehru went around encrusting even thicker coats of whitewash so that they could pretend a façade of Hindu/Muslim unity against British colonial rule. After Independence, Marxist Indian writers, blinded by their distorting ideology, repeated the big lie about the Muslim record. Militant Islam sees India as 'unfinished business' and it remains high on the agenda of oil rich Muslim countries such as Saudi Arabia, which are spending millions every year trying to convert Hindus to Islam.

At the end of a long and distinguished career Orientalist William Muir (1819-1905) declared:

... the sword of Muhammad and the Quran are the most fatal enemies of civilisation, liberty, and truth which the world has yet known ... an unmitigated disaster parading as God's will ...

Hammond (2010) concludes:

Islam cannot survive freedom. The Quran cannot survive intense scrutiny and critical investigation. In this technological age, Islam's days are numbered. Although they can hijack Western technology to use against the West, the foundations of Islam are rotten to the core and cannot stand.

Hammond hopes that Islam can be subdued by Christian prayer and missionary work, but the present authors believe this view is naively optimistic.

In his book *The Legacy of Jihad,* Boston physician Andrew Bostom wishes that his children and grandchildren may "thrive in a world where the devastating institution of *jihad* has been acknowledged, renounced, dismantled, and relegated to the dustbin of history by Muslims themselves."

Chillingly, Harris (2007) concludes:
Islamic jihad has demonstrated an astonishing adaptability to different historical and material conditions – and in the post-9/11 epoch, there is no reason to believe the spirit of jihad cannot be adapted to challenges of modernity.

In the West we assume that democracy is the answer to problems posed by fanaticism but Harris (2007) points out that in the Muslim world the most tolerant people are ruling elite and the rich, "whilst the religious class and the bulk of the population have been precisely those who are most fanatically opposed to Western ways - - thus the spread of democracy in Muslim countries will end by empowering those who are most opposed to the very modernization that the West wishes to bring about in Islamic culture."

Muslims reared for conflict

Francis Fukuyama's book *The End of History and the Last Man* argues that alpha males are the cause of all conflict and that as they are gradually eliminated the world will become increasingly peaceful.

Harris (2007) argues that this only applies to the West thanks to Liberal Democracy which:

"is eliminating the alpha males from our midst, and at a dizzyingly accelerating rate. But in Muslim societies, the alpha male is still alive and well. While we in America are drugging our alpha boys with Ritalin, the Muslims are doing everything in their power to encourage their alpha boys to be tough, aggressive, and ruthless. We teach our boys to be good students, to aim at getting good jobs with large, safe corporations, to plan prudently for their retirement. They want their boys to become holy warriors. We are proud if our sons get into a good college; they are proud if their sons die as martyrs."

Another major factor in Muslim conflict is that 40% of Arabs live in poverty, so that jobless young Muslim men without prospects see reason in fighting to improve their lot.

Islamic hate messages

In April 2015 Islamic State jihadists put videos of prisoners being beheaded by militants in Libya on Twitter.

In an article in Melbourne's Herald Sun newspaper on 19 April 2015, journalist Andrew Bolt pointed out that:

- All the 21 Australians jailed for terrorism offences this century had been Muslim.

- ASIO was investigating 400 Muslim threats

- There are less than 500,000 Muslims in Australia, and more than 400,000 Buddhists, but not one Buddhist has been convicted of a terrorist offence.

- "At least five prominent Australian journalists and cartoonists have been subjected to serious death threats by Islamists, requiring two to move home."

Israel and Palestine

The authors see the foundation of the state of Israel in 1948 as marking the beginning of 'World War 3', and the ongoing conflict between Israel and Palestine is the longest running conflict in the Middle East.

The West continues to hope for a "two state solution", but some believe that only a 'one state solution' is practical, that is, a single state in which Muslims, Jews, and Christians live side by side. It is most unlikely that this would work, or that Israel would accept such a proposal. Indeed, it would probably result in even greater conflict in the long run.

Egypt and Tunisia

According to Aid (2012):

The U.S. intelligence community had been reporting for years that popular unrest with the Ben Ali and Mubarek regimes was building, but according to a senior U.S. intelligence official, nobody at DNI headquarters at Liberty Crossing foresaw that mass street demonstrations would lead to collapse of both the Tunisian and Egyptian regimes. The thinking among the intelligence analysts at the time was that the massive police and security services of both countries were more than capable of suppressing any public unrest. The analysts were wrong.

Well even we authors of this book are not infallible, and we are Mohrons, members of the new religion for which the 9th Law is that the prophet of Mohronism is Murphy of the very well-known Murphy's Law. And that law is 99% accurate about human history being a disaster more often than not.

Iraq and Syria

Iraq, having been involved in a great deal of conflict since the 1980s, as noted in Chapter 15, it continues to endure almost daily bomb attacks made by the competing Sunni and Shi'ite factions.

To compound matters greatly, Islamic State now control much of Iraq, early in 2015 having inflicted a humiliating defeat on the Iraqi Army when taking over a city in northern Iraq, despite being its forces being greatly outnumbered.

 According to Aid (2012):

Classified intelligence reports reviewed by the author reveal that the two top Syrian intelligence services, Syrian Military Intelligence and the General Intelligence Directorate, continue to covertly permit Iraqi to freely operate from its soil. Syria's not-so-secret involvement in the war in Iraq between 2003 and 2008 was considerable. According to the study done for the Marine Corps Intelligence Activity by the Center for Naval Analyses, "Inside Syria [Iraqi] insurgent leaders could take refuge, financiers could organize money flows into Al Anbar [province], foreign fighters could transit en route to Al Anbar, and insurgent cadres could even establish a few training camps. The Syrian government seemed to turn a blind eye to much of this activity, although they never allowed insurgents to truly mass inside their territory.

No – the latter would not be discrete would it. But it all continues to sound like you can't trust the Arabs, not the Muslims, that is.

On Iraq, Aid (2012) says:

In another ominous potent of things to come, the U.S. government's relations with Nuri-al-Malaki's Iraqi government have been slowly slipping because the Baghdad regime has been quietly moving away from the United States toward close ties with Iran. Iran's ability to influence the policies of the Iraqi government is a source of heated debate within the U.S. government and intelligence community, although nobody disputes the fact that the Iranian intelligence services are striving to ensure that the policies of al-Malaki are to Tehran's liking.

So business as usual, the Arabs and/or Muslims stick together to some extent, at least, and often to a considerable extent.

Iran

At a Melbourne club where a group of Vietnam veterans meet on Friday and Saturday nights for a "few beers" the vets agreed with the first author one night recently that Indonesia was a potential threat to Australia, as was the strong possibility of Iran developing nuclear weapons sooner rather than later, and that we (the West) would one day have to "nuke" Iran.

This would, of course, bring us nearer, probably, to the end of World War 3, what this book is all about.

Aid (2012) says on Iran: *The CIA has no station inside Iran since Washington broke diplomatic relations with the regime after militants stormed the U.S. embassy in Tehran on November 4, 1979.*

. . . . Not only does Iran maintain a sizable embassy in Dubai, complete with a large complement of intelligence officers, but according to a leaked State Department cable, banks in Dubai currently hold about $12 billion of Iranian government money, which the Tehran regime secretly uses to finance terrorist groups, its overseas weapons purchases, and its clandestine acquisition of nuclear technology.

Israel deplores the latter situation, as it should.

Writing about the 2015 US-led agreement with Iran to limit its nuclear activities and reduce sanctions against, the editorial column in the *Herald-Sun* on 16/7/2015 concluded:

The deal will cover the next 10 years. They will be anxious years as the Middle East remains not only a powder keg but, as Israel fears, become a nuclear one.

In the *Weekend Australian* of August 8-9, 2015, foreign editor Greg Sheridan wrote:

Obama's deal with Iran is the worst possible deal. It will in the long run likely make the Middle East far more unstable. More important, it makes the prospect of the spread of nuclear weapons throughout the Middle East much likelier.

Number of militants on the increase

The Federally Administered Tribal Areas (FATA) is a semi-autonomous tribal region or proposed province of Pakistan in north-western Pakistan, bordering Pakistan's provinces of Khyber Pakhtunkhwa and Balochistan to the east and south, and five of Afghanistan's provinces to the west and north. The Federally Administered Tribal Areas comprise seven tribal agencies (districts) and six frontier regions, and are directly governed by Pakistan's federal government through a special set of laws called the Frontier Crimes Regulations (FCR).

The territory is almost exclusively inhabited by the Pashtune, who also live in neighbouring province of Khyber Pakhtunkhwa and are mostly Muslims.

According to Burke (2011):

Equally, the Pakistanis' declaration of victory in the FATA also appeared premature. There are plenty of signs that any respite would be temporary. Only 600 of an estimated 10,000 militants in South Waziristan were thought to have been killed, and, more importantly, most of the multitude of groups that had sprung up over previous years remained mobilized.

Islamic State

According to ABC2's 'Foreign Correspondent' program (8 PM, 19/5/2015):

Hundreds of young Western-educated women are running away from home to marry radical Islamic fighters and live in the self-declared 'Islamic State' in Syria.

IS claims it has 550 "women inside IS."

IS denies the many atrocities for which it is well known, claiming its activities are in accordance with shariah law.

IS videos have been released showing girls as young as 9 being married to IS fighters, others being used as sex slaves.

Islamic State propaganda says that it wants to join its caliphates in Syria and Iraq, also posting a film clip on the Internet in which a young convert says:

We will not rest until a black flag is flying over every land.

An article in Melbourne's Herald Sun newspaper on 20/5/2015 said:

Islamic State militants searched door to door for policemen and pro-government fighters and threw bodies in the Euphrates River in a bloody purge after capturing the strategic city of Ramadi [in Iraq].

About 500 civilians and soldiers have been killed since the final push for Ramadi began last Friday.

The Taliban

According to Aid (2012):

Left unsaid in the estimate was that It is now widely accepted inside the U.S. intelligence community that, barring a complete collapse of the Taliban from within, it is probably not possible to defeat them militarily, no matter how many more American troops are sent to Afghanistan. Not only were the Taliban continuing to gain strength and expand the scope and intensity of their operations, but their underground "shadow governments" were now probably dug in too deep to be uprooted, especially in the rural areas of southern and eastern Afghanistan.

He goes on to say:

Pakistan remains an even more complex and perhaps intractable problem. According to Ambassador Richard Holbrooke, President Obama's special adviser on Afghanistan, "Pakistan may be a knot that we may never to be able to untangle." The intelligence community's view was that the security situation in Pakistan, while significantly better than it was in 2009, was nowhere near as good as President Obama's progress report made it out to be.

So, we are afraid to say, as others have of late, the terrorist problems around the world, including in India and its neighbours, will continue for decades at least.

Returning to Afghanistan, Aid (2012) says:

So in the fall of 2010, the emphasis secretly shifted to negotiate a peaceful settlement of the Afghan conflict with the Taliban, while at the same time keeping up the military pressure on the Taliban through an intensified campaign of commando raids that targeted senior insurgent field commanders. The expectation was that these commando raids would induce the Taliban leadership in Pakistan to come to the negotiating table.

. . .

And just when officials in Washington and Islamabad thought that relations couldn't get any worse, they did. In June 2011, CIA officials alleged that someone in the Pakistani government or ISI had leaked to the Pakistani Taliban that the United States intended to launch drone strikes on one of the Taliban's two bomb factories in northern Pakistan. This led to yet another round of bitter incriminations between the U.S. and Pakistani government and intelligence officials. Senior officials in Washington told congressional officials that, in their opinion, Pakistan could no longer be trusted with any sensitive classified information.

So who can you trust in the Middle East these days?

More powerful weapons for jihad

As Burke (2011) notes, "most Taliban commanders did have watches – along with, by the end of 2009, an array of sophisticated military equipment that few amongst them had even heard of a few years previously."

In the few years since then it has become increasingly obvious that Iran may well be able to secretly produce nuclear weapons within a year or two, despite US and UN vigilance aimed at preventing this.

In addition, in early 2015 it became clear that Islamic State were putting a lot of effort into recruiting top scientists to develop advanced chemical and biological weapons.

Remembering the crude chemical weapons used by Saddam Hussein to slaughter some 50,000 Kurds in northern Iraq, one can only shudder at what might be to come as WW3 heats up with the use of 'NBC' weapons by Islamic terror groups as sophisticated, widespread, and powerful as Islamic State in Levant or ISIL, now usually referred to as IS for simplicity, or ISIS when referring to Islamic State in Syria.

Disturbingly, recent reports (June, 2015) that ISIS has begun collecting radioactive material from hospitals to make 'dirty bombs' have caused concern.

Such reports occurred a few years ago, then the concern being al-Qa'ida, but ISIS, of course, is hardly unconnected in thinking and operations from 'AQ.'

As for dirty bombs, in the fictional book *The Variant Virus,* which introduces secret anti-terrorism agent Simon Sinclair, terrorists sprinkle hijacked radioactive waste on London from helicopters (Mohr, 2012c). In the present book Tables 25.1 and 26.1 give some idea of the massive nuclear and biological warfare research programs and stockpiles of the USSR and USA circa the 1970s and 1980s.

With the appearance of new 'superbugs' such as the highly lethal Klebsiella pneumonias, carbapenamase-producing bacteria (KPC) which can resist the strongest antibiotic treatments, the prospects of biological warfare are set to become even more frightening than hitherto.

Solutions

Some of the measures that might be taken against Islamic extremists and terrorists include:

[1] Anti-radicalization programs.

A new program aimed at stopping 'vulnerable' teenagers from joining Islamic State was initiated in Melbourne in May 2015 with federal government funding. The program was developed by an anti-terrorism expert and aims to counter the social media propaganda of terrorist groups such as IS.

30. CONCLUSIONS

In August 2015, however, a former deputy of the Australian arm of Jemaah Islamiah said that Australia was at risk because of ineffective deradicalization procedures, blaming this for a nephew going to fight for IS in Syria.

The present authors, however, believe that it would be better to carefully scrutinize Mosques, other Islamic group meeting places, Islamic shops (especially bookshops). Then the BS spouted by religious and other leaders could be carefully assessed, as indeed could the sanity of the leaders themselves, and action taken if need be.

[2] A change in dress codes?

There was considerable negative public reaction to a Melbourne school making a class of girls wear the hijab for a day, supposedly to see what doing so feels like.

There was considerable public outrage over this was misguided exercise, some suggesting that the girls should have been told to wear a crucifix as this was more appropriate in Australia.

Perhaps a more sensible suggestion would be for students to get hold of the book *World Religions* (Mohr & Fear, 2015) and learn a little about how most of the world's religions were 'concocted', often by a lone man claiming unwitnessed conversations with God, for the purposes of obtaining money, status, influence and power.

As for dress – since Muslims have all too often controlled "non-believers" excessively, and often cruelly, it would make sense to ban the hijab and burka. After all, we don't normally like masked people coming into shops with loose clothing – all too easy to be a criminal with an automatic rifle concealed under their loose robes.

Then, if we choose to follow the precedents set by Muslim conquerors all too often over 15,000 years, those women who did wear hijabs etc. could be beheaded which would save them the expense of such headgear.

[3] Passport confiscation.

In April 2015 the US military targeted an Australian fighting in Syria for assassination because of his association with Jabhat al Nusra, al-QA'ida's official affiliate in the ongoing conflict in Syria.

Around the same time another Australian in Syria fighting for al Nusra posted on the Internet a statement ridiculing the Islamic State terrorist group for it having lost the city of Idlib to al Nusra. Idlib was the second major city in Syria captured by al Nusra in a year.

In Australia there is growing concern about more than a hundred young men having gone to the Middle East to fight for Islamic State and other terrorist groups.

Several Australian women have also gone to fight for IS or support them by marrying the men of ISIS.

On 18 April 2015 the Melbourne Herald Sun newspaper reported that 30 Australians had been confirmed to have died fighting for Islamic State.

As a result of such reports the Australian government has placed travel bans on several young Muslims suspected of radical tendencies, preventing them from leaving the country.

[4] Be smarter ourselves.

An example of this is a Finish couple who were taken hostage by a terrorist group and then sold on by that group to al-Qa'ida who produced a 2013 video propaganda message using pictures of them.

While this farce was going on they had the intelligence to note that one of the masked men dealing with them did not have black hair. His hair was long and lightish, however, and they kept just one strand of it that had fallen out and been left stuck in the pages of a book which they had been given, no doubt to read some loony message

After they had escaped and/or been released from their ordeal they gave this strand of hair to authorities who sent it for DNA testing. This was promptly done and the results circulated, thus arriving at the appropriate security person's desk in Australia on 27 September 2013.

It turned out that this enabled that particular villain/terrorist to be identified as an Australian who had joined ISIS et al. in 2012-2013 and he was subsequently killed in a drone strike.

The Finish couple got it right, at least to some extent, and are now well known in Finland, and the wife is now running for election to the Finnish parliament.

The husband bottom-lined it all about the Australian terrorist he had helped ID, and who was killed not long ago in a drone attack:

Probably the world is in a better place without him.

As for measures in Australia, Melbourne's Herald Sun newspaper reported on 8 June 1015 that:

A new law enabling police to force would-be jihadis into deradicalisation programs and ban them from the internet is being examined by the Victorian Government.

The unprecedented crackdown would allow police to apply for Community Protection Intervention Orders (CPIOs) – similar to intervention orders – for anyone deemed to be radicalised, even if they are not planning terror attacks or seeking to fight overseas.

That all sounds very fine, but we are inclined to agree with Rita Panahi, who writing a column in the 8/6/2015 issue of the same newspaper says, in speaking of a supposed expert in these matters, one 'Prof Kessler':

But unlike some of his colleagues in academia who have jumped on the anti-terror gravy train, Prof Kessler, who has studied Islam, including militant Islam, for more than 50 years, can see that deradicalisation is a strategy doomed for failure.

[5] Air campaigns.
In April 2015 a US counter-terrorist drone strike on an al-Qa'ida base killed an American al-Qai'ida terrorist who had threatened a major attack in Melbourne, Australia. He had been close to al-Qa'ida's leader Ayman Al-Zawahiri and a key member of the organization's propaganda machine.

The man, Adam Gadahn, had converted to Islam in 1995 and after the terrorist attacks in Europe in 2005 he released a video saying: "Yesterday London and Madrid. Tomorrow, Los Angeles and Melbourne, Allah willing. And this time, don't count on us demonstrating compassion."

An al-Qa'ida operations leader was killed in a second drone attack on the same day.

In September 2015 Australia expanded its air campaign in Iraq to include targets in Syria, joining the US and other allies in a campaign to weaken IS.

[6] Mercenaries and Special Forces.
The USSR failed miserably after years of trying to curb the Taliban etc. in Afghanistan. Indeed, Kim Philby, the greatest spy in history who had been a double agent for the USSR inside MI6 until he escaped capture by flying to Moscow to live, warned the US against invading Afghanistan, saying that such an invasion would not be successful. The US, indeed, learnt the hard way in Iraq in 1991+ and 2003+, as well as then in Afghanistan.

The alternative of sending thousands of US, UK, Australian etc. troops to Iraq to train the local army has not worked, as evidenced by the Iraqi Army fleeing a much smaller advancing ISIS force in Iraq in April 2015.

Brutal forces like those of ISIS are best dealt with by Special Forces and highly experienced mercenaries.

Perhaps the best example of the latter was 'Mad Mike Hoare's legendary 5 Commando group in the Congo in 1964, the movie *The Wild Geese* being loosely based on the exploits of this group, and Mike Hoare being the 'military advisor' in the making of this movie (Smith, 2012).

Mike's men were ruthless, Smith's book showing photographs two of them shooting a rebel as he stands helpless waiting for them to do so.

In taking a town they used a method of going through it invented by the Germans in WW2. They would go through the town, a pair of men coming to each side of each door and throwing with left and right hand a grenade into the room to 'clear it'.

30. Conclusions

If there were women and children inside, you see, there might well be terrorists hiding behind them who would eventually kill them anyway, having killed you.

With their successes Made Mike's men gained a fearsome reputation, apparently, for one day when a village with 2,000 armed rebels inside heard that Mad Mike's men had arrived on the outskirts of the village, the rebels dropped their weapons and ran for their lives.

Little did they know, perhaps, Mad Mike only had about 40 or 50 men in that team and did not himself go out on missions normally, if at all.

While movies can 'glamourize' war, and such people as Mad Mike, the realities of conflict are generally gruesome in the extreme, and Smith's book *Mad Dog Killers,* which tells the story of the exploits of Mad Mike Hoare's 5 Commando, makes this clear, intentionally or otherwise (Smith, 2012).

The latter is more nearly how to deal with such ruthless groups as ISIS, that is, fight fire with fire.

Indeed, the armed forces of most major countries always have special groups such as the British Special Air Service (SAS) because:

Regular troops as the British learned in North America in the 18th century have an almost impossible task when fighting an elusive foe who can, chameleon-like, fade into the natural background, and who avoids at all costs any form of traditional set-piece battle. Ambushes and traps, the torture and mutilation of prisoners, the quick hit-and-run raid, the use of hostages and blackmail, hijackings and the slaughter of civilians who might be in the way or just in the wrong place at the wrong time – all these became part and parcel of a new form of total warfare which the conventional armed forces of the world are largely unable to cope with (Quarrie, 1985).

Besides the SAS, Great Britain also has the Parachute Regiments (Para), The Royal Marine Commandos (RMC), the Special Boat Squadron (SBS) and 'Raiding Squadrons' for special, quick and smaller scale operations.

In the Falklands War, for example, 1SBS made a diversionary raid on Port Stanley while 2Para were taking a key ridge for observation purposes. Then four raider craft carrying 2SBS and 2SAS sneaked into Port William, the estuary of the Murrell River. They were detected and repulsed by heavy fire, but while sitting this out under cover 2Para successfully entered Stanley and took it.

The US and many other countries, of course, also have commando and other special units which they use to good effect occasionally.

Our point here, however, is that there will never again be trench warfare as in WW1 in which up to 200,000 men were killed in a day. Nor will a million US troops ever land on foreign shores to win a war, as they did in Europe in WW2. The conflicts since that time have almost always involved terrorism and response by smaller forces using pinpoint bombing etc.

The back cover blurb of a book about mercenaries by journalist James Brabazon reads:

In a fly-blown bar in West Africa, British reporter James Brabazon found himself being briefed on covert military plans to overthrow the government of Equatorial Guinea – a tiny country fabulously rich in oil- by one of Africa's most notorious mercenaries, his friend Nick du Toit.

The botched coup and its tragic consequences left a host of guns-for-hire victims of their own avaricious schemes and ruthless double-crosses. Mark Thatcher, only son of the former British prime minister, was famously implicated in the plot. In a twist of fate James Brabazon remained free, while Nick du Toit was sentenced to thirty-four years in a violent and depraved Black Beach prison.

MY FRIEND THE MERCENARY is both an account of James's courageous journey into the bloody Liberian civil war – where, with Nick as his bodyguard, he was the only journalist to film behind rebel lines – and the inside story of an astonishing coup attempt. It is a brutally honest book about what it takes to be a journalist, a survivor and a friend in the morally corrosive crucible of war (Brabazon, 2010).

We will leave it at that except for one further quotation from the text of this book:

The RUF was infamous for its extreme atrocities. The mutilation of civilians was a favourite tactic. Their fighting units went by the names of Blood Shed Squad, Burn House Unit and Kill Man No Blood Unit – this latter group prided itself on beating people to death without a drop of blood being spilled. The Born Naked Squad stripped their victims naked before killing them. So it went on. Their military campaigns were known by a series of cruelly honest code names, too, including Operation Burn House, Operation Pay Yourself and the brutally self-explanatory Operation No Living Thing.

The book goes on to recount the sorts of expenses incurred in hiring cars etc. that this journo had in his foray into the dark depths of African political conflict, and tells of how he (Brabazon) managed to escape from capture by the African terrorists with the help of his friend Nick, who as noted above ended up given a long stretch in jail when he was captured later in the story.

[7] Real democracy.

In the last century or so the West have always sought to replace 'bad', dictatorial and tyrannical governments with democratically elected ones, as will be obvious if one reads much of this book. As Aristotle claimed long ago, today we always have *oligarchy*, not democracy, and this is more obvious in the US and UK in particular.

What we should really aim for, however, is 'real democracy', and what we mean by this is summarized in Appendix B, and this would certainly reduce conflict because it gives people at the grass roots an opportunity to vent their feelings at the ballot box and elect a local member who would be truly independent of any 'party line' and might thus actually do what the people of his electorate wanted.

[8] Other measures.

Other measures of dealing with disputes not involving conflict of any kind, however, are discussed in Appendix A.

[9] Protectorates.

Finally, in dealing with the vexatious problems of the Middle East we should not go so far as to 'nuke' the whole area, as a friend of the first author suggested recently.

Instead, we recommend that Iraq and Syria be taken over as UN mandated protectorates, just as Palestine was a UN-mandated protectorate under British control from the 1920s to 1948 (when Israel was created and WW3, in effect at least, began). Then, just as many people are now predicting decades of further conflict and terrorism in the Middle East, we would predict that such mandated territories would remain as such for 20 – 30 years, if not more, giving a new generation of Muslims an opportunity to become a little more enlightened and tear out the most offensive and violent pages of their copies of the Koran, if not abandon that evil religion altogether.

Media comments

With Iran on the verge of obtaining nuclear weapons, and the brutal Islamic State terrorist group still controlling much of Iraq and Syria, and also now putting a lot of effort into developing advanced chemical and biological weapons, WW3 looks set to heat up.

In an article in Melbourne's Herald-Sun newspaper on 10/6/2015, journalist Simon Benson reported:

The country's first national security chief has warned that the new and unprecedented threat of terrorism in Australia could be with us for decades – possibly for a generation to come.

He went on to say:

The number of people supporting Daesh (Islamic State or IS), compared to 18 months ago, the number of people travelling [to join them], *is rising.*

The editorial comment in the June 29, 2015, edition of *The Australian* newspaper began:

"Islam's time of peace turns deadly in three countries
A better military strategy is needed to defeat the caliphate.

A year on from the so-called Islamic State's declaration of a Sunni caliphate, the series of barbaric attacks in the pasts few days, far from the jihadists' stronghold in Iraq and Syria, is a reminder of the group's increasingly ubiquitous reach and the challenge it poses to every nation in the world."

It concluded with:

"Mr Essebsi (Tunisia's president) has acted by closing 80 mosques where preachers have radicalized followers. As he says, a global strategy is needed to combat an organisation that now has 35 affiliated groups in 17 countries and jihadist recruits from 40 countries."

Closure of mosques and other centres which encourage radicals could be hoped to reduce Islamic extremism and, indeed, in September 2015 there were public protests against local government approval of plans to build a mosque in the Victorian provincial city of Bendigo.

As Tom Elliot wrote in the *Herald-Sun* on 7/8/2015:

Want to open a mosque here? As long as you can get it past the local council you are free to do so.

Try to open a Christian church in much of the Muslim world, however, and death threats, fire-bombings and mob rule will result.

Another concern is that there are twice as many students attending Islamic schools in Australia as there were only 8 years ago, another sign that Islam and its 6th pillar of jihad are growing globally at a frightening rate.

On Wednesday 17 June, 2015 an article in the *Herald-Sun* newspaper began:

Put all jihadis on trial

DUAL-nationality Australians fighting for Islamic State abroad should be returned here to face trial before being stripped of Australian citizenship, says shadow attorney-general Mark Dreyfus.

The article concluded by quoting Australia's PM, Tony Abbott saying to the Parliament:

If you leave this country to fight for a terrorist army in Syria or Iraq, you are committing the modern form of treason and we don't want you back.

In August 2015 Australian government authorities reported that, in a period of only about 10 months, 336 would-be terrorists had been intercepted at airports when embarking on journeys to Middle East hotspots.

Indeed, the problem of Islamic radicalization of youth has become so bad that programs have been introduced into some Australian schools to try and prevent it. Nevertheless, in late 2015 there were reports that children as young as 14 might be forced to wear tracking devices to prevent them making terrorist attacks in Australia.

Disturbingly, in July 2015 it was reported that boys as young as eight were being taught how to behead a hostage using plastic dolls for practice. Then in October it was reported that boys as young as five were being recruited by Islamic state and "taught to kill."

On Monday June 29, 2015 a front page article in *The Australian* newspaper began:

"Terror threat 'will outlast ISIS'

Islamic State's influence in Australia has become so powerful that the threat of terrorism will long outlast the conflict in Syria and Iraq and will remain for at least a generation."

In the *Herald*-Sun on 11/9/2015 Tom Elliot wrote:

Recent comparisons have been made between IS and Nazi Germany.

He concluded, however, that while ISIS might succeed in forming an extremist Sunni Muslim nation in regions of Iraq and Syria, it lacked the ability to *"project substantial force – conventional or otherwise – overseas."*

He also noted that the ASAD regime in Syria, which had used chemical weapons, should also be dealt with, but concluded that *"recent history tells us that Western intervention in the Middle East is doomed to either failure or unintended consequences.*

And a longer-term analysis of military strategy suggests that air power alone rarely achieves a decisive result."

Harris (2007) points out that:

The West is now in the position of a player in a game of chess who finds himself constantly on the defensive, waiting for the move of the far more aggressive player that he is pitted against. We have completely lost the historical momentum - -.

Like a chess player on the defensive, we no longer have the option of forming our own strategy: We have our hands full in reacting to the unexpected moves of our opponent.

There is, indeed, no doubt that sporadic bombing of ISIS targets in Iraq and Syria is not enough, and that follow-up ground forces are then needed to clear areas of militants.

Similar tactics are needed in Nigeria and elsewhere to combat Islamic terrorism.

At present, however, the signs are that ISIS is still recruiting heavily, particularly in Egypt, Algeria, Yemen, Saudi Arabia and Afghanistan, and still gaining ground. The signs are equally grim elsewhere in the Middle East, particularly Iran, Palestine and Lebanon, and also in much of North Africa.

World War 3, therefore, has a long way to run and it is imperative that the Western allies seek to end it as soon as possible by both military and diplomatic means before it gets out of hand with the use of NBC weapons.

All the indications are, however, that Islamic terrorism, or *Islamofascism* as the late Christopher Hitchens called it, is likely to spread globally as millions of refugees flood into Europe from Syria, Iraq and Africa.

As a result, many Jews are leaving Europe for what they believe is the comparative safety of Israel, a strong parallel with the late 1930s.

Similarly, Jewish schools in Australia now need armed guards because they fear local jihadists and ASIO is currently investigating 400 terrorist threats. Such threats are set to increase with Australia having undertaken to settle 12,000 Syrian refugees.

The top five sources of refugees are all Muslim but in Australia Muslims make up a disproportionate proportion of prison populations and all the 21 people jailed in Australia for terrorism were Muslims. Nine of these were born in Lebanon or to Lebanese families and gun crime in the Lebanese enclaves of Sydney is now rife.

In the *Herald-Sun* on 21/8/2015, columnist Andrew Bolt concluded that, if Syria with a population of 23 million can produce 4 million refugees, then if Islamic State takes over Iraq (population 33 million), Afghanistan (30 million), or Egypt (82 million), then "millions more refugees will join this invasion of Europe, including parents of tomorrow's jihadists. After a decade or two of that, how safe will Europe be for Europeans – and us?"

On September 7 his column pointed out that many of the Afghan and Somali refugees Australia had taken in had joined bikie gangs and jihadist groups, and that there had been clashes in Sydney between supporters of Syria's Assad regime and those of the Free Syria Army.

On September 14 his column said:

Nothing that might make you fear the consequences of this great river of people is given much coverage. Even news in April that Muslims on a boat to Italy murdered Christian passengers was played down.

Citing several recent Muslim-related riots in Europe, he added:

All [European nations] *have struggled to assimilate large Muslim minorities, and all have battled increasing jihadism.*

They have learned that mass immigration from the Middle East is now more like colonization - - .

In the *Weekend Australian* of August 29-30, 2015, Troy Bramston wrote:

The threat to humanity from Islamic State is different to the threat from Hitler. - - - What we are seeing today is the collapse of the nation-state in the Middle East and Africa, and Islamic State imposing its own rule of terror against religious minorities in actions akin to genocide.

In the *Weekend Australian* of September 12-13 David Kilcullen reported that as many as 9 million Syrians had been displaced by conflict, 2 million of them going to Turkey, and another 2 million to Lebanon and Jordan. It also reported that Israel, Saudi Arabia and Turkey "all see Iranian expansionism – and the violence and destabilization that come with it – as an even greater threat than Islamic State. For Israel this is an existential threat, a fact underlined this week when Iranian Supreme Leader Ali Khamenei claimed in a public speech that the 'Zionist entity' would no longer exist within 25 years."

The same edition, however, carried an article with the headline:

Destruction of Islamic State is the first step on the road to Middle East solution.

As conflicts continues, if not widens, in the Middle East the millions of Muslims refugees from Syria, Iraq etc. may destabilize neighbouring countries, as well as much of Europe and the West, including Australia, the editorial column of the *Herald-Sun* of 23/10/2015 carrying the headline:

Terror grows in the suburbs.

The article cited Abdul Numan Haider's attack on two policemen in 2014, and the "sophisticated network responsible for radicalisation of other teenagers and young men" that he had been caught up in as a danger to Australia.

It also cited the Lindt café siege in Sydney where a self-proclaimed sheik took 17 people hostage, forcing them to hold up an Islamic flag in the window, and resulting in the death of two hostages when police had to resort to storming the building.

Most tellingly, however, the article pointed out that:

The list of active Australian terrorists fighting in Iraq and in Syria, where Islamic State is now being pursued by RAAF Hornets, is a long one.

In September 2015 ASIO's director-general said that "two-thirds of all actual and foiled terrorist attacks against Australians since 9/11 had occurred in the past 12 months.

He concluded: "It's pretty clear that the fight against terrorism is going to be a long and difficult one."

Indeed, 2014 had seen a spike in terrorist activities globally with 13,000 attacks resulting in the deaths of 32,000 people, the most lethal year of the 45 for which records have been kept.

On September 15, 2015, the Lebanese education minister said that Islamic State was sending trained jihadists undercover as refugees to Europe via Turkey and Greece to attack targets in the West.

A letter published in the Herald-Sun newspaper on 13/6/15 began:

Vietnam all over again?

REMEMBER Vietnam? I do, I was there as a helicopter gunner. America continually bombed areas of suspected enemy location, but it was a lost cause and a waste of good men. If NATO countries think bombing suspected Islamic State locations will have the desired result, they must be dreaming too.

The letter concluded: *This IS death cult has no intention of stopping until its quest is achieved. NATO needs to quickly get troops in there on the ground and in large number and with air support. Stop pussyfooting around, a heavy hand is required immediately.*

An article by former treasurer Peter Costello in the *Herald-Sun* on 15/9/2015 said:

IS could be quickly defeated in a land campaign, but no country is volunteering to lead and commit the forces required to do it. If the campaign is restricted to air warfare, it is not so much a campaign to defeat IS as a campaign to contain it.

On 27/9/2015 *The Age* newspaper reported:
In one of the most ambitious deals yet struck between the combatants in the multi-faceted war in Syria, supporters of President Bashar Assad will essentially trade territory in two parts of the country, stop bombing one another's civilians and pledge to observe a six-month ceasefire.

In preceding days a consensus had been developing with the view that, at least in the short term, Assad should play a role in efforts to bring peace and stability to Syria, so that the West should join with Russia in supporting him.

This is a positive sign that gives some hope that Islamic State might be defeated in Syria, and hopefully then in Iraq. Nevertheless, defeating other militant Islamic groups in the Middle East and Northern Africa is likely to take decades.

Ending World War 3

Ending global Islamic terrorism will be difficult and may take many more years. Some solutions were proposed in the book *World War 3, When & How Will It End?* (Mohr, Fear & Sinclair, 2015), those proposals including many of the 'solutions' discussed in the present chapter such as 'real democracy'.

The August 10, 2016, edition of *The International Express* said that, according to the Metropolitan Police Commissioner, another terrorist attack in the UK was certain to occur before long, the page 12 editorial comment saying that:
Protecting borders must be a Government priority.

Melbourne's Herald-Sun newspaper reported on 5/7/2016 that: *Would be terrorists are being caught up in airport stings as they try to join extremist groups overseas.*
Security agencies secretly cancel the passports of would-be foreign fighters, allowing them to go to airports where they are intercepted, questioned and have their electronic devices scanned for information.

The article said that 170 passports had been cancelled since June 2014, and that since then 500 people had been taken off planes by security officers of the Border Force.

The same newspaper reported on 3/8/2016 that a new counter-terrorism intelligence service was to be established to provide ASIO with an early warning system for possible terrorists trying to leave or enter the country.

On August 13 it was reported that Australia's intake of Syrian refugees had been slowed by increased security checks.

Elected to Australia's senate at a federal election on 2/7/2016, well-known anti-immigration personality Pauline Hanson called for an end to Muslim immigration and a ban on new mosques, also saying:

You can't deny the fact that in these mosques they have been known to preach hate towards us. It's not me, it's our society that are on the streets against the building of mosques.

About Islam she said:

We're talking about a political ideology. They would say it is a religion - - and they say it's a religion of peace. We know that's not true either.

About Australia's Racial Discrimination Act which forbids anything which is "reasonably likely ... to offend, insult, humiliate or intimidate another person or group of people" because of their "race, colour or national or ethnic origin," Senator Derren Hinch said:

I'm offended and insulted that they say I can't say anything that will offend or insult.

Here he was in agreement with Hanson who had said:

We are entitled to freedom of speech and freedom of expression, saying that the laws were *stifling people's right to have an opinion.*

A reader agreed with this in the Herald-Sun of 4/8/16:

Free speech is only free until you offend someone, or a group.

A reader of the Weekend Australian also agreed on 6/8/16: *She* [Hanson] *is in direct touch with the concerns and fears of ordinary people, who are all too often ignored by our superiors.*

In conclusion:

There should be major revision in shariah law and Islamic thinking to reduce their intolerance and violence. In particular, a revised edition of the Qur'an in which references to such nefarious activities as jihad are removed is badly needed.

Democratic government should be introduced throughout the Middle-East, along with formation of independent nations for such disaffected groups as the Kurds and Palestinians. Initially, elections in such new nations should be supervised internationally to ensure that they are democratic.

More important right now, perhaps, Muslims leaders and preachers should be encouraged, if not required, to speak out at every possible opportunity against Muslim violence and terrorism, wherever it may occur. To monitor this, therefore, Pauline Hanson's suggestion of CCTV cameras in mosques might make sense. After all, there are 2 million CCTV cameras in London, nearly all of these in public places such as streets, parks and the lobbies of large buildings.

A letter published by the Herald-Sun on 8/7/2016 read:

Haven't radical Islamists killed us infidels with planes, pressure cooker bombs, suitcase bombs, improvised explosive devices, knives, pistols, rifles, grenades, truck bombs, suicide vests, stones, rockets, and even chucked us off tall buildings?

Isn't the ideology the problem, and not the weapon of choice?

A column by Rita Panahi in the same newspaper on 13/7/2016 said:

- you cannot blame the continual fighting and sectarian violence on Western imperialism, the Iraq war or the state of Israel.

The truth is that Islam desperately needs some reformation. Railing against the West for its racism, decadence and immorality will not bring peace to the Middle East or other regions torn apart by sectarian violence.

Whilst IS has lost ground of late, the Taliban now controls more territory than at any time since before the invasion of Afghanistan, so an end to 'WW3' is not yet in sight. The authors hope, however, that some of the ideas in the present book, and also in their previous book *World War 3*, will point in the right direction, perhaps the most urgent of these being that a new, 'friendlier' edition of the Koran is badly needed.

Without this, young Muslims will continue to find encouragement in the Koran's many incitements to jihad and join such evil organizations as IS and al-Qa'ida, or commit 'lone wolf' or small-group attacks in such countries as Australia. If such attacks continue, calls for banning of Muslim immigration, and even banning of mosques and the religion itself, will grow louder around the world.

Indeed, circa 18/7/2016, TV host Sonya Kruger echoed Pauline Hanson's call to end Muslim migration to Australia, saying: *I want to feel safe. There is a correlation between the number of people who are Muslim in a country and the number of terrorist attacks,* adding: *You're not allowed to talk about it.*

Andrew Bolt wrote in the *Herald-Sun* of 15/8/16 about the need to at least 'free up' Australia's Racial Discrimination Act, saying: *At last Australians are finally refusing to be treated like scum, too stupid and vicious to be free to speak,* and noted that 600,000 had voted for Pauline Hanson's One Nation Party at the federal elections of the previous month.

On a historical note, *The Weekend Australian* on 30/7/2016 printed a recent article from *The Times* about the upcoming centenary of the *Balfour Declaration* [which was briefly discussed in the last section of ch. 6] which said:

The Balfour Declaration set the scene for a century of conflict but it also contains within it the germ of a two-state solution.

We, as noted more than once earlier, see the final outcome of that declaration, namely the creation of the state of Israel in the UN-mandated British Protectorate of 'Palestine' in 1948 as the main seed of WW3, i.e., the seemingly endless spate of Islamist jihad and terrorism that has plagued the Middle East and more recently the world since that time.

We do, however, agree that it was meant, of course, to be a 'two-state solution', one which failed because of high levels of Israeli-Palestinian conflict, for example the 5 day war of 1967 which saw Israel claim control of a great deal more territory which it retains control of to this day.

If Israel can belatedly be persuaded to hand back those regions 'stolen' from the Palestinians in 1967, however, that would go a long way towards restoring peace in that region, and it can only be hoped that some of the many territorial disputes elsewhere in the conflict-ridden Middle East will also be settled peacefully in the not too distant future.

Helpful too, one hopes, are plans by the US and Russia to increase investment in new hi-tech military equipment to help combat hostile nations and terrorists.

During August 2016 media commentators concluded that:

[1] After 5 years of civil war in Syria between Sunni rebels, IS, the government, and US & Russian forces, there is no end in sight to the slaughter and mass emigration.

[2] Aleppo could be termed the "Syrian Stalingrad".

[3] Terrorist attacks on the West have "steadily" increased over the last 15 years and more than "half-measures" are needed to deal with the ongoing jihad of IS etcetera.

On the latter point we can't agree more that even stronger attacks on IS are needed, along with restriction of Muslim migration and religious practice in the West.

Whilst much of the territory overtaken by IS in the last decade in Syria and Iraq has now been retaken by government forces and their allies, the Taliban still controls much of Syria, and, as shown by Tables 29.1 − 29.4, Islamic terrorism committed by dozens of terrorist organizations continues unabated around the world, continuing a violent history that dates back to the origins of the Muslim religion.

We hope, therefore, that this book will encourage people to work towards reduction of the propaganda, advertising, religious ravings etc. that brainwash so many people into becoming consumer zombies, political zealots, and Islamists and jihadists.

Recommendations

With Islamic State still in control of much of Syria and Iraq, and likely to gain further ground elsewhere, there is a growing body of opinion, shared by the present authors, that current bombing campaigns against IS must be backed up by special forces on the ground to deal with any remaining resistance.

Russia has had ground forces operating in Syria, and in late September 2015 President Putin told CBS television: "We are trying to establish some kind of coordinated framework" [to resolve the conflict in Syria]. In early October Russia began cruise missile attacks launched from offshore ships on ISIS targets in Syria.

Iran, however, still remains a potential nuclear threat in the future, and efforts must be made to reduce that threat. Indeed, some consideration must be given to global nuclear disarmament, though this, of course, would be difficult to enforce, but perhaps far less costly than maintaining massive nuclear armaments such as those of the US and Russia.

In much of the world, including the whole of the Middle East, Indonesia, Pakistan, much of Africa, and parts of India, many Islamic terrorist groups remain active, and combating these is likely to remain a problem for decades to come.

Indeed, jihad being the 6th pillar of a vengeful and backward religion, it seems likely that Islam's long history of violence, oppression and jihadism is likely to continue indefinitely unless fundamental changes are made within Islam itself. Such changes could include a revised and more liberal edition of the Koran, banning the hijab and burka, strict restrictions on Muslim migration, and perhaps even a tax on Muslims to help pay for combating Muslim extremism and terrorism.

Such a tax would be comparable to that imposed by Islam on non-Muslims for centuries, but perhaps trade sanctions on countries harbouring Islamic extremists might be a better and less disruptive option.

In the recent book *Inside IS – Ten Days In The Islamic State* German journalist Jürgen Todenhöfer, who had spent 10 days embedded with IS in Iraq and Syria, said that the West is "drastically underestimating the power of IS" who he called "a nuclear tsunami preparing the largest religious cleansing in history" with plans to kill "several hundred million people."

"They now control land greater in size than the United Kingdom and are supported by an almost ecstatic enthusiasm the like of which I've never encountered before in a war zone."

In late September 2015 the Jakarta chief of police was reported as saying that Australia was an obvious target for Islamic extremists: "But you are accommodating asylum-seekers, including those coming from the conflict areas. The main ones today are from the Muslim world: Afghanistan, Pakistan, Iraq. They are seeking asylum but ... they still have this emotional connection with the Muslim world."

At the end of September 2015, Russian President Vladimir Putin called for "genuinely broad alliances against terrorism, just like the one against Hitler."

He said: "Similar to the anti-Hitler coalition, it could unite a broad range of forces that are willing to resolutely resist those who just like the Nazis sow evil and hatred of human kind."

The bottom line is that strong measures must be taken by several nations, particularly the US and Russia and their allies, to reduce the level of Islamic conflict substantially and, hopefully, largely eliminate it eventually.

There should be major revision in shariah law and Islamic thinking to reduce their intolerance and violence.

Democratic government should be introduced throughout the Middle-East, along with formation of independent nations for such disaffected groups as the Kurds and Palestinians. Initially, elections in such new nations should be supervised internationally to ensure that they are democratic.

Appendix A

REDUCING FUTURE CONFLICT

Herodotus

According the back cover of *Herodotus, The Histories* (tr. de Sélincourt, 1954):

Herodotus's Histories is the first great prose work in European literature. Its main theme is the heroic and successful struggle of a small and divided Greece against the mighty empire of Persia – with its underlying conflict between the absolutism of the East and the free institutions of the West. Herodotus has been called the Father of Lies as well as the Father of History; but it was a feature of his method, when evidence was lacking, to record popular belief, and the result of one of the most entertaining books in the world.

Herodotus was born between 490 and 480 B.C. in the Dorian town of Halicarnassus. He spent a few years of his earlier manhood travelling through most of the known world, ranging from Palestine, through northern Africa, and up to southern Russia. When older he retired to Thurii in Italy, and there he revised and expanded his great book.

According to de Sélincourt:

The plan of History is grand and simple. Herodotus announces it in his opening paragraph; it is to trace the events which brought Greece into conflict with Persia, with a full description of that memorable struggle, and within the framework of the story to record what is worth remembering in universal history, - or, in other words, all the information he has been able to collect, historical, geographical, sociological, and legendary, about the whole of the known world.

Herodotus relied on existing writings and oral testimony, the first Persian invasion having been just before he was born, and the second when he was still a child. Apparently he spent plenty of time gleaning the information for his writings from people he encountered during his extensive travels, later reflecting and revising his thoughts.

Some of his fellow men thought he gave too much credit to Athens for repelling the Persian invasions, but de Sélincourt opines that Herodotus is remarkably "large-minded" and impartial.

Book One of his great book says that Persian historians blame the quarrel between the Greeks and the "Asiatic peoples" on the Phoenicians, people "originally from the coasts of the Indian Ocean" who made many trading voyages, some of them migrating to new lands.

In Argos, when they were selling their wares at a fair, some women visited it, one of them being a king's daughter. Then a few of the Phoenicians, after talking amongst themselves, "made a rush at them." Most escaped, but the king's daughter was captured and taken away on a ship and raped.

This was "the first in a series of provocative acts."

Then "some Greeks - - - carried off a Persian king's daughter, thus giving them tit for tat". Another similar act by the Greeks inflamed the situation further, particularly as demands by the Persians for reparations were ignored.

Herodotus concluded that *the only sensible thing is to take no notice* when a woman is abducted, arguing that the fate of just one individual does not justify the escalation of the ensuing dispute into a full scale war in which a great many people are killed.

There is some sense in this, and, of course, we are all too familiar with hostage situations around the world today, a 'bad many' of which are not resolved satisfactorily, but rather end in the rape and murder of victims, often after a long period of imprisonment and abuse and torture.

The bottom line here, of course, is that throughout recorded history mankind has been conducting acts of terrorism, war etcetera, the concern expressed in this book being that of WW3 ending badly, very badly indeed.

Reducing future conflict

Measures needed to reduce future conflict include (Mohr, 2014):

[1] To reduce conflict in the world and, indeed, improve the overall quality of life for the general human population, Mohr's *Attitudinal Model of Conflict* should be understood as widely as possible (Mohr, 2014). Then it might be hoped that people will:
(a) Base their attitudes on rational thought, observations, and facts, not prejudice.
(b) Try to understand people of different backgrounds.
(c) Make 'positive' contact with other peoples to reduce, or at least understand their differences.
(d) Be more 'democratic' in their judgment of others, that is, consider the views of others when forming their own.

[2] <u>Education</u> of our children should not be the long drawn-out bore that it is now. Four or five years of incarceration in day care and kindergarten, and then twelve more at school is far too long. In the first few years home-based learning, perhaps in small groups with a special teacher gives much better results (Packard, 1978)
Then 10 years at school should be more than sufficient for the average child (Mohr, 2012a).
Indeed, because of growing public dissatisfaction with the US education system, many US children are home-schooled and often do much better as a result (Penn, 2007).
At school far more emphasis should be given to teaching life skills. They should, for example, be taught how to deal with bullying and bad bosses, how to develop realistic career goals, about consumerism, and about the 'time value of money'.

Finally, education at all levels should be less of a series of lectures by a 'parade of clowns' and, at least after the first few years, should more along the lines of 'here is the textbook, study this chapter this week and then we shall have a class discussion and question session on it'. A more mature, two-way, equal status approach such as this should be far more effective and much better preparation for life.

[3] <u>A fair go for all</u>. There needs to be a much fairer distribution of wealth in societies so that corrupt executives cannot make up to 1000 times more than those that do the actual work of producing saleable products.

[4] <u>Ethnic harmony</u>. Tolerance and understanding between different races, religions and ethnicities should be encouraged. Historically disadvantaged indigenous peoples such as the Australian aborigines should also be given a 'fair go' in society (Broom, 1980).

[5] <u>Population control</u>. Our population is exponentiating and it is now at least twice what it should be if everybody is to have a reasonably good standard of living. China's one-child policy, for example, has helped it advance greatly economically. Elsewhere, as Carlo Cipolla implored, there also needs to be more emphasis on 'quality not quantity' (Cipolla, 1974).

[6] <u>Protect jobs</u>. Globalization of trade should be reduced because, for example, shipping countless different makes and models of cars around the world cannot be economically sensible. In addition there should always be modest tariffs to protect local jobs.

A 4-day week, perhaps of 36 hours, should be made the norm. This could prove more efficient and would greatly improve quality of life.

Income splitting before tax should be allowed for married couples to allow one parent to stay at home to care for and oversee the crucial early education of children.

[7] <u>Resource conservation</u>.   Resource scarcity is a likely source of future conflict. As of 1997, for example, in the 1500-mile expanse of the Japanese archipelago there wasn't a single major oil field and the rest of Northeast Asia was no better off with North Chinese and Indonesian fields approaching exhaustion (Calder, 1997).

More energy-efficient buildings and cities are needed to preserve crucial finite resources such as oil. Thus, growth of 'megacities' full of wasteful air- conditioned multistorey buildings and crowded freeways should be curtailed, and smaller regional towns encouraged instead.

[8] <u>Control the arms industry</u>. A highly excessive 8 million new small arms are sold each year, more than 60% to civilians (Thomas, 2007).   The arms industry should be drastically reduced, land mines totally banned, and biochemical and nuclear weapons outlawed.

[9] <u>Terrorism</u>. Leaders of religions used as a justification for terrorism should be compelled to speak out openly and repeatedly against use of their religion as a *basis* for terrorism.

[10] <u>Greater UN power</u>. Every nation should contribute on a per capita basis, adjusted for their economic circumstances, towards a large UN armed force which could be used to deal with minor conflicts and deter larger ones.

Nations could save far more than this cost by greatly reducing the size of their armed forces to a level sufficient to deal with little more than domestic emergencies.

A UN court should also be established to judge grievances between countries and impose economic sanctions and fines.

Finally, to make the UN more democratic, the power of veto given to a few countries should be removed.

To implement such measures large societies must be structured, however, and must have governance and, for this to have any hope of significantly reducing human conflict, it would need to be 'real democracy', not the increasingly ineffective democracy seen in the corrupt, outdated, and predominantly two-party 'revolving door' Westminster system (Mohr, 2014c).

Finally – we urge readers to get hold of the first author's books that mention the *Contact Hypothesis* (Mohr, 2012a, 2012b, 2012d, and 2014), particularly the latter.

Contact hypothesis, as he now puts it, says that the *ethnic difference* (E) between two groups, can be written most simply as:

$$E = aD - bC$$

where C = *contact* between the groups, and D = *differences* (cultural etc.) between the groups. Then, as Mohr has it in *The History & Psychology of Human Conflict*, "positive contacts" (friendly) *reduce* E, and will also reduce D, the differences between the 2 groups over time. That is, you stay polite, don't fight (however) over just about everything possible – but focus on the positives and try and live without conflict, hatred, war and mayhem such as we have now.

Intel Wars

Aid's book of this title gives an excellent idea of what goes on in 'Intel Wars' these days, and has been quoted a few times earlier in this book, so to save you the reader flicking to the References at the end of the book here are the details for it again:

Aid MM, *Intel Wars, The Secret History of the Fight Against Terror,* Bloomsbury, New York (2012).

On this issue it may be some consolation to the reader to take note of an article in Melbourne's Herald-Sun newspaper on Saturday 13/6/15. It was headed *Terror Twits* and began:

"*TWITTER* will tip off suspected terrorists and criminals using its service if police ask it for information about them, the *Herald Sun* can reveal."

To hear this is some consolation to the present authors, though we note that, as is not uncommon the journo and editor have got it a bit wrong in the above sentence – the point is that the POLICE can be tipped off about terrorists using twitter if they so desire. If the police, intelligence services etcetera were all equally incompetent we would be in far more serious danger than we already are.

Conclusion

Earlier in this appendix we mentioned education as being one of the areas in which we could attempt to deal with the issues of conflict, terrorism, war etc. – for example by discouraging 'copycat' behaviours whether drugs or terrorism.

Islamic jihad, of course, is a growing global problem thanks to the many Muslim terrorist groups around the world, and the many radical Muslim preachers, who preach violence against unbelievers.

The Koran pays scant attention to 'turning the other cheek', placing far more emphasis on jihad. The sacred Sahih Muslim urges Muslims to make nonbelievers submit to Muslim rule:

Invite them to [accept] *Islam; if they respond to you, accept if from them and desist from fighting against them. If they refuse to accept Islam, demand from them the Jizya* [the tax on unbelievers] . . . *If they refuse to pay the tax seek Allah's help and fight them.*

In an infamous statement in 2014 Islamic State quoted holy scripture more than 25 times, and ordered Muslims around the world to kill unbelievers – to "smash his head with a rock, or slaughter him with a knife, or run him over with your car."

In a sermon at the Al-Abrar Mosque in the Gaza Strip on Friday 9th October 2015, Sheik Muhammad Sallah waved a knife and shouted for Muslims to stab Israeli Jews, ordering them to: "Attack in threes and fours, and cut them into body parts. Some should restrain the victim, while others attack him with axes and butcher knives."

The Sheik gave the Prophet Muhammad's slaughter of a Jewish tribe in Khaybar in 629 as an example to justify his recommendation.

Indeed, in following days there was a wave of knife attacks by Palestinians against Jews in Jerusalem, a Hamas spokesman calling them "heroic" and saying: "The intifada is intensifying."

Appendix B

REAL DEMOCRACY

Relatively minor conflict between individuals in society cannot be avoided at times but can, with improvements in education and government be much reduced.

Larger scale conflict between groups of various sizes ranging from competing criminal gangs to competing nations is, however, a different matter as it is usually the leaders that instigate conflict.

In part, the problem here is that the 'meek do not inherit the earth', as the Christian Bible says. Far from it, for it has almost always been the most assertive and dishonest 'alpha types' with type A personalities that have led us by the nose to believe various and sometimes absurd religions and to fight for them if so directed.

Similarly, of course, political leaders use propaganda and lies to convince people to support them and, if need be, fight for whatever cause they see fit to fight for.

It would help, therefore, if we had *direct democracy* so that the populace can vote on major issues, hopefully preventing leadership groups from summarily committing nations to conflict.

One reason this is needed is seen in the Westminster system where parties have 'safe seats' that are given to people with more money and/or influence. Another problem is that party members must vote in unison as directed. A further problem is that ministers are chosen by the party leader, whereas they should be elected by the party.

Yet another is that in so-called democratic countries big business is able to make huge donations to political parties in return for more favourable treatment, for example, lower company taxes. The USA, for example, is effectively run by a higher echelon of long-established wealthy families who run large businesses. These businesses include the arms industry which makes massive profits from arms sales because, as long as even just a few minor wars are going at any one time, that encourages arms sales on a global basis. We have to be suspicious, therefore, about the motives of countries that have large arms industries and also a habit of almost always being involved in one war or another.

All this is not, of course, democratic. We should be represented by independent representatives in each electorate who have empathy for the concerns of people at the grass roots of society.

In addition, direct democratic voting should be allowed for all major issues to ensure 'government by consent.'

In situations of national emergencies that require rapid response, however, this is not practical.

The only solution, therefore, is to have what I will call *real democracy*, that is, truly representative democracy, features of which would include:

[1] Government should be by a parliament of elected representatives for each region of a state or country. These representatives should be elected as independent individuals not associated with any political party or group, and they should only be allowed one or two terms.

[2] People wishing to be selected for a pool of 20-30 prospective candidates for election would have to meet age and other criteria and pay a modest fee. As part of the selection process they would also be interviewed by electoral authorities to help assess their suitability. In Australia, for example, these interviews would be held at the Australian Electoral Commission offices in the federal electorate within which the prospective candidates resided.

[3] The candidates for election in each region should be chosen from the pool of prospective candidates by a panel of 15 – 20 people chosen randomly from the population of the region, but according to certain selection criteria such as age, selection of panel members thus being comparable to the way in which jury members are chosen.

As part of the selection process the prospective candidates would give a short public speech and be interviewed by the selection panel. Thus the selection process would be comparable to that used to 'preselect' candidates to represent a party at elections in the Westminster system, but would entail selecting circa six candidates.

[4] A new selection panel would be chosen for each election. The overall process is illustrated in Figure B.1, the prospective candidates, of which there might be many, being interviewed to obtain a pool of 'prospective candidates' from which the candidates for election are chosen by the selection panel process.

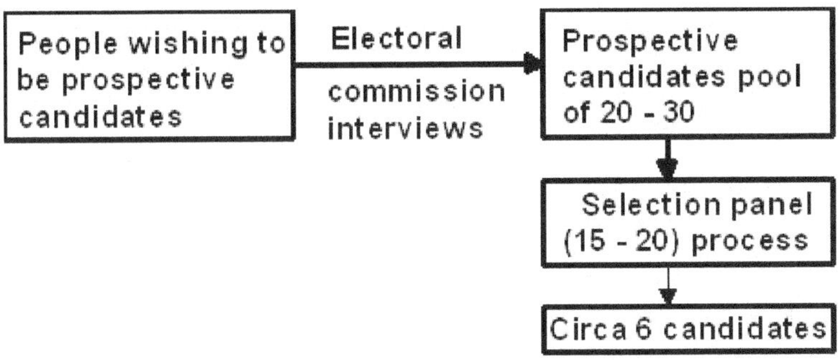

Figure B.1. Selection of candidates for election.

[5] Members of parliament would elect a chairman and groups of members to deal with each of the main areas of government, for example finance, education and health. The chairpersons of each of these groups would be elected by the members of the groups.

[6] Elections of parliament would be every 3 – 4 years.

[7] The public at large would be allowed to vote on major issues such as taxation rates and foreign policy by referendum, and such referenda should also be able to be held when a certain number of people call for it.

[8] How members of parliament voted on each motion would be recorded in the newspapers etc. so that their electorate could judge whether their views were being represented appropriately.

[9] A record of how members of parliament had voted on all motions would be kept at the electoral offices of members and a copy made available to the public for inspection.

[10] Members of the public should be able to record how they wished the local member to vote on a particular issue at the member's electoral office.

A more truly democratic system of government such as this would be less open to control by a single leader and just a few of his or her friends.

It is this sort of oligarchical or 'clique' situation that has been at the heart of man's endless history of corruption and conflict, whether the form of government was ostensibly a monarchy or a so-called democracy.

It is only through 'real democracy', as outlined above, that the world might have any hope of lasting peace in the future.

We gripe elsewhere about oligarchy – on Melbourne's talk-back radio station 3AW at 8:59AM on 16/6/2015 talkback host Neil Mitchell and a caller discussed "are we selling off too much of the farm." Of course. The 'not free lunches' given to the pollies by big and transnational biz have just about given away all state and federal assets so in the West there will be more 'Great Depressions'/GFC's (same thing) to come.

Australian politics became a bit more democratic with the creation of 'The Australian Democrats', the founder Don Chipp being a disgruntled former member of the Liberal Party. The Democrats did one good thing we well recall, that is, when 10% GST was introduced by the Howard Government (despite having previously promised not to do so) they forced the amendment that 'essential' or basic food not be included, as good result for poor people.

It also became a bit more democratic when Pauline Hanson, with a little help of a couple of other people who later betrayed her, launched the *One Nation* party which had immediate and astonishing success in winning 7 senate seats in Queensland, and a couple more in other states.

Rupert Murdoch, who some believe runs the country, now with the help of his sons, usually backs the Liberals, but not always – after an argument with them circa 1980 his media pushed successfully, as usual, for Labor Candidate Bob Hawke. Thus, no doubt at the urging of the Libs hierarchy, he had his press get rid of the troublesome One Nation, and the redheaded (dyed – it made her more noticeable) Pauline.

As a bit of an aside – note that Julia Gillard, our first woman (not female – not specific enough – one could mean a dog etc.) PM, also went red (appropriate!) at the hands of the halfwit hairdresser that she was foolish enough not to dump in favour of somebody within Labor ranks to help protect her back.

Back to Hanson – besides being backstabbed from within, she did make an initial very bad impression on Aborigines etc. with her maiden speech in parliament in which she raved for a page or two in a rather racist fashion, enraging Aborigines and those sympathetic to them. She wrote the speech herself and did not have anyone censor it, or write it for her, as she should of course have done (Hanson, 2007).

As for corruption in politics, Michael Moore's book *The Washington Connection* (Moore et al., 1977) gives a good account of that in the US, for example how the arms biz influenced mistakes like the Vietnam and Korea fiasco's discussed in Chapter 14.

As for stupidity, Moore points out the blunders of policy that exacerbated the 1970s OPEC oil hike crisis.

As for the BS 'econobabble' of always pretty 'thick' pollies and economists, the latter was an example of this, as is the stupidity of not taking measures to slow the rise and rise of China's economy, for example by having at least small tariffs on some locally manufactured goods in the US and like countries with far higher wages, and whose greedy CEO's move manufacturing wherever the slave labour is cheapest.

In 2009 China overtook Germany as the world's 3rd largest economy (Heywood, 2011). Thanks to their hybrid one-party government and 'unprivatized' government businesses, China is likely to continue doing well while in the West the antiquated and farcical 'revolving door' Westminster system of yelling clowns on both sides creaks ever more loudly.

Heywood's textbook has a chapter entitled *Nuclear Proliferation and Disarmament* (Heywood, 2011), an important issue in the context of the present book, and one on which a good deal has been said and written, but not much done – we opine that not only nukes and landmines, but most weapons should be banned!

REFERENCES

Aarons M, Loftus B, *The Secret War Against the Jews,* Mandarin Press, Melbourne (1999).

Abelson H, Ledeen K, Lewis H, *Blown to Bits, Your Life, Liberty, and Happiness after the Digital Explosion,* Addison-Wesley, New York (2008).

Aid MM, *Intel Wars, The Secret History of the Fight Against Terror,* Bloomsbury, New York (2012).

Alibek K. *Biohazard,* Arrow Books, London, 2000.

Batra R, *Surviving the Great Depression of 1990,* Bantam/Schartz, Sydney (1988).

Bell R, Hall R, *Impact: Contemporary Issues & Global Problems,* The Jacaranda Press, Brisbane (1991).

Ben-Menashe A, *Profits of War, The Sensational Story of the World-Wide Arms Conspiracy,* Allen & Unwin, Sydney (1992).

Bethe HA, *The Road from Los Alamos,* Touchstone Books, New York NY (1991).

Black E, *IBM and the Holocaust,* Little Brown, London (2001).

Blondel J, *Voters, Parties, and Leaders,* Penguin, Harmondsworth (1963).

Brabazon J, *My Friend The Mercenary,* Text, Melbourne (2010).

Brook-Shepherd G, *Iron Maze, The Western Secret Services and the Bolsheviks,* Pan, London (1998).

REFERENCES

Broom L, Jones FL, McDonnell P, Williams T, *The Inheritance of Inequality,* Routledge & Kegan Paul, London (1980).

Brown A, *The Rise and Fall of Communism,* The Bodley Head, London (2009).

Buchanan JM, Tullock G, *The Calculus of Consent,* The University of Michigan Press, Ann Arbor (1974).

Burgan M, *On The Front Line, Spying and the Cold War,* Raintree, Oxford (2005).

Calder K, *Asia's Deadly Triangle, How Arms, Energy, and Growth Threaten to Destabilize Asia-Pacific,* Nicholas Brearley Publishing, London (1997).

Carey J (ed.), *The Faber Book of Science,* Faber and Faber, London (1995).

Caselli F, Coleman WR, *On the Theory of Ethnic Conflict,* paper posted on the Internet (2012).

Chambers Dictionary of World History, Chambers Harrap, Edinburgh (1993).

Cipolla, CM, *The Economic History of World Population,* 6th edn, Penguin, London (1974).

Clark G, *In Fear of China,* Lansdown Press, Melbourne (1967).

Clarkson W, *The Valkyrie Operation,* Blake Publishing, London (1998).

Colborn T, Dumanoski D, Myers JP, *Our Stolen Future, Are We Threatening Our Fertility, Intelligence, and Survival? – A Scientific Detective Story,* Dutton, New York (1996).

Cowie HR, Collins MB, Ryan DB, *Imperialism, Racism and Re-Assessments,* Nelson, Melbourne (1994).

Crough G, Wheelwright T, Wilshire T (eds), *Australia and World Capitalism,* Penguin (1980).

Dabscheck B, Niland J, *Industrial Relations in Australia,* George Allen & Unwin, Sydney (1981).

Davies, D, *An Introduction to Clinical Psychiatry,* Melbourne University Press, Melbourne (1971).

Dees M, *Gathering Storm, America's Militia Threat,* Harper Perennial, New York (1996).

De Sélincourt (tr.), *Herodotus, The Histories,* Penguin, London (1954).

Doyle D, *Inside Espionage, A Memoir of True Men and Traitors,* St Ermin's Press, London (2000).

Dreyfus S, Assange J, *Underground,* Heinemann, Sydney (2011).

Forbes HD, *Ethnic Conflict: Commerce, Culture, and the Contact Hypothesis,* Yale University Press, New Haven (1997).

Goodall (van Lawick-Goodall), Jane, *In the Shadow of Man,* Houghton Mifflin, Boston (1971).

Hamlyn (publisher), *The Sores of Civilization,* Marshall Cavendish, London (1970).

Hammond P, *Slavery, Terrorism and Islam,* Frontline Fellowship, Cape Town (2010).

Hanna FP, *Women in Islam,* Horizon Publishing Group, Sydney (2015).

Hansen, P, *Untamed & Unashamed, The Autobiography,* JoJo Press, Melbourne (2007).

Harris L, *The Suicide of Reason, Radical Islam's Threat to the Enlightenment,* Basic Books, New York (2007).

Heywood A, *Global Politics,* Palgrave Macmillan, London (2011).

Hodges A, *Alan Turing, The Enigma,* Vintage, London (1985).

Hughes-Wilson J, *Military Intelligence Blunders,* Carroll & Graf, New York (1999).

Ikenson, B, *Ingenious Inventions, How They Work and How They Came to Be,* Black Dog & Leventhal, New York (2004).

Jay P, *The Crisis of Western Political Economy*, The Australian Broadcasting Commission, Sydney (1981).

Jencks C, Smith M, Acland H, Bane MJ, Cohen D, Gintis H, Heyns B, Michelson S, *Inequality: A Reassessment of the Effect of Family and Schooling in America*, Penguin, Harmondsworth (1975).

Jones S, Israel P, *Others Unknown: The Oklahoma City Bombing Case and Conspiracy*, Public Affairs, New York (1998).

Knightly P, *Philby, KGB Masterspy*, André Deutsch, London (1988).

Larsen RJ, Buss DM, *Personality Psychology, Domains of Knowledge About Human Nature*, McGraw-Hill, NY (2002).

Lifton RJ, *Destroying the World to Save It: Aum Shinrikyo, Apocalyptic Violence, and the New Global Terrorism*, Metropolitan Books, New York (1999).

Mackenzie KR, *The English Parliament*, Penguin, Harmondsworth (1950).

Masoff J, *Oh Yikes! History's Grossest, Wackiest Moments*, Workman Publishing, New York (2006).

Massoulié F, *Middle East Conflicts*, Interlink Books, New York (2003).

Maxwell N, Yahuda M, Wheelwright T, Jayawardena C, The Chinese model: politics in command, in *Political Economy of Development*, Australian Broadcasting Commission, Sydney (1977).

McCormack MH, *What They Don't Teach You at Harvard Business School*, Fontana/Collins, London (1986).

Miller J, Engelbert S, Broad W, *Germs, The Ultimate Weapon*, Simon & Schuster, New York (2001).

Mohr GA, *Finite Elements for Solids, Fluids, and Optimization*, Oxford University Press, OUP Oxford (1992).

Mohr GA, *The Pretentious Persuaders, A Brief History & Science of Mass Persuasion,* Horizon Publishing Group, Sydney (2012a).

Mohr GA, *The Doomsday Calculation: The End of the Human Race,* Xlibris, Sydney (2012b).

Mohr GA, *The Variant Virus: Introducing Secret Agent Simon Sinclair,* Xlibris, Sydney (2012c).

Mohr GA, *The War of the Sexes: Women Are Getting On Top,* Xlibris, Sydney (2012d).

Mohr GA, *The History & Psychology of Human Conflict,* Horizon (2014).

Mohr GA, *Elementary Thinking For The 21st Century,* Xlibris, Sydney (2014b).

Mohr GA, *The Pretentious Persuaders, A Brief History & Science of Mass Persuasion,* 2nd edition, Horizon Publishing Group, Sydney (2014c).

Mohr GA, Fear E, *World Religions, The History, Issues, & Truth,* Xlibris, Sydney (2015).

Mohr GA, Mohr PE, Mohr RS, *Brainwashed Zombies: Religious, Political & Consumer Persuasion,* Amazon-Kindle (2018).

Moore, Michael, *Stupid White Men ... and Other Sorry Excuses for the State of the Nation,* Penguin, Melbourne (2002).

Natkeil R, *Atlas of 20th Century History,* Bison Books, Greenwich CT (1982).

Nojumi N, *The Rise of the Taliban in Afghanistan,* Palgrave, New York (2002).

Odle F, *The Picture Story of British Inventions,* World Distributors, Manchester (1966).

Packard V, *The People Shapers,* Nelson, Melbourne (1978).

Panniker KM, *Asia and Western Dominance,* p. 116, Allen & Unwin, London (1959).

Penn, *Microtrends, The Small Forces Behind Today's Big Changes,* Allen Lane, London (2007).

REFERENCES

Philby R, Lyubimov M, Peake H, *The Private Life of Kim Philby*, Fromm International, New York (2000).

Plowman D, Deery S, Fisher C, *Australian Industrial Relations*, McGraw-Hill, Sydney (1980).

Prados J, *Vietnam, The History of an Unwinnable War, 1945-1975*, University of Kansas Press (2009).

Quarrie B, *The World's Elite Forces*, Octopus Books, London (1985).

Sampson A, *The Arms Bazaar*, Coronet Books, London (1977).

Sauerbruch F, *A Surgeon's Life*, André Deutsch, London (1953).

Self P, *Administrative Theories and Policies*, 2nd edn, George Allen & Unwin, London (1977).

Smith I, *Mad Dog Killers, The Story of a Congo Mercenary*, 30 South Publishers, Solihull, England & Pinetown, South Africa.

Snow RL, *Terrorists Amongst Us, The Militia Threat*, Perseus Publishing, Cambridge MA (1999).

Soros G, *The Bubble of American Supremacy, Correcting The Misuse of American Power*, Weidenfeld & Nicolson, London (2004).

Spencer J, *A Nineteenth Century Life*, Liveright Publishing Corporation, New York (2013).

Suter K, *All About Terrorism, Everything You Were Too Afraid to Ask*, Random House, Sydney (2008).

Sweezy PM, *The Theory of Capitalist Development*, Dennis Dobson, London (1946).

Taylor L, Walton P, Industrial sabotage: motives and meanings, in *Images of Deviance*, S. Cohen, p. 219, Penguin, Harmondsworth (1971).

Thomas M, *As Used on the Famous Nelson Mandela, Underground Adventures in the Arms and Torture Trade*, Ebury Press, London (2006).

Time-Life Books, the editors of, *Fists of Steel,* Time-Life Books, Alexandria VA (1988).

Time-Life Books, the editors of, *Storming to Power,* Time-Life Books, Alexandria VA (1989).

Watson P, *The Modern Mind, An Intellectual History of the 20th Century,* Harper Collins, New York (2001).

Weil A, *Terrorism,* Saddleback Educational Publishing, www.sdlback.com (2013).

Wheen F, *How Mumbo Jumbo Conquered The World,* Public Affairs, New York (2004).

Whittell G, *Bridge of Spies, A True Story of the Cold War,* Simon & Schuster, London (2012).

Wonnacott, P. & Wonnacott, R. Economics. McGraw-Hill, New York, 1979.

Yeltsin B, *Against The Grain, An Autobiography,* Summit Books, New York (1990).

Young DJ, *December 1941, America's First 25 Days At War,* Pictorial Histories Publishing Co., Missouri, Montana (1992).

Zubok VM, *A Failed Empire, The Soviet Union in the Cold War From Stalin to Gorbachev,* University of North Carolina Press (2007).

General reference sources

Chambers Dictionary of World History, Chambers Harrap, Edinburgh (1993).

Collins National Encyclopaedia, Collins, London (1966).

Egerton-Eastwick RW (ed.), *The Oracle Encyclopaedia,* George Newnes, London (1896).

Encarta Book of Quotations, Pan MacMillan, Sydney (2000).

Encarta Encyclopaedia 1999, Microsoft Corporation, 1998.

Encyclopaedia Britannica CD 99 (1999).

REFERENCES

Encyclopaedia Britannica Ready Reference 2003.

Mindscape World Atlas & Almanac, The Learning Company Inc., Crawley, West Sussex (1999).

Natkeil R, *Atlas of 20th Century History,* Bison Books, Greenwich CT (1982).

The Oxford Dictionary of Quotations, 4th edn, Oxford University Press, Oxford, 1992.

The Oxford Interactive Encyclopaedia, The Learning Company, 1997.

Philips' New World Atlas, George Philip & Son, Ltd, London (1934).

Power Quotes, Daniel B. Baker, *The Business Library,* Information Australia (1992).

The SBS World Guide, 4th edn, Reed Reference Australia, Melbourne (1995).

The World Almanac and Book of Facts 1998, World Almanac Books, Mahwah NJ (1998),

1999 World Book Multimedia Encyclopaedia, World Book Inc. (1998).

Wikipedia.

WORLD WAR 3

The book examines the history of human conflict concisely, including modern terrorism that continues to spread globally.

- ➢ An overview of man's long history of conflict.
- ➢ Urban crime and conflicting groups in society.
- ➢ Tribal, ethnic, religious and political conflict.
- ➢ Territorial and imperialist conflict.
- ➢ The two World Wars.
- ➢ Terrorism and revolution.
- ➢ The threats of nuclear and biochemical warfare.
- ➢ Conflicts of 'democratic' vs. 'socialism'.
- ➢ Islamic terrorism and jihad and World War 3
- ➢ Proposals to reduce conflict.

G. A. Mohr published more than 35 books, including:

A Microcomputer Introduction to the Finite Element Method
Finite Elements for Solids, Fluids, and Optimization
The Pretentious Persuaders, A Brief History & Science of Mass Persuasion
Curing Cancer & Heart Disease
The Variant Virus, Introducing Secret Agent Simon Sinclair
The Doomsday Calculation, The End Of The Human Race
Heart Disease, Cancer, & Ageing: Proven Neutraceutical & Lifestyle Solutions
2045: A Remote Town Survives Global Holocaust
The History & Psychology of Human Conflict;   The War of the Sexes
Elementary Thinking for the 21st Century
The 8-Week+ Program to Reverse Cardiovascular Disease
The Scientific MBA;   Mohr's Law of Hierarchies
The DIY Cardiovascular Cure;   Combating Cancer
Elementary Thinking for Modern Management
The Psychology of Life;   The Psychology of Depression

Also with R.S. Mohr/Richard Sinclair & P.E. Mohr/Edwin Fear:

The Evolving Universe: Relativity, Redshift and Life from Space
World Religions: The History, Psychology, Issues & Truth
The Brainwashed: From Consumer Zombies to Islamic Jihad
Human Intelligence, Learning & Behaviour
New Theories of The Universe, Evolution, and Relativity
The Psychology of Hope;   The Population Explosion
Brainwashed Zombies: Religious, Political & Consumer Persuasion
Human Conflict: An Attitudinal Psychology Model
World Religions: From Animism to Mohronism
The Psychology of Hope: The Psychology of Success